W9-AYA-367

Someday All This
Will Be Yours

Someday All This Will Be Yours

A HISTORY OF INHERITANCE AND OLD AGE

HENDRIK HARTOG

HARVARD UNIVERSITY PRESS

Cambridge, Massachusetts

London, England

2012

Copyright © 2012 by the President and Fellows
of Harvard College
All rights reserved
Printed in the United States of America

Library of Congress Cataloging-in-Publication Data

Hartog, Hendrik, 1948–
Someday all this will be yours : a history of inheritance and old age / Hendrik Hartog.
p.   cm.
Includes bibliographical references and index.
ISBN 978-0-674-04688-7 (alk. paper)
1. Inheritance and succession—United States—History.   2. Older people—
Care—United States—History.   I. Title.

KF771.H37   2011
346.7305′2—dc22   2011014356

To my children

Contents

Someday All This Will Be Yours

Over the Hill

One morning in February 2000 I sat reading in the library of the University of California's Boalt Hall Law School. I was in Berkeley because my nearly ninety-one-year-old mother lived in a retirement community in San Mateo, thirty miles away, on the other side of San Francisco Bay. I was on leave from teaching, and I had decided that it would be good to spend some extended time with my mother, more than the quick long weekend every other month that I had reluctantly devoted to her over the previous nine years. But I also knew that, over the whole short month of February, I would go crazy if I stayed with her or too near her. So, I rented a small room in Berkeley, alternately traveling one day over the Bay Bridge to sit with her and walk with her and take her places—to stores, the beach, the San Francisco apartment of her quarrelsome eighty-nine-year-old sister—and the other day reading and exploring in the Berkeley law library.

I was looking through the first volumes of the *New Jersey Miscellany,* an obscure and unofficial series of New Jersey case volumes published through the 1920s, because I was curious about how routine property law cases were handled at a moment of early suburbanization. The *Miscellany* included cases that were without much doctrinal significance but did sometimes tell interesting and relatively detailed stories. I lingered, as I turned the pages, on a number of early auto accident cases, early zoning cases, and a couple of cases in which children challenged a father's will because of the "undue influence" of a new and much younger wife. Then I came across *Lotz v. Rippe* (1924).

In *Lotz*, a vice chancellor, that is, a judge sitting in the New Jersey Court of Equity, declared void an elderly woman's will, which gave all her property to her two daughters. Instead, he ordered that her house be conveyed to her nephew. Annie Rippe, the elderly woman, had long lived in West Long Branch on the Jersey shore, in a house with a small farm attached. Her nephew, John Martin Lotz, lived with her. At first, prior to the death of Annie's husband, John was paid ten dollars a month plus his board for his work as handyman and gardener. Later, after the farm land had been sold, leaving only "an ordinary house of eleven rooms," he went out to work as a carpenter and paid her five dollars a week for his board and continued to do chores about the place without pay. Her sole income was from the sale of vegetables, produced largely through her nephew's work, and from a few permanent and summer boarders. The work of running a boarding house eventually became too much for her. In 1919 John proposed, with the support of Annie's daughter Addie, that if Annie Rippe would promise to give him the property in her will, he would take care of her and the property, make sure she stayed comfortable, and keep a roof over her head. In effect, to speak somewhat anachronistically, her house would become her retirement home. She agreed. They all went to a lawyer, who drew up a will that gave John the property after Annie's death. For the next four years he did all of the work he had promised, made "improvements" to the property, and took care of the boarders, as well as of her. However, in 1923, without telling him, Annie Rippe went to a lawyer and made a new will, one that gave all her property to her two daughters and revoked her previous will. And then she died.

Her will was admitted to probate without any notice to John since he was only a nephew and was not mentioned in the document. Eventually, however, he learned that he was not getting the property (the sisters had probably begun or at least had threatened to begin eviction proceedings to get him out of the house). He then found a lawyer who brought a petition to the equity court. The petition asked for "specific performance" of her promise, based on his performance in doing as he had agreed. Because of the work he had done and his reliance on her assurance, Annie had become bound to convey the property to him in her will. When she changed her will to exclude him, he became entitled to the intervention of an equity court.

The sisters resisted. Their lawyer argued variously: Their mother had the right to change her will (they introduced evidence that she had a reason for doing so, as John Martin Lotz had occasionally used offensive language in his aunt's presence). If there had ever been an agreement at all, it was void because it was an oral contract, and oral agreements for land violated the Statute of Frauds, a long-standing law that required all land transactions to be in writing. Third, her earlier promise to make a will in his favor had been founded on his "undue influence" over her.

However, Vice Chancellor Foster gave John Martin Lotz exactly what he had asked for. He had done as he had promised; he had cared for his aunt; his "performance" of that care, in combination with the revoked but written will, proved that there had been a valid and enforceable contract between them. Perhaps it was the daughter's "undue influence" that had produced the second will. Whatever had caused Annie to change her mind, not to give him the property would have been to reward his aunt's fraud. That is, she had benefited from his labor but, near the end, had tried to avoid paying him for it as she had promised to do. End of case.

Work and care for property. You do this (take care of me), and I promise to do that (give you property at my death). A primordial transaction found perhaps anywhere and everywhere and in any time and every time. Furthermore, at least in the New Jersey vice chancellor's rendition, this transaction had produced an enforceable contract.

Yet for me, a former property law teacher, the opinion seemed odd. The story of the case—of a promised inheritance in exchange for care—was a familiar one to me. I had taught versions of the story that lay behind the case throughout my years as a property law teacher. However, in the conventional law school rendition of "the law" used to decide such situations, the nephew would have lost. Indeed, a year before the decision in *Lotz,* Benjamin Cardozo, the chief judge of the New York Court of Appeals and the most eminent state court judge in the United States, had decided *Burns v. McCormick,* a decision founded on a story almost identical to that in *Lotz.* In addition, *Burns v. McCormick* quickly became a canonical and casebook reprinted repository of reasons that younger caretakers, particularly young family members who had been convinced to stay home and care for elderly relatives, would lose when they tried to enforce elderly relatives' unwritten (oral or "parol") promises to make wills.[1] I was confused by the vice chancellor's blithe rejection of doctrinal understandings that I had thought were unquestioned in the 1920s. Moreover, I was particularly struck by the form of the opinion in *Lotz:* its unqualified acceptance of the nephew's rights, as well as the absence of any case citations or doctrinal discussion. To Vice Chancellor Foster, this was an easy decision based on the evidentiary record before him. He felt no obligation to invoke authority for his decision. He claimed, implicitly, that he was reproducing a well-established and uncontroversial understanding of legal doctrine.

Lotz v. Rippe was only a starting point for the project that became this book, a small case of no further significance in this history. (Just as my life as my mother's "caretaker" is of no further significance, except as suggesting an initial contrast between the legally entangled family caretaking characteristic of old age care in the past and the structures of commercialized care and retirement and claimed independence which often seem to define the lives of elderly people today.) Nonetheless, from *Lotz* I began a project that led me deep into nineteenth- and early twentieth-century New Jersey law. Soon I would learn that both the result in *Lotz* and the result that I would have predicted as a law professor were always present and available for judges who faced such legal cases. There were always several right answers as judges and chancellors confronted rich and indeterminate evidentiary records of family quarrels and enmeshed relationships, which they necessarily shaped by picking and choosing their way through thick fields of inconsistent legal doctrines.

In any event, from that small case I have moved backward and forward through a body of New Jersey cases, many decided in the New Jersey Court of Equity by chancellors and vice chancellors, but others decided in other state courts. Some occurred in the New Jersey Prerogative Court, which dealt with appeals from probate decisions—decisions about what happens to property after a property owner's death—made in county "orphans' courts." Others were decided in the New Jersey Supreme Court, which heard appeals of civil suits for damages, and in the New Jersey Court for the Correction of Errors and Appeals (often known as the Court of Errors), which served as the court for final appeals from all other courts in the state.[2]

Eventually, after many false starts, I assembled a database of well over 200 New Jersey cases decided between the late 1840s and the early 1950s. In addition, for approximately sixty of those cases (mostly cases appealed to the Court of Errors) I was able to work with full trial transcripts.

All of those cases rested on the same underlying transaction: As in *Lotz*, they began, at least in the legal imagination and in the memories of some of the witnesses, with a promise by an older property owner to a younger person—usually a child or another younger relative but sometimes an employee or a neighbor. "Someday," an old man or woman had said, which might mean "when I am done with it" or "when your mother dies" or "soon," "all this will be yours!" "When I die, I will leave you the land," or "I will pay you for your time and effort," or "you will inherit everything," or "you will be treated as my own child." "But until then, you must stay with me and work," or "stay with me; care for me." Or, "Don't leave me!"

Because the older persons had not kept their promises, legal cases came into being. The younger persons, who had received nothing or had certainly not received what they had expected, were left to sue. To win in court the younger persons needed to prove that there had been a promise and that they had done the work on which that promise had been conditioned. However, more often than not, the younger persons lost in court and were left with nothing.

Such cases dealt with the contested claims of family members (often children, nephews and nieces, and informally adopted children but also related or unrelated housekeepers) to property (often land but just as often unpaid wages), which were based on promises made by older parents and other elderly relatives in exchange for care. In exploring the law—the legal doctrines and the judicial institutions—that helped produce these stories, my focus is as much on the family members who made the promises, worked both together and against one another, and brought the cases, as it is on the courts and the lawyers who litigated. The cases that resulted were almost always understood as routine legal business. As far as I can tell, no lawyers specialized in such cases. No lawyers appear to have made a name for themselves by their advocacy in these cases.

The goal is to explore an intimate transaction—care for me, and you will get my property—and the cases, legal doctrine, and legal culture that the transaction produced. By working through how and why such agreements were made, as well as the consequences for the individuals who made them, we learn much about the moral and legal lives of nineteenth- and early twentieth-century family members, labor conflicts within families, responsibility for and care of old people, the legitimate and illegitimate uses of family property and wealth, and the internal economy of family work.

The New Jersey cases produced by these arrangements stand as an unsystematic but thorough sampling of thousands of similar cases—founded on similar underlying transactions—that occurred in other state courts in nineteenth- and twentieth-century America.[3] Not one of these New Jersey cases is important by the conventional measures that lawyers, legal scholars, and political scientists use. They are largely forgotten today. They established no precedents of continuing significance or public prominence. In their own time a few of the 200 would be cited for particular doctrinal points in cases decided in other states. They also produced a sequence of legal doctrine and argumentation that later lawyers and judges used in briefs and opinions throughout the 1930s and 1940s. Yet in their own time both lawyers and judges saw them as part of the routine work of the legal system.

In the aggregate they expressed a doubly private body of law. They were private in the categorical sense that they were not public law. That is to say, they dealt with relations between two or more "private" individuals, not relations between private individuals and the agencies and institutions of the state. They were cases produced within the law of wills, of contract, of property, and of the practices of equity. They were also private because judges and lawyers almost uniformly understood them as not implicating large policy questions. The opinions rarely challenged existing understandings of regulatory or constitutional law. Fundamental (and fundamentally contradictory) public policies and public commitments coursed through the cases—the freedom of property owners to change their mind (testator's freedom), the capacity of adults to bind themselves by contract, the presumption that those who work for others do so for pay, the special uncommodified character of relations between family members, the contradictions in public definitions of who is and who is not part of the family, the absence of children's public duty to care for a parent, the need to reduce to writing agreements for important transactions, the special responsibility of courts (and especially courts of equity) to uncover and prevent "fraud," among others, but no one acted as if these cases established or remade public policies.[4]

Most such cases involved the claims and the resources of middling people, including many farmers, but also small merchants, laborers, tugboat captains, butchers, and contractors and builders. The property at stake was often quite small in quantity and value, sometimes miniscule. Indeed, the value of the property at stake must often have been considerably less than the litigation costs for the family members. Obviously, if there were no property (wealth) in a family at all, there would have been no litigation. Still, it is equally clear that the situations that produced litigation were less likely to come into being where significant wealth existed. Rich old people were less likely to look to children and other family members for direct care because they would not have needed to use a promise of future property as an alternative to ordinary wages in the present. The rich—young and old—were more likely to shape their family strategies in careful consultation with lawyers.

In many of the stories told in testimony, lawyers often appear as advisors to elderly persons who had been asked to reduce a series of promises to a formal written document (a will or a deed). However, few younger caretakers—children or other relatives or employees—ever consulted an attorney before the death of the old person or the end of the relationship. Lawyers became central to those stories only when the claims and conflicts ended up in litigation.

The core legal problem that brought these documents into existence was how (including when, whether, and why) to claim rights to some or all of the estate (the property) of a dead (or a soon-to-be-dead) person who had not named a specific individual as the recipient of property in the decedent's will. One might call this John Martin Lotz's problem. Behind that abstractly stated legal problem was the reality (or at least the claimed or imagined reality) that work had been done and lives had been shaped by promises to convey property at death. There had been what lawyers today call "reliance." In addition, behind that reality lay a swirl of social expectations about old age and about how, in a world without social security, retirement benefits, or pensions, it was possible to have a good, or at least a decent, old age. Call those collectively Annie Rippe's problem. In life, the now or soon-to-be-dead older persons had had particular goals shaped by their legal and economic situation. Those goals characteristically had to do with, first, how to engage and mobilize family members in one's care and well-being as one declined physically and perhaps mentally and, second, how to control and to keep those family members attentive and caring.

The cases and transcripts I am relying on—revolving around situations where younger persons sued because they had not received legacies or properties they believed had been promised to them in exchange for care work—were surely representative cases in the sense that legal actions of this sort were part of the ordinary work of state courts throughout the nation. However, what did they represent in terms of the history of family life and family caretaking? Were the practices detailed in the opinions, briefs, and testimonies common, normal, everyday?[5]

One can imagine these cases as the unhappy and unsettled endings to family stories about care, alongside four alternative endings that did not ordinarily result in litigation. In one presumptively happier ending, an older person fulfilled a promise by will or by *inter vivos* (that is, before death) conveyance, and the younger person (the potential litigant) was satisfied; therefore, there was no litigation. In a second alternative story, an older person had not fulfilled a promise, but the younger person "lumped" it, did not sue, perhaps to maintain family harmony, perhaps out of ignorance, or perhaps because of a negotiated settlement with siblings and other family members. In a third, there would be no litigation as an ending because a younger family member had offered care and work to an older person out of "love" or customary obligation without looking for compensation or requiring promises or commitments. And in the fourth alternative ending, probably the least happy of all, there would be no family conflict over property because there was no family property. In that situation, certainly in the public imagination, the poorhouse loomed. None of these alternatives, all of indeterminate size and significance, would necessarily leave any record in the case law.

The cases explored here, by contrast, always concerned situations that involved some property (although often relatively little). In these not uncommon circumstances, older persons failed to fulfill a promise and younger persons—the adult children—had not accepted that what the older persons had not done was "right" or their right not to do. One should not be surprised that people chose to litigate when such situations occurred. The moment of parental death was one that was widely understood as a distinctively legal moment in the life course. Inheritance, probate, and the transfer of familial assets were paradigmatic moments when everyone knew they had to deal with the law. Situations involving land and other valuable properties and their final disposition were ones in which, perhaps above all others in everyday life, potential litigants had an enormous incentive to sue. Surely, many family members drawn into litigation must have often wished that their story instead had one of the alternative endings. (If only sister Kate had not insisted on her rights, or if only dear old Dad had not avoided writing the will. Why could we not have all just gotten along?) Still, in this individualistic and capitalistic legal culture, such legal conflict was normal, although unpleasant, for family members. It remained a predictable event in a family's history. Family members would find many disincentives to sue because of the disruption to or destruction of familial relationships. However, by the time litigation was initiated, often the family was already in deep conflict. The possibility of a negotiated settlement may have been long past.

These are examples of what legal anthropology has labeled "cases of trouble." A case of trouble reveals norms of the legal culture (i.e., what ought to have happened) even as it is by nature a case about claimed violations of norms and tests of the power of norms, as well as a case about individuals who did not easily or comfortably embody or conform to the identities the norms prescribed. A case of trouble may explore how courts and other decision makers reconciled or chose between contradictory norms.[6] By attending closely to the ways litigants, witnesses, lawyers, and judges talked about what had happened within families in such cases, one can learn a great deal about what might be called the "conditions of freedom" within those families and within the legal culture.[7]

What the trial transcripts of these cases also offer are extraordinary details about what actually went on within households and about family work and caretaking. There are other available sources of information on the social history of care: diaries, memoirs, oral histories, prescriptive literatures, sermons, medical reports, statistical and demographic studies, and governmental and nongovernmental inquiries. Where appropriate, I have looked to these. What is distinctive about such trial transcripts, though, is the sustained exploration that each side in litigation devoted to the question of what work had actually been done. Of course, most of what was said in testimony was self-serving and often hearsay, at best efforts to reconstruct events and conversations that had occurred many years before. Still, so long as one reads with sufficient care and a critical eye, one gains from these transcripts a kind of access to the conflicted and fraught situations that lay behind or, more accurately, before the disputes in court. On one side, on the side of the child or younger person who claimed to have earned an inheritance, it was always important to describe exactly what work had been done and how, because the work itself, in combination with promises, might produce entitlement, a right to compensation. On the other side, it was usually important to minimize, diminish, or otherwise challenge the work for exactly the same reasons. In the end, the results were rich and detailed (and tested) testimony about who did what, how they did it, how it was solicited, how negotiations over family work occurred, and how the nature of the work changed over time as families aged and reconstructed themselves and as generations and individuals jockeyed for position within those families.

There is a certain bloodlessness to the history of care as it has often been written about. Care itself is a neutral word that can hide the rages of the demented and of their caretakers, and the struggle to keep a house clean when one has to live with an incontinent old man or woman, the chaos of everyday life. "Care" may be made (as "parenting" often is) into a natural event or process, predictable in its place within the life course. In much recent writing, it has become indicative of the oppressions of women who became caretakers, in part because of its apparent dreariness (at least as compared to the excitement of our own lives). Still, one may lose the sense of lives unhinged by needs and demands. The apparent inevitability of care—its position as a site for inevitable dependency—can also obscure the negotiations between and within generations, the ways in which needs, desires, opportunities, promises, and work joined to form life plans and ambitions.

Not in these transcripts, though. To work with these materials it is necessary to confront the particularity of the situations described and of the stories told. *Lotz* is not a representative case. It is a story about one nephew who lived under distinctive circumstances with his aunt, who made a deal with her and apparently with her daughters, and who shaped his particular life through those relationships and the work he did. All of the cases about daughters, sons, housekeepers, or adopted children became, through the matrix of petitions and complaints and the testimony of supportive witnesses, particularized and distinctive. It was never "work" in the abstract that testimony described. It was mopping or mucking out the stable or improving the property by "ditching" or dealing with a father who could not help but mess the sheets. For complainants and plaintiffs, what was important were the ways their lives had been shaped and changed—made distinctively and peculiarly different—by the promises of parents and other older people.

In part, we are concerned with normal and everyday ways of soliciting or managing family work as revealed by or expressed in court documents. However, we are even more interested in the everyday, normal, known ways of recourse to law in the face of family conflict and uncertainty. We are also interested in the moral discourses that legal actors—including litigants and witnesses, as well as lawyers and judges—produced in trying to make legal and cultural sense out of promises made, commitments made and abandoned, work done, and lives molded by other family members. Courts provided the hope of corrective justice for particularized wrongs committed by other family members. They offered the peculiar finality of a legal decision, a finality that might become something that approximated a kind of "peace." In addition, they offered a chance to tell one's story even as they also molded and categorized those stories.

One true wonder of these records—as social history—is in their inability to be reduced to a representative norm. It is important to remember that a trial is a record of words spoken. Sometimes those were words that would never have been written within a Victorian or post-Victorian society. There are flashes, moments, when something like an otherwise hidden reality—about dementia, incontinence, love, the work of care, and the annoyances and pleasures of intimate relations—comes tumbling out.

As I explored this unfamiliar world of family dealings and conflicts around old-age care, I learned that in important ways older people and adult children in the 1930s and early 1940s dealt with each other much as their grandparents and great-grandparents had done in the mid-nineteenth century. To put the point slightly differently, those who negotiated over care, caretaking, and family work within families in 1850 did so in ways that would have felt recognizable to those negotiating over the same issues in 1940.

As a result, I began to understand the project that became the book as an exploration of a structure or field of practices that reproduced and sustained itself over time.[8] I gradually came to place more weight on the continuing singularity of the practices of this period as belonging to a long historical era and less on the modest changes in those practices during those years.[9]

What do I mean by a "field of legal practices"? I am not describing a unitary field of legal doctrine. Rather, I am concerned with practices involving negotiations over family work and caretaking and the uses of inheritance as an inducement. These rested on both official and folk understandings of property law and contract law, as well as on expectations of love and duty within families. Parents, children, neighbors, and other relatives all thought and spoke about what would happen in the law. They made predictions about what the courts would do, in fact.[10] Although those predictions were often incorrect, both the young and the old knew a great deal of rough-and-ready law. What is more, their conversations and their negotiations revealed internalized and sometimes sophisticated understandings of legal norms. They understood testator's freedom; they understood notions of "undue influence"; many of them understood the core premise of the Statute of Frauds: that all land transactions needed to be in writing (even illiterate individuals seem to have understood that). Adopted children knew the fragility of promises that they would be treated like blood relatives. Elderly parents knew that they would no longer have control over property once it was conveyed to and possessed by others.[11]

In the ethnically diverse world of late nineteenth- and early twentieth-century New Jersey, those whose conflicts ended up in the case files spoke many different languages and came from many different immigrant communities and ethnicities. (They were overwhelmingly white and of European origin, and, of course, there had to be some property in the family.) Early and late, many of the litigants and witnesses had Dutch or English names. Later there would be Germans, Scandinavians, German and eastern European Jews, Italians, Irish, French, Russians, and more. Many had come from agrarian communities that severely restricted any right to choose who would inherit property. In much of Europe, in those agrarian communities, clear customary rules would have determined responsibility for elder care. The transmission of wealth from one generation to the next was more or less fixed, not subject to negotiation.

Such inherited practices of care and inheritance occasionally came up in the course of the testimony. One can read lawyers, judges, and chancellors working to fit those practices within familiar Anglo-American legal understandings. Yet the overwhelming impression these case files produce is of the immigrants' adjustment to the hegemonic legal culture, their internalization of Anglo-American legal norms. Property-holding members of those communities—older men and women—apparently learned quickly to use the vocabulary of rights and exclusivity of Anglo-American law. They did so with canniness and sophistication. In particular, they learned to value and to mobilize the norms implicated in the Anglo-American legal notion of "freedom of testation." Older people knew they had the right to pick and choose among potential heirs; they knew they could disinherit almost anyone, including lineal descendants and close kin. They knew that possession of property meant the power to make choices. They also knew that their future well-being depended on their successful mobilization of the power to choose, which property gave them.

The law mattered for these parents, children, other family members, and neighbors. Years before litigation appeared on the horizon, the law shaped the way they talked about caretaking, family obligations, and individual freedom while negotiating, planning, and fighting with each another. Many talked law all the time. Nearly everyone relied on the power of contract law to organize private relations, including familial relationships. Everyone knew that it was only through law that property would be transferred and held. Their attention was focused on a particular moment in the life course, the prospective death of a parent, when law mattered for many otherwise law-abiding and law-ignoring Americans.

When that law talk led to litigation, it implicated a diversity of often contradictory legal doctrines and understandings: equity law, the law of "undue influence," doctrines connected to the Statute of Frauds, and a good deal of contract doctrine. What doctrines were mobilized in any particular case depended as much on the competence, sophistication, and attention of the lawyers involved as on the internal logic of the law or the "felt necessities" of the facts of the case.

This was a legal field almost entirely constructed through the doctrinal categories of private law, in particular of property and contract. During these years, public power was rarely mobilized directly to confront or discipline wrongs done within families. As far as the constitution of the family was concerned, there were few public law alternatives to private law remedies. The local community overseers of poor people and the other institutions of English and early American community life, including church bodies, which had once claimed the right to discipline family members and enforce their family responsibilities, had fallen into desuetude in the face of dramatically increased mobility, which regularly removed young and old from the jurisdiction of community institutions. At the same time, neither the states nor the federal government were yet in the business of structuring or mandating old-age care. Large corporate institutions had not yet discovered elderly people as a market force. Individually held property was the only security against the risks that old age promised.[12]

The field never generated significant policy debates or legislative struggles. Nor was it the subject of sustained judicial pronouncements. Occasionally those who were committed to the rationalization of law and legal doctrine—legal academics—noticed this emerging field of practices.[13] However, for the most part, policy makers and legal academics alike paid it little mind.

Still, this complex of private law, legal rules, and doctrines, in combination with inherited and changing understandings of family obligations, became for many older people and their adult children a field in which to improvise and construct ways to solicit, manage, and reward family work. Within that field, old age could be provided for, even as it was also fought over. Within that field, family members worked and fought and schemed as they also sustained inherited and emergent understandings of duty to each other. Within that field, culturally, economically, and biologically constituted "needs"—care, dependency, health, support, love—were planned for, negotiated over, fought over, and distributed. Within that field, struggles over adulthood, economic independence, contractual freedom, and individual responsibility became a part of the constitution of family life and solidarity.

At least some of the time, these practices—that field—would have achieved the functional goals of care and continuity of relations and the transfer of property to those whose work had been solicited. Moral obligations and love joined with legal rights, duties, and expectations—including the threat and the prospect of litigation—to produce ways of managing generational transitions and the needs of old people and other dependents.

Yet, anger, disappointment, and family disarray were also the results of those practices. It may be that the tensions and conflicts that the field generated were so great that eventually parents and children alike happily gave it up when new ways to manage and to pay for old-age care appeared over the course of the twentieth century.[14]

In 1872, the now forgotten poet Will Carleton first published one of the most popular poems of the late nineteenth century, "Over the Hill to the Poor-House." The story the poem told, versions of which were later transferred into song and theater and several silent movies, was not really about a poorhouse (that is, about a publicly funded institution that housed poor and homeless people and, in particular, poor, homeless, and isolated old people). Rather, it told a story of the abandonment of a parent by cruel children. The poorhouse was only where the story ended.

The female protagonist of the poem was a recent widow "of seventy, and only a trifle gray/ . . . smart an' chipper, for all the years I've told,/ As many another woman that's only half as old." However, she had been left without property—a disaster—and so she had to find one of her children to live with.

She was, as she recounted, "ready and willin' an' anxious any day/ To work for a decent livin' and pay my honest way; For I can earn my victuals, an' more too, I'll be bound, / If anybody is willin' to only have me 'round."

Nonetheless, as the poem details, not one of her five available adult children, all of whom had established independent households, wanted to have her "'round." (There is a sixth child, in prison, who will appear in a later poem.) In one instance, she and a daughter-in-law had words. In another, her daughter felt there was not enough space in the house. When the widow moved in with her oldest son, Thomas, his children treated her without respect. "But all the child'rn was on me——/ I couldn't stand their sauce——/ And Thomas said I needn't think I was comin' there to boss." She wrote to two other children, who lived near one another "out West," that is, far away. One wrote back that "'twas too warm there for anyone so old." The other "had an opinion the climate was too cold." Her children "shirked and slighted" her. They "shifted" her about. They "well nigh soured" her, and they "wore" her "old heart out."

And then one of her children committed the final indignity. The widow was put "on the town." She was made an object of public charity, and so she ended up in the poorhouse.[15]

The poorhouse may not have been what the poem was about, but the image of an abandoned old person trudging wearily toward an unwelcome public institution became one of its two lasting contributions to modern American culture, mobilized in later debates over social security and public welfare. The poorhouse became an icon of all of the dangers of old age and dependency in industrialized America. (The poem also apparently introduced the phrase "over the hill" to convey being past one's prime or advanced in age.)[16]

What the poem also etched for its readers was the curious asymmetry of the parent-child relationship. As Carleton's aged narrator put it, "I'd have died for my daughters, and I'd have died for my sons. And God He made that rule of love; but when we're old and gray I've noticed it sometimes, somehow, fails to work the other way." Parents had to love their children, and that meant that they had to care for them. Children did not have to reciprocate. They were free of obligations. They were free to turn their parents out, to put them away, to refuse them, to ignore them, to move away, and it was because of that freedom that older people ended up in the poorhouse.

Was that really what happened? Some readers wrote Carleton to challenge his conclusion. "It is too cruel," said one. "There never was such a case in the world," exclaimed another. A law judge wrote him a critical letter and said that if he wanted to succeed in literature, he had better learn to "write naturally . . . according to human nature." How could it be, according to the judge, that an old lady was "living at the public cost when she has children to support her"? The story had to be wrong; children could not—legally or morally—escape responsibility for their impoverished parents. However, Carleton pointed the judge to cases that proved the truth that the poem revealed. The judge investigated and acknowledged that Carleton was right. At least legally, if not morally, children really were free to abandon their parents.[17]

Carleton was correct, as a matter of brute law. Yet, everything we know about late nineteenth- and early twentieth-century America suggests that few older people ended up in the poorhouse. Most children did not abandon their needy parents. Indeed, many older people succeeded in convincing someone younger to live with and care for them.

Still, "Over the Hill to the Poor-House" describes in concrete detail a fear widely shared throughout the legal culture, a fear that served as a goad to legal action. The poem suggests one possible but terrifying ending to a predictable family story, an ending shaped by the legal freedoms of adult children and the absence (to write in a somewhat anachronistic mode) of any public support for the elderly—aside from the poorhouse—that would substitute for care by one's children. The notion that one's children would leave because they could and that one would be left all alone was a fertile anxiety for elderly participants in the legal culture.

There was, in this world, one way to solve the problem. One needed to act, as Annie Rippe had acted. One needed to use what one had in ways that would mobilize the sustained care and attention of younger people. The old had to deal directly with their adult children, including nephews and informally adopted household members, if they were going to secure the support and care—the labors—of those adult children. They needed to use the promise of an inheritance. Otherwise, they would just be left alone, and no one would care. And then the poorhouse loomed.

As Will Carleton knew, the core identities of those within this legal and familial field were not the husbands and wives that have captured the attention of most histories of family law; nor were they the parents and (young) children and the increasingly present state officials, who have been emphasized in histories of child custody law and of the development of child protective services.[18] Instead, in the poem, as well as in cases, our attention is drawn to two characters, shadowy figures within family law as it has ordinarily been conceived: the adult child and the elderly person.[19]

Adult children were not legally bound to remain and to work for their parents. Nor were they obligated to care for the old. Adult children were, paradigmatically and legally, free individuals, "emancipated," to use the technical term. Having grown out of the parents' family, they had become persons who might establish new families. Adult children had taken responsibility for their own lives. Once a child became an adult, in theory the parent-child relationship evolved into a relationship between contractual equals, unlike the husband-wife relationship, which was defined by inequality and by continuing duties and rights that could end only with death or divorce. There was no reason in law why adult children could not negotiate with their parent, deal with a parent as one individual to another, and rely on the parent's promise to pay for work. Furthermore, there was little—perhaps nothing—to keep an uncaring or careless adult child from allowing a parent to go over the hill to the poorhouse.

Nonetheless, experientially, culturally, and at times legally, adult children were still likely to feel obligations to their parents. They were sometimes still "children" and thus bound to work and to obey parents or parentlike figures. Adult children—those older than twenty-one years of age, sometimes even middle aged—who stayed on to live in their parents' households might discover that they were not fully emancipated even if parents had promised to pay for the work, for the "services rendered."

Many women and some men would have known from an early age that if their parents survived into old age, it would be because they would have to care for their parents. There were no retirement systems, no means of social security, and no pensions to speak of. Retirement usually meant turning over one's responsibilities to a child or another younger person. Everyone knew that a successful old age, that is, a period of cared-for old age without the need to work as one had in earlier years, required the mobilization and attention of family members. Women and men would have known that care of the old was more than just the purchase of commodified services. A distinction drawn today between caretaking (i.e., the work of managing and purchasing care for those who can no longer do it for themselves) and caregiving (i.e., the intimate, direct physical and economic care that middle-class people today expect others to do for dependent people) would have made no sense at all.[20] Life "at home" for many younger people would include the continuing intimate bodily care of a perhaps demented or incontinent, often needy, and certainly demanding older person, who usually also remained the owner of that home. Additionally, for many children the predictable care of one or both parents and of parental properties would also have been central to their own life plans. They looked to the rewards of inheritance as the planned payback for caring for the old. The notion, integral to the tax code and to ordinary language today, that inherited wealth is "unearned" would have seemed nonsensical to them.

Some daughters and fewer sons would never have experienced any separation from parental households. They would have stayed on for years after their chronological childhoods. In important ways, those daughters and sons would have remained "unemancipated" even though they were also adults. For others, a period of separation, of a life lived on one's own or of a new household of one's own, would have been interrupted or stopped by a more or less sudden return to the parental home because of a parent's demand or need for care. That demand or need, while perhaps resented, would also have been a predictable feature of life because everyone lived in a world in which one's family was the only recourse when such needs arose. For still others, a new home would—sooner or later—have to be shared with a mother or father (or with another elderly relative). Many new wives, in particular, would have discovered (if they did not already know) that marriage to somebody's son meant sharing space with and eventually taking care of that son's parent or parents.

Also, there were many young people who "served" within households as poor relations, as "adopted" children, or as straightforward employees. For them, caregiving was not just a sudden imposition on an independent real life. It was their ongoing, their real, their only working life.

Still, one should not overstate the differences between the emotional experiences of adult children a century ago and those today. If the testimony in law and equity cases about caretaking by the young of the old reveals anything, it is that then, as now, adult children would have known family life as fundamentally contradictory. Throughout the previous century, between the mid-eighteenth and the mid-nineteenth centuries, a market revolution may have led many young men and women to seek their fortunes away from the homes of their parents as it also reduced the significance of landed wealth as an organizing feature of family life. Yet, well into the twentieth century, even as New Jersey became more urbanized and less rural, the ambitions of many young men and women remained tied to their expectations of inheritance. Daughters still brought husbands home to live with their parents, just as many sons brought wives home. The core resource at issue in family negotiations was usually not pay or cash or the short-term profits of a family enterprise. Rather, it was almost always an inheritance, family property, to be distributed at death. Land—more precisely, the family home—often remained what was wanted most.[21]

By the second quarter of the twentieth century, there existed a legislatively articulated and publicly enforced law of adoption. Until then, however, many children and other younger people joined (or were joined to) households through a variety of mechanisms ranging from articles of apprenticeship and labor contracts through a continuum of explicit and informal adoptions. Many of those children, whatever the terms under which they arrived within households, became permanent parts of families. They might have stayed from bonds of love and gratitude, but they also remained because of the promise or the hope of inheritances.[22]

Nearly all adult children would have understood themselves as born (or placed) into families, those complex collectivities that were inescapably part of their psyches. Moreover, most would have lived much of their lives within those families. They would never fully escape them even after growing up and making new families. Insofar as adulthood meant growing away from families of origin, it would have been a tentative and incomplete separation. At any moment many might find themselves thrust back into childhood and into relationships that mimicked those that had preceded their adulthood. One need hardly add that the return into those relationships sometimes made them feel resentful and angry.

However, adult children were also free adult individuals, even within their families. They might have felt burdened by their responsibility to take care of their elderly parents, but that sense of obligation would have been what lawyers call a "mere" expectation: emotionally felt and perhaps intensely experienced but not one that could be coerced, imposed, or required (legal treatises of the time called it a "natural" obligation). No one—certainly not needy elderly parents—could make them do anything they did not want to do. Grown children could always leave if they chose not to stay and take care of their parents. No one could throw them into jail for doing so. No parents could drag them back if, as adults, the grown children chose to ignore them—their needs, their wants, and their cares. No parents could insist that they be provided with a home if an adult child would rather not offer one. No parents could keep an adult child in service if the terms of service were unsatisfactory. If adult children left and, in doing so, ignored the needs of their elders, those children might be marked as unloving and uncaring. However, they knew they had the right to be unloving and uncaring, ungrateful and callous, and to lead their own lives. That right was one meaning of what it meant to be a free American.[23]

Why the adult child has had little presence in American family history has a great deal to do with the assumption that American family life is and has long been organized around the nuclear family, which means that adult children are understood as having left home, married, and created new families when they became adults. Children ceased to exist as members of households when they grew up.[24] Then too, the inherited relational legal categories of "the law of persons"—particularly husband and wife and parent and (infant) child—have tended to define the realm of the family. The adult child is, definitionally, outside of those categories (which exclude much else about family life and history, including how siblings interacted with one another, grandparents, and the elderly, as well as the roles of more distant kin).[25]

I suspect, though, that the absence of the adult child from family history may have most to do with a widely shared and continuing intuition that the solidarity that joins an adult child to a family "of origin" stands in fundamental tension with individualism and individual freedom. Much recent historical writing challenges simple versions of that intuition. Scholars have explored how life within the modern family became increasingly premised on "the special responsibility that each person has for his or her own life."[26] They have detailed how, over time, the property-based powers of fathers and husbands were challenged and often destroyed as wives and unemancipated children were gradually acknowledged as the possessors of separate legal identities. Women and men—as wives and husbands and sometimes as "children"—became free contractual actors who could be punished or held liable for their actions but could not be prevented from exercising their inherent freedom as individuals to pursue their own lives. Scholars have revealed how, over the course of the long nineteenth century, young children also came to be understood as individuals in formation, who, as persons with special and individual needs, could make claims on the state for care and intervention.[27] Still, for all the recognition of such changes, much literature remains focused on "the family" as a special domain in which the individual was restrained and family members—that is, wives and husbands, as well as parents and small children—engaged with each other out of "love," that is, without an expectation of pay or of immediate compensation.[28]

Competent and knowing nineteenth- and early twentieth-century lawyers and judges certainly knew better even as they participated in and contributed to the ideological discourse of the family. They knew families to be filled with adults who were not household heads, adults who might or might not be the biological children of household heads. Webster's mid-nineteenth-century dictionary defined "the family" as "The collective body of persons who live in one house, and under one head or manager; a household, including parents, children, and servants, and, as the case may be, lodgers or boarders."[29] Such a definition, while it reveals an expanded population of the family, still masks the definitional difficulties that courts confronted in the situations that asked them to determine who was inside or outside the family and thus who was entitled to the benefits and obligated to perform the duties that came from being inside the family. Most important, it hides from us what a family was, which was a place where work occurred. This definition of the family would have seemed too obvious for words.

To survive and flourish, family members mobilized their own work and that of others. In a time before labor-saving technologies, when a decent life depended on living with others (with diverse skills) who could all work together, a family was, by its very nature, a complex enterprise in which everyone needed to work. Some of that work was directly and conventionally economic, wealth producing: farming, clearing land, cutting wood, working in stores, pooling wages, and "doing the books" (keeping records), particularly when only some family members were likely to be fully literate. Some of that work today would be labeled "care work": nursing the sick and the elderly, taking care of the younger children, cooking, cleaning, doing the laundry, being available to listen to and to talk with others. However, much of what family members did blurred the line between the two. Young men (and some young women) gave up jobs elsewhere to take care of family enterprises (and family members) so that family wealth would not dissipate. A young man cared for his father by taking over farming tasks or the family store or business so that his father could "retire." He also cared for his father by bringing home a wife who would do more direct care work. After a mother died, an older daughter gave up an opportunity to marry or to work away from home to take care of younger siblings; her willingness to do so allowed her father to continue his remunerative work.

It is impossible to understand family work and struggles over inheritance from the nineteenth century into the twentieth century without taking account of the relentless and noisy ideological insistence on the separation of "the family" from the world of work. Much nineteenth-century legal and social thought was committed to a vision of the family as something other than a realm for individualized economic strategizing and conflict, as not the workplace. However, it is important to emphasize the extent to which that vision grew within and out of a legal culture that had to deal constantly with the conflicts over family work carried on by individual family members, many of them adult children.[30]

What was a family? According to one familiar answer found throughout the public culture of nineteenth- and early twentieth-century America, a family was an institution where work occurred because of ties of love and care, not because of greed or economic calculations. Another answer, again a familiar one, described the family as an institution that provided resources and care for young children and for the elderly and the dependent, for those who could not work productively. (In this latter sense the family was an institution that has since been partially replaced by social security and public and private pensions.) Almost no one, on the other hand, except in the context of litigation, spoke publicly of the family as a location for dealing and bargaining by rational, self-interested actors. Those who participated in such negotiations and legal conflicts over family work probably only rarely disagreed with the public culture. They may often have hidden from themselves the contradictions inherent in what they were doing.

Here, however, families are studied as locales or arenas filled with men and women who held interdependent but conflicting life plans and identities.[31] The focus is on families within which competent parties negotiated and fought with each other over promises, inducements, commitments, and obligations and over differing understandings of needs and duties. For the most part those parties assumed that care and work within families needed to be paid for, although the currency used—love and guilt, as well as cash and land—varied dramatically. Much of the time family pay would be delayed until death, when inheritances would be used as a form of accounting and compensation. However, when care and work were not paid for or when they were paid for inadequately or incompletely, conflict and litigation would ensue.[32]

Meanwhile, the elderly were both a ubiquitous and a growing presence within nineteenth- and twentieth-century household life. However, like adult children, the old have remained relatively hidden in histories that continue to imagine that families were constituted by marriage and by the presence or absence of young children. It remains convenient to conceive of the old as a new "invention" and that they were not a significant part of any historical era until just yesterday. To put it differently, it is an implicit assumption that in the past death usually solved any problems that old age might have created if older people had lived longer.[33]

The problem of how to mobilize care for the elderly is as much a feature of every human society as is how children should be raised. However, in a nineteenth- and early twentieth-century society defined by mobility and free labor, securing that presence, attention, and work posed particular difficulties. The characteristic answer of many earlier societies to the problem of elder care, which was to draw (often coercively) on the labor and the resources of the next generation, was tested and challenged in the nineteenth-century United States in the face of a free labor market and widened geographic mobility, as well as reduced fertility. In some cultures, perhaps, older people could have relied on their status as heads of families, as patriarchs and matriarchs, to secure their needs and wants. In some cultures, resources predictably flowed upward from the young to the old. For most in the United States, by contrast, a characteristic family bargain for young men in many traditional cultures—wait and obey and eventually you will inherit, and then you can make your children wait and obey— had become much less attractive. One lesson of capitalism is always this: Why wait (for the death of a father), especially when so many possibilities appeared to lurk elsewhere, away from home and family?

For young women, too, distance, the presence of mobile and marriage-able young men, and a growing (but, of course, still comparatively limited) job market weakened the control of the old.

At the same time, the needs of the old did not lessen in nineteenth-century or indeed in early twentieth-century America. A relatively growing population of the elderly led somewhat longer lives and came by the late nineteenth century to expect a period of life not defined by daily and pervasive labor. However, everyone knew that such a period—call it, as they did, retirement—depended on the resources and the work of other family members. Older people may or may not have wanted the young in their households, and they almost certainly did not want to have to live in the households of their children or other younger relations. Still, they knew, as did all competent members of the culture, that care, when it was needed, ordinarily came from children and other relations. In a world with few labor-saving devices and in which only very wealthy older people would have possessed the disposable income that would have allowed them to purchase servant-based care, both care and retirement almost always required the direct presence, the attention, and the work of adult children (or of others who could substitute for adult children), that is, of free individuals who might otherwise have moved away from parents to wherever the jobs (and husbands) were.[34]

What did older people do with their properties? How did they use their accumulated resources to construct and to implement plans for old age in order to avoid going "over the hill to the poor-house"?

The answer to both questions was, of course, that they did many different things. What an older person did depended on the shifting negotiating positions and family circumstances of the old and the young within the family. It depended on the norms and practices of the communities within which the older person lived. In addition, the care and retirements that older people constructed reflected their individual familial, economic, and emotional situations. Some of the old, like some of the young, were quarrelsome; some were childlike; and some misunderstood their bargaining positions. Some felt bound by their language; others were profligate with promises. Some demanded too much—care, attention, loyalty—and received nothing. Others broke promises they had made. Some relied naïvely on cultural expectations of care or on love. Some felt abandoned and resourceless. Gender norms shaped strategies and behavior, as did the potential or actual availability of a spouse as an alternative caretaker. Some daughters could be imposed on or fooled into staying on, but other daughters rejected or avoided gendered cultural expectations. Men with property could often remarry younger women when their wives died, thereby threatening the inheritance of the children from the earlier marriage. A surprising number of older people turned to "strangers," that is, to nonrelations—to lessees, neighbors, handymen, or housekeepers—when their children became unavailable or unwilling or were nonexistent, offering an inheritance in exchange for care and work. The freedom that possession of property gave to the old was both an individual and an individualized freedom. A committed nominalist could find 200 different choices among the 200 odd cases in the New Jersey case records, and these are only the situations that ended up in court.

Given the availability of remunerative work elsewhere, why did younger people work for their elderly parents and other older relatives? By the mid-nineteenth century, it had clearly become an inadequate answer to say simply that they had stayed because they were members of a family. When older family members with some wealth made promises to younger family members without wealth in order to get the help or work they needed and wanted, they treated those children and others as contractually competent individuals. Sometimes children became, in effect, employees; more often they became partners or purchasers of "future interests" in property, with time and labor as the consideration, the quid pro quo. Later on in those families' lives, when the promises and negotiations between older property owners and adult children were challenged in litigation over compensation and inheritance, many judges and lawyers reconstructed family members as participants in a labor negotiation who bargained hard with one another. The younger people had worked for the old because the old had offered them the functional equivalent of a labor contract. Each "side," in this rendering, had calculated closely and carefully over individualized self-interest and had worked to get the best deal, to extract the most, from those they were negotiating with. That vision of canny and hard bargaining probably exaggerated what had usually gone on, but it was also not a vision without roots in an experiential reality.

When attention is focused on the elderly and the adult child, the period from the mid-nineteenth to the mid-twentieth century stands revealed as a paradoxical moment in American (and, indeed, Western) family history. One might call it the moment when, for significant numbers of Americans, contract created or re-created the family as a corporate unit.[35] From the perspective of older persons, the ability to distribute their wealth through inheritance became both a measure of individual freedom (as one early case put it, "The power of disposing of property is an estimable privilege of the old")[36] and a way to impose (or perhaps to create) traditional obligations. From the perspective of the young, inheritance became both an occasion for contractual freedom (one made a choice to go home and thus to forego other opportunities in the wider world because of the deal one had made) and an opportunity to receive what one was entitled to because one had done as one ought as a good and loving child or family member. One effect of such promises was often to make people assume or to reassume (or to act as if they assumed) ascriptive roles within a hierarchical, noncontractual family. Sons contracted to be "sons." Daughters contracted to be "daughters." Not infrequently other relatives, nonrelatives, or distant relatives who were hired as employees or brought in as "help" became like "sons" or "daughters" over time. Almost all of the contracting meant to produce something other than a business enterprise or a partnership. At minimum, the goal was to create or re-create a familial or family-like relationship; the hope was that a "real" family would result.

Often those older people who made promises in order to benefit from the work of other family members did so in part because the promise of future family property was the only resource they possessed. They lacked a cash flow—or even any cash at all. They may or may not have intended to commit themselves by promising to convey family holdings and wealth to the particular individual whose work was being mobilized. They may or may not have wanted those family holdings and wealth to become a legacy for the next generation as a way to construct "the family" as a continuing institution, in part defined by its "properties." Nonetheless, they needed to do something to mobilize the care or the support that occurred only within a family. And bought "love" was perhaps better than no "love" at all.

The same held for those without wealth: the adult children whose labor was their resource and the "employees" in the labor negotiations. The reason they stayed or came home to work was complicated and often based on contradictory motives. They wanted recognition for their individual work and contributions; they wanted to make a good deal and to advance economically, but they also wanted to be or to remain part of a family.

In the chapters that follow, I begin by exploring the ways older people used promises—not transfers or executed contracts, but promises—to keep the young close. This first part of the book is organized around what I call the King Lear problem, the problem of not giving up control and power and property too early, in the context of a mobile and free society—America in the nineteenth century—that drew children and other younger people away from the old. In the later chapters of the book, I explore the moral and legal strategies of younger people, the promisees, who had not received what they thought they had been promised, what they thought they had worked for. In the middle, in between those two parts, I focus on what happened when needs overwhelmed strategies, when things fell apart.

Part One

Planning for Old Age

Keep also as much of your property, if you have any, in your own hand as is necessary for your own support, and make not yourselves dependent on the most affectionate and obedient children. They will be more affectionate and more respectful when you are not dependent.

Archibald Alexander, "Reflections on Old Age," in William Edward Schenck, ed., *Nearing Home,* 1868

Chapter One

Of Helplessness and Power

In 1849 James W. Davison was in his mid-sixties. He and his wife and a variety of other relations lived on a farm of approximately one hundred acres on the border between Middlesex and Monmouth counties in central New Jersey. By then he had given four older sons nearby farms of roughly similar size, although of somewhat lesser value. He had four daughters who still needed marriage "portions." He was, so others portrayed him later on, no longer energetic, and he suffered from some kind of speech impediment (perhaps as a result of Parkinson's or one or more small strokes, to speak the language of twenty-first-century medicine). Only his immediate family could understand his words, which meant that he was unable to conduct ordinary business with strangers.[1]

He needed help. Like other property owners in nineteenth-century America, he secured that help by making a promise.

His youngest son, James (Jimmy), was about nineteen and still living at home, and it was to this son that James W. Davison made the following promise: "If I paid off the girls and kept him and my mother, I could have the farm when he was done with it." At least that is how in 1860 son James remembered his father's 1849 promise. Son James also remembered that he had agreed to these terms. James stayed on for the next ten years of his life, and he worked full time and hard on his father's farm. He did so, in the rendition of William Leupp, who would become his lawyer, "in full reliance [on his father's promise] . . . that in so doing he was making some provision for his own settlement in life . . . as well as discharging the duty of a son towards his parents."[2]

What did "keeping" his father mean? James's work made it possible for his father to give marriage portions to several daughters: $700 to two of James's older sisters, $900 to a third, and $1,200 to Ida, the youngest sister, who, like James, had stayed on to take care of their parents and who married only in 1858, when she was twenty-three. (It might be that Ida, too, had responded to a promise, perhaps for a larger marriage portion, in return for staying and putting off marriage.) James made improvements to the property, including "ditching" the land. He negotiated with outsiders and collected debts for his father. His mother died in 1855. He himself married early in 1857 to Jane Perrine, a neighbor's daughter. It may well be that marrying, in effect finding a woman who could replace sister Ida and his mother as a caregiver, was a central aspect of what it meant for James to "keep" his father. It, too, was probably part of the implicit deal.

When he married, James Davison built a small house on the farm at a cost of $300 to $400. He and his bride lived in the small house for a few months until his sister Ida left their father's house to live with her husband. Then the couple moved into the larger house because his father, James W. Davison, needed them, particularly Jane.[3]

For a decade, James "kept" his father as he had promised to do. However, in June 1859, something happened. Or did not happen. Whatever did or did not happen, the result was chaos.

According to the old man, he watched one afternoon as his daughter-in-law went into a room in the "back house" with one of his grandsons, James Davison Herbert. James W. went out of the kitchen door and around the smokehouse, and then he lit his pipe and walked back. As he watched, "they was in the back house and James Herbert was by her and busy with her." He had seen them, he was convinced, "in a position that left no doubt on his mind of a criminal intimacy." "Jane appeared to be setting on the seat," and James Davison Herbert was "on his knees before her."

James W. Davison was a good church member, and he would not have his home turned into a bawdy house. Jane would have to leave. She was, he declared, "nothing but a damned bitch[,] and he wanted her to take her things and go."[4]

Both Jane and James Davison Herbert denied that anything "improper" had occurred, and apparently no one—in the family or in the community—believed James W.'s story. Everyone took James W. Davison's story as an old man's fantasy. According to Jane, who was then three months pregnant, she had long felt uncomfortable in James W. Davison's household, ever since Ida had married and moved away. She did not like being the only woman in the house. She had asked James several months earlier whether he would hire a woman to help her out around the house. She had even offered to pay the woman's board herself. "She didn't want her to do no work—she wanted her company." Meanwhile, James W. followed her around while she worked, talking about how James "wasn't good for nothing" and saying that an old man "wasn't like [an] old woman," that he still could satisfy her. Jane had told him that "she didn't want to hear more of his blackguard talk[;] she had heard too much of it." She also complained to James, who thought he had handled it by telling his father to stop talking like that.

According to James W., he had not followed Jane around and made improper proposals even though Jane had given him "reason to do it." One Sunday, so he reported in testimony, he was reading in his bedroom when she came in. There was "no body about the house but us two, and [she] squatted down on her hunkers right above me but I said nothing. Then she got up and come to me and had little Peter [her son] and she held him out before me and asked him who that was and I held my hands out to the boy to come to me. I had always handled him a good deal and he had got so he liked to come to me. Then she set him on my knees." Later, he reported, she had told her husband, James, "that I had took hold of her." But he "thought Jane was as willing to come to me as the little boy." According to James W., he had "scolded" his daughter-in-law the next day. "Says I this kind of work is not right. . . . I told her if I had went into her room I wouldn't blame her, but she came into my bedroom."[5]

At first, James Davison had thought his wife should just put up with his father's talk, as did Jane's own father.[6] Still, once James W. accused Jane of adultery with his grandson, James defended his wife. He confronted his father, who insisted Jane "was a 'whore'—he said she was a damned bitch of a whore." James W. also apparently questioned the legitimacy of his son James's children. (James testified that "there was something said about my children by my father, I don't remember exactly, he made some statements about my children which I don't wish to repeat, don't know as there is any good in it.")[7] After that, James, Jane, and their children moved to Jane's father's place. James also warned his father that he would do what he could to stop him from spreading his stories.

But there was no stopping James W. Davison. James Davison Herbert testified that he ran into James W. in the smokehouse. "Granddaddy," he asked, "are you going to stick to what you said?" "Yes, I'll have to now." A few days later Peter Perrine, Jane's father and a neighbor, went to the Davison house to reason with James W. In that conversation, James W. apparently promised that if Jane delivered a child before April of the next year, he would concede that he had "belied" her. Later he denied offering that concession. Perrine threatened him with suit for slander if he continued spreading the "disgraceful" story. James W. said he could "kiss his ass." He said the same thing to James, when James again confronted him.[8]

Peter Perrine and James went to one of James's older brothers, John, to ask him to help restrain their father. James told John he was thinking of charging their father with slander. John told him he "wouldn't do no such a thing." He recommended that James go back and continue to live in the little house he had built on the property and hire a woman to care for their father in the big house, and, implicitly, to wait for their father to die. However, James did not believe he could stay on the property as before. "He said he couldn't do it. He said he had worked some eight or nine years then, and might work as much more, and the old man would turn him away[,] and he would get nothing." He thought about taking his family and going elsewhere; at the same time he also discussed with others how to formalize his relationship with his father by taking a lease or making an agreement to farm the place "on shares." He also continued to consider whether to bring a slander suit against his father.[9]

Still, after a few days, James, Jane, and their children moved back from Peter Perrine's house into the small house. For the rest of the summer, James continued to work his father's farm, while James Davison Herbert and Hulick Cavalier, an eleven-year-old nephew who also lived with them, brought meals to James W., who lived alone in the house. During that time James W. also continued to tell others what he believed he had seen his daughter-in-law do.

One day older brother John and another brother, Reuben, came to see James while he was threshing grain at Peter Perrine's farm. Reuben said he thought that he could get $2,000 out of their father if James would agree to leave and not sue. The money was meant to cover both James's lost wages and his willingness to drop the suit. (Later, during cross-examination, Reuben said he thought the sum was more than James deserved because he had had his board and clothing throughout the previous decade.) James rejected the offer. One also suspects that the offer infuriated him and drove him toward further actions.[10]

In September, to vindicate his wife's "character and honor, and evince her innocence," James Davison brought slander charges against his father, James W. Davison. James W. was arrested, and then he had to find men who would stand security for him so that he would not be jailed.[11] He went to find his son Joseph, but Joseph was not at home, so he went on to Reuben's place. Reuben agreed, and the two of them went back to find Joseph. The three of them rode on to a lawyer's office, where the two sons agreed to secure their father's presence at trial. Then they drove back to Joseph's place, where James W. was to stay for the night since he now felt afraid that he might be poisoned if he went home. "If they would do one thing they would do another."

In the wagon, on the way back to Joseph's place, the old man made Reuben an offer. Would he take the farm and "keep him"? Reuben said no; he was afraid "they [presumably, the local community] would all be affronted about it if I took it." (The offer was at first made only to Reuben because at that moment Joseph was "in the woods. He had got out to answer the call of nature.") However, the next day Reuben went over to Joseph's place and talked the matter over. The two of them decided to take the place together. At the later trial, Reuben offered the following reconstruction of that decision: He and Joseph had not accepted their father's offer out of a desire or an expectation that they should get more of their father's estate. He and Joseph were afraid that, if they did not take formal title to the property, the property would be lost in a judgment against their father. (Evidently, the two brothers presumed that their father would lose the slander case.) They did not wish to harm their brother James (although they were obviously willing to keep him from recovering damages in his suit). "My father wished me to take it, to keep him," was how Reuben put it. Their overarching goal was to maintain and to care for their father. When asked whether he believed the property would ever be theirs, Reuben answered in the affirmative—if there was anything left after paying for James W.'s care. (Meanwhile, their father, when told of their decision, was relieved. "He said if he had all New York he couldn't help himself. I[t] would do him no good. . . . [I]t would do him no good as he couldn't help himself.")[12]

Back the three of them then went to the lawyer's office, where the father conveyed his farm to Reuben and Joseph for $5 paid by each and a promise by each to maintain him for the remainder of his life. That included obligations to pay the expenses of his last illness and his funeral, including a "decent" headstone. The next day, September 21, 1859, James received the following notice:

To Mr. James Davison, junior.

Take notice that your service is not wanting on my farm, now conveyed away to my two sons, Reuben and Joseph Davison; and I have given them immediate possession of the same; and if you continue thereon, I shall hold you as a trespasser, and proceed against you according to law; and, further, I shall not want any more of your help to gather in my crop, at present on said farm.[13]

Eviction proceedings began almost immediately. During the fall, Joseph and Reuben came to take possession. According to James, Joseph threw down fences that he had put up, took "his" horses, "his" apples, "his" corn, and "his" other "things" out of the barn and then sold all of them at auction. When James tried to "forbid" him from throwing out "his" hay, Joseph said, "What the hell do I care for you[r] forbidding?" James gave up and left the property, including the small house he had built for his family.[14]

However, in May 1860 James presented a petition to the chancellor of the New Jersey Court of Equity. His father had made a contract to give him the property at death, and James had fulfilled the terms of the contract. He had given up years of his life to serve his difficult father. He and his wife had worked hard and well, and now his father and two brothers had cheated him out of what he had earned. He had no remedy at law since there was no written contract, and his oral agreement with his father violated the Statute of Frauds. Thus, as a formal matter, his brothers had legally evicted him. Only a court of equity could declare fraudulent and void the transfer of the land from James W. to Reuben and Joseph, who were in no sense "bona fide purchasers" of the property. Both of them had ample notice of James's preexisting claim. He also needed the "extraordinary" powers of equity to declare that he would be entitled to the property on his father's death.[15]

A court of equity justified its intervention into a legal situation—its power to act, its jurisdiction—by invoking and describing the inadequacies of common-law damage remedies.[16] Thus, James Davison's petition had to describe him as evicted legally. Equitable remedies became necessary because the common law, as applied to the distinctive facts of a particular case, would produce or reinforce injustice. Equity jurisdiction existed for situations in which there were either no legal rights or inadequate ones or in which legal rights—that is, those identified with the common law—were being mobilized for unjust or fraudulent ends. A chancellor (the judge who presided over a court of equity) clarified the need "to do" equity by explaining how "legal" rights were being mobilized wrongfully or unjustly. For those who demonstrated their need or right to an equitable remedy, a court of equity offered particularized remedies, discretionary remedies, in place of the generalized justice that was the mark of common law jurisprudence.[17]

Much of the testimony James Davison's lawyer produced in support of James's petition went to the quantity and quality of his work. (For everyone who testified, Jane's work was either incorporated into James's or not considered legally relevant.) Robert D. Davison, a next-door neighbor, testified that James had done all of the work on the farm for the past ten years and that the farm was now in much better shape than it had been before James took over. The husband of one of James's sisters reported that James "worked harder than I would like to work." Allison P. Jamison, first married to James's sister Mary and then, after her death, married to sister Ida, agreed. According to Sarah Davison, a seventy-two-year-old cousin, James "always treated his father right; he always did what was right; and I never heard or saw anything amiss in his conduct. In sickness you know there is a great deal to do, and he always did what he could do—night and day."[18] According to another witness, whenever he wanted anything, James W. told him to go to James. James W., on the other hand, was "about doing nothing." Allison Jamison could remember him only gathering a little corn. Furthermore, when asked by neighbors about any business relating to the farm, James W. always referred them to James. James W.'s own witnesses agreed that James W. no longer did any work on the farm.[19]

In their responses to James's petition, Reuben, Joseph, and James W. all admitted that James had worked for and with his father on the farm, although James W. insisted that he (James W.) was still "accustomed to a laborious and active life" and that until two years ago he had "continued without intermission to work and be actively employed in and about the business of the said homestead farm and participated in the manual labor done on said farm." They acknowledged that James had acted as his father's agent, but that was solely because of James W.'s speech impediment or "nervous disorder." When they identified him as an agent, they meant that he was a species of servant, not someone entitled to an expectation of ownership.

What was the meaning of James's work on the farm and for his father? According to Reuben, Joseph, and James W., James Davison had remained on "the homestead" "voluntarily and of his own accord," not because of a continuing and binding agreement. Indeed, when asked whether he had ever asked James to stay, his father testified: "No. I tried to coax him to quit." James was always at liberty to leave, and, if he had done so, he would not have "violated or infringed any agreement." That he stayed did not demonstrate the existence of an agreement. He stayed because he evidently "found it more for his convenience . . . and comfort to do so." Also, presumably because he harbored "the hope that his . . . father would by will give him . . . the said homestead or some part of it." The work he had done was nothing more than the work that any family member would do as part of a going enterprise. Even his occupancy of the small house was always with the permission of James W., "at his will and pleasure and was liable to be terminated at any moment he chose." Reuben, Joseph, and James W. also offered into evidence instances of James's "rudeness, violent temper and gross incivility" (including an argument that had ended with James's pushing "the old man" on to the stove), as well as moments when he had seemed to concede that he was living on the land on speculation, without any real entitlement or any binding contract.[20]

However, after several days of testimony, Chancellor Green ruled in James Davison's favor. The chancellor summarized the testimony, giving much more credence to James's witnesses than to those produced by the defendants. He noted that James W. had made a will in 1856 that declared that he had already given all of his sons except the complainant "their portions" in personal and real estate and had made "advancements" to his elder daughters. In this will, the whole of his remaining real and personal estate went to his two youngest children, James and Ida (then still unmarried), who had stayed home with him, and he gave the farm specifically to James. Yet, three years later, "without any failure of service," James was "turned out of possession without remuneration for his services, and the entire real estate of the father [was] transferred to his brothers." The chancellor found that he did not have to decide whether this "change of purpose" was the result of "the painful difficulty" between James W. and Jane or the result of "the contrivance" of Reuben and Joseph. Either way the result was a situation of "peculiar and extreme hardship" for James.[21]

Did that "hardship" entitle James Davison to relief? On the one hand, "the rule" was "well settled" that if James had worked "gratuitously" (i.e., merely out of a "hope" that he would eventually receive a legacy from his father), he had no right to compensation, no matter how extreme the hardship. His father retained his right to change his mind. That is what testator's freedom meant, and testator's freedom was a core value in the law. In this case, however, James had proven that he had "rendered" his services because of a "distinct understanding" that he would receive the farm on his father's death. His father had told witnesses that his will was "as good as a deed" and that the only reason he had not conveyed the property immediately to James was that "he had been advised by a friend not to put all his property out of his hands in his lifetime." The fact that, as the defendants' own witnesses conceded, James had been offered $2,000 to abandon his slander case and "in satisfaction of his interest in the farm," suggested that there was a preexisting contract between James and his father. Otherwise, "it is difficult to understand why so large a sum should be offered in satisfaction of his claim." That the contract had not been written down made it more difficult to prove its terms. Nonetheless, the fact that it was an oral contract did not, according to the chancellor, constitute a valid objection to its enforcement. James had "served" his father "upon the faith of the contract . . . faithfully, and to his father's satisfaction." There had been "part performance" on the complainant's part, and part performance took the case out of the operation of the Statute of Frauds.

The court thus decreed that James was entitled to the farm on his father's death. That meant at minimum that the deed conveying the farm to Reuben and Joseph was "set aside" immediately "as fraudulent and void."

The chancellor concluded his opinion with the probably vain wish that the conflict within the Davison family might be "amicably adjusted." The father remained entitled to "the enjoyment" of his farm for the rest of his life and to the "services" of his son James (although one wonders whether anyone thought that Jane should have to continue to take care of her father-in-law). If the father refused to accept James's work and help, it might be necessary for the court to make "further directions" both for the management of the farm and for the care of the father, who could evidently no longer feed himself or take care of the house. Yet for the moment the court put off ordering any further specific performance.[22]

As happens so often, several mysteries followed that apparent conclusion. Who did live with and care for the old man for the four years he would survive beyond the chancellor's decree in February 1861? What happened to the slander suit? One assumes it was settled. In any case, it does not appear in any of the surviving records. James's new lawyer eventually filed a bill for costs with the court in August 1864. Did that mean that the family had continued negotiating for three more years?[23]

James W. Davison died on May 16, 1865, at age eighty, and he was buried in the cemetery of the Perrineville Presbyterian Church. His son James must have "quieted" his title in the "homestead" soon thereafter. In the 1870 census, James Davison is recorded as the head of the farm household. None of the three children who were identified as part of his household at that time, Hannah, Mary, and Rebecca, would survive to adulthood. Meanwhile, James and Jane Davison continued to have children. Of the nine or ten children that Jane gave birth to, the only ones to survive infancy were born in 1870, 1872, and 1877. James would die in 1898; Jane would live on into the new century. In a 1902 biographical register appended to a history of the New Jersey coast, their son John, born in 1872, was described as "one of the youngest, yet most prosperous, farmers in Middlesex county," with seventy-five acres of "highly productive land." He had apparently married a cousin, the daughter of John J. Perrine. His father, James Davison, was described as having been "a man of excellent repute, a practical farmer[,] and a true and worthy citizen."[24]

Davison v. Davison was one of a number of legally similar cases that appeared fairly suddenly in the mid-nineteenth century. In these cases, adult children or others who cared for those who were old or had a disability sued for compensation for the work they had done (or claimed to have done). Prior to about 1850, one barely sees evidence of such conflicts in the case records. The earliest published U.S. case in which a child sued in equity to enforce an oral contract relying on "part performance" (as James Davison had sued) occurred in 1832 in Delaware, and in that case the child lost. The first case in which a relative won, while making such a claim, was in New York in 1846.[25] However, between 1848 and 1861, when *Davison* was decided, eight New Jersey cases were brought by children and other relatives who had expected to be remembered in the wills of older people for whom they had worked. From then on, the flow of cases was continuous until the 1950s.[26]

In nearly all of those cases, as in *Davison,* the "complainant" (or petitioner or plaintiff) comes across as a sympathetic subject with whom a twenty-first-century reader will naturally identify. It does not take a lot of work to turn the youngest son, James, into the hero of a folktale inhabited by archetypal characters drawn from an agrarian past: a chosen and mistreated son, a foolish father (old man), an innocent wife, and scheming brothers. Although there are debts, lawsuits, and a wider commercial world lurking around the periphery, the testimony produces an impression of a closed world of family and neighbors, indeed a world in which many of the neighbors are also family members. In addition, the chancellor becomes something of a fatherly "good king," who, while doing the discretionary work that is the distinctive mandate of courts of equity, sets the disordered world aright and thereby allows the story to end with a happy resolution.

Indeed, part of the allure of such cases is their apparently universal, folktale-like qualities. Sons and daughters (or, as in *Davison,* a son and a daughter-in-law) were given difficult tasks (taking care of needy parents, maintaining and improving property, staying home when they would rather leave). They faced expected and unexpected difficulties—tests—as they worked out a destiny defined by those tasks and by private obligations situated within families. They needed to overcome burdens identified with the land, with parents, with siblings and others. When courts ruled in favor of those situated as James Davison was, it feels morally satisfying. When courts did not, as often happened, it offers us a familiar opportunity to distinguish morality and right judgment from "the law" made by fallible people.

Alternatively, one might imagine *Davison v. Davison* through a historically conventional understanding of American kinship and family structure. This is an understanding that situates parents' responsibilities for their children and the overarching significance of the marriage bond at the center of what the family "means," as well as one that emphasizes the individual freedom of the child within the family, particularly the male child.[27] The story of the case might be restated then along the following lines: James was an adult young man in the late 1840s. As such, he would expect to establish his own household by marrying and having children. Within the legal culture of the Anglo-American world, he would not have understood himself as bound to remain with or be responsible for the care of his father and mother. As a free young man living in an expanding capitalist America, where the labor of such young men was in constant demand, he would have stayed on to take care of his parents only if there were an agreement, an exchange, giving him something special for the work and time he dedicated to their care. When he agreed to remain with his parents, he had burdened himself by undertaking exceptional tasks that he had no duty to assume, tasks that as a result could be understood only through the lens of contract. Like other adult young men in that culture, he would have felt entitled to have a home of his own once he married, a separate space in which to live with his wife and children. When James's sister Ida moved away and his father's care demanded that he and his wife move back into his father's house, that, too, would have been understood as an additional burden that gave evidence of his claim to be living and working there because of an agreement with his father.

Did that mean that he was therefore entitled to receive the "homestead" farm even after he had decided to sue his father? Or did his decision to initiate legal proceedings constitute a breach of the contract, so that his father was entitled to give the farm to others, in this case to his brothers? Those questions, certainly as Chancellor Green answered them, presumed a particular understanding of what family meant and of what marriage required of a man and his wife. Jane Davison would certainly have known that, as James's wife, she would be responsible for the household, for the cooking and the cleaning, and perhaps that would have required some tolerance of a difficult father-in-law. Indeed, putting up with in-laws was probably part of her understanding of what it meant to be a wife. Still, what she had had to put up with from James W. obviously went too far and was not part of the bargain. By contrast, James W., Joseph, and Reuben Davison all characterized James as having dishonored the family when he brought an action for slander against his father. Insofar as they would have acknowledged that James's work for his father implied any contract with his father (which, of course, they denied at trial), such a contract could not have survived such a breach of his obligations to protect and sustain the family's honor. Whatever promises James W. had made to James were obviously contingent on James's loyalty to James W., and James had proven himself disloyal. However, from the chancellor's perspective, as well as James's, marriage again trumped other relationships. Marriage separated James from his family of birth and required a distinct and intense form of loyalty that weakened other kinship ties. James's connections with his father and his other kin were far less important than his relationship with his wife, who was entitled to his trust and protection. In addition, at least according to the chancellor, James Davison should not suffer for having done exactly what the legal culture asked him to do as a husband.

Of course, framed either through the lens of a folktale or of an imagined American nuclear family structure, we bleach out many of the characters that shaped the conflict in the case. *Davison v. Davison* was not simply a story of struggle between a father and his adult son. Others—siblings, cousins, nephews, brothers-in-law, a father-in-law—swarmed through the testimony. Perrines and Davisons had intermarried for generations (and would continue to do so). Almost everyone who testified was a relation of some sort. Moreover, the questions of what it meant to belong to a family and what was expected of a family member were inescapably present. James's long-standing relations with his brothers are hard to disentangle from the mess that was *Davison v. Davison*. In this case, as in many others, the underlying conflict was both between parent and child and between contending and competing siblings. At law, brothers and sisters were not locked in formal relationships, as husband and wife and parent and child were. Legally speaking, they were strangers to one another. Yet, these legal "strangers" were obviously enmeshed in each other's lives. The Davison brothers all lived close, on land given them by their father. Also, they all felt at least some responsibility for his care. Meanwhile, Peter Perrine spent a great deal of time "advising" all of the various Davisons on how they should behave. He clearly assumed that Davison family business was his business as well, both before and after his daughter's marriage into the family.[28] In addition, what of the young men living with the Davisons? James Davison Herbert, who was both a grandson of one James and a nephew of the other, was identified in the trial as living with James Davison (the younger) under articles of agreement, perhaps an apprenticeship, perhaps in a less formalized "placing out" arrangement. Why Hulick Cavalier, another young nephew, was living with James and Jane was never articulated in the testimony. He may, like so many children in mid-nineteenth-century households, have been an informally adopted child. However, he certainly had not been legally adopted, and no one described him as "belonging" to

James and Jane. These two young men were never identified as servants or help, but they were also not entirely part of the family, whichever "family"—James's or James W.'s—one chooses to focus on.

Most of all, in making the story about James Davison, the son, who is, after all, the winner in the case, we lose the ability to see the family as James W. Davison worked to construct it. Plus, James W. Davison becomes nothing but James Davison's problem. Now, it is important not to deny a messy reality. By the end of the 1850s, James W. Davison had become a problem for himself, for James Davison, and for several others. He was a widower who could no longer care for himself. He was dependent and physically needy, and he may have been somewhat demented and a bit paranoid. However, a decade earlier, in 1849, when his aging had first become a problem for him, he had handled it by making use of a variety of cultural, economic, and legal resources. The case of *Davison v. Davison* was a direct result of plans he had made then and implemented over the next decade.

What happens when we shift our point of view from the child to the parent? Our attention moves away from James W. Davison's helplessness, as it was by the time the case came to trial. Instead, we explore his earlier strategic behavior: the ways he mobilized the work and care of his children by his use of the promise of inheritance. Our point of view shifts away from the familiar image of a child struggling to achieve independence from parents. We focus instead on a parent who had resolved to prepare for old age.

To reach old age, that is, to survive after age sixty in reasonable health, was a legitimate expectation for someone like James W. Davison, who was a moderately well-off farmer of the mid-nineteenth century. Indeed, if one survived the various risks of infancy, young men and women, say at age fifteen, could look forward to a life that would predictably stretch forward well into their sixties and possibly beyond. For families like the Davisons, death was still an ordinary presence in a way that we might find unendurable. Still, it was the death of children (James and Jane would lose at least six children, none of whom reached adolescence) that typified the ordinariness of death in life. Middle-aged men and women faced fewer risks.[29]

Old age was not merely a demographic fact, a percentage of a whole population, or an experience for a small though growing fraction of the population, although it was all those things as well. In 1849 old age was also, as it had been for centuries in the Western world, an alluring but dangerous prospect, a hoped-for achievement, one that shaped the lives of men and women while they were vital and competent and in relative control of their own affairs. Old age offered the possibility of "retirement," a word that did not mean exactly what we intend by it today (it certainly did not suggest an expectation that the retirees would "consume" their accumulated property) but that did suggest respite from a life of hard work, of a happy period in which one did not have to struggle to survive, of a time when others took over daily labors (without denying one's continuing power as the possessor of property).[30] In a world of private lives, private life plans, and private law, old age became a goal, a (perhaps *the*) culturally legitimate reason for accumulation, investment, and strategic planning. Yet old age also threatened decrepitude, disability, dementia, and despair. How to make it the former and to prevent (or at least delay) the latter were tasks that required planning and the mobilization of whatever resources one had accumulated by middle age.

In an age before labor-saving devices made it imaginable for an older person to live alone, before social security and public and private pension systems allowed men and women to "earn" the right not to work after a particular age, and before the existence of a thick market of institutions and entrepreneurs dedicated to marketing services and care to the middle- and upper-class elderly, the core need was the direct labor and attention of others. Who were those others? Except for the very rich and the poor, the answer was almost universally family members. And inheritance was the hook that mobilized the attention and the work of those family members.

However, drawing on the labor of children required planning. Male children no longer assumed that staying home and serving parents was the best option in terms of their own economic futures. Daughters, likewise, married men who lived in and moved to places far from their parents (and an increasing number of daughters would leave home with or without marriage to search for work themselves). Parents, the soon-to-be-old, could not rely on custom and culture to secure a good and cared-for future or to keep caregivers close.[31]

Instead, many, like James W. Davison, engaged in a complicated dance to draw the young in to the labor of care, a move that was fraught with risk. On the one side lay what one might call the King Lear problem: If property were transferred too quickly, too finally, too securely, then one placed oneself at the mercy of one's children. Nothing protected one. One could not trust to love or duty alone. A lyric of the popular song version of "Over the Hill to the Poor-House" made the moral explicit: "The boys grew to manhood. I gave them / A deed for the farm, aye, and more. / I gave them this house they were born in, / And now I'm turned out from its door."[32] Only a foolish man or woman, someone like Lear, gave up the power and security that property offered. Once property was gone, one faced the indignity of living within a child's household or, worse yet, living alone.

Sermons and advice manuals emphasized the same point. Archibald Alexander, who taught at the Princeton Theological Seminary through the first half of the nineteenth century, advised the old to keep "as much of your property, if you have any, in your own hand as is necessary for your own support, and make not yourselves dependent on the most affectionate and obedient children. They will be more affectionate and more respectful when you are not dependent." William S.

Plumer, a Baptist theologian, wrote in a similar way: "If you have property, retain exclusive control of enough to keep you from want. A dependent old age may be unavoidable, and when it is, should be borne submissively. But it is a great trial. If men will treat you well without property, they will also if you have your own means. The reverse of this is not *always* true." In 1868 Henry Ward Beecher advised the old to show "foresight" in preparing for old age and not to depend on Providence. He believed "it would be better that the father should not be dependent upon his children at any period of his life." There might, he allowed, be "something beautiful . . . in the thought of a parent leaning on the shoulders of those whom he has reared." On the other hand, there was "something more beautiful in the thought of a man leaning upon his own staff." The editor of the *American Farmer* editorialized as follows in 1892: "No matter how good, how affectionate, how tender, or how generous children seem to be, never, as you value your own happiness and their future peace, put all your property into their hands, trusting to them to give you whatever you need for your subsistence. . . . Do not imagine that putting everything out of your hands, leaving you free, will give you any permanent pleasure. . . . Let your children make their way as you made yours. It will be time enough for them to have what is yours when you are finally through with it all." Seven years later, a magazine column designed for farmers' wives made the same point in different words: "I wish I could reach the ear of every aged person whether man or woman. I would say this: do not put your property out of your hands. As long as you live keep what you have in your own name, be it much or little. . . . It is a most conclusive way of assuring careful and considerate treatment to have the reins in your hands as regards property."[33]

Yet, on the receiving end of that advice, old people (or middle-aged people contemplating their hoped-for old age) knew that their children had economic options and opportunities, many of which would draw them far away, options and opportunities that would make them unavailable as caretakers. The culture taught children to resent and to resist assertions of parental power. Ordinarily, young men did not willingly subordinate their lives and their ambitions within a parental domain. Leaving home, in effect leaving parents to fend for themselves, had become a cultural norm.[34] Daughters' situations were surely different. Yet not so much.

Sentimental songs endlessly recycled images of the lost world of the "old folks" at home, but the point of those songs was never that one ought to have stayed and cared. Rather, it was all about a regret or an ambivalence about choices made. As everyone knew, freedom and happiness meant moving away. The 1852 "Young Folks from Home," published as a companion piece to Stephen Foster's "Old Folks at Home," began this way: "Young folks from home, how gaily speed de hours." Then, in the second verse is this observation: "Young folks from home, how happy dey all seem." In almost all such songs, old folks would be returned to, but only at the end, at death, too late.[35]

One might well imagine that for older people such songs described nightmare scenarios and stood as warnings. There was nothing good about being "old folks" *alone* at home. There was nothing good about young folks getting back home in time for a funeral. One wanted a full household of family members dedicated to one's continuing care and support. One needed ways to convince younger people to stay at home—your home. However, one needed to convince them to stay without giving up one's property, one's security.

How to make them stay and not just for a little while? How to do that while retaining control and without giving up property? These were tests of old age.

In 1849, at about the same time that James W. Davison made his promise to his youngest son, a forty-nine-year-old Ruth W. Buzby was working at securing her own care for the future. Her story, as it also worked its way toward a legal conflict, reveals another version of how older persons might use their property to good advantage.

In 1819, when Ruth was nineteen, she had married Asher Buzby, who was about six years older than she was. They had farmed in Mannington in Salem County in southern New Jersey. They were both members of the Society of Friends. Between 1820 and 1827 she gave birth to at least four children, two sons and two daughters. One of the sons died in infancy; the second, Nathan, died in 1853, shortly after he had married, while his wife, Lucy, was pregnant with a son. That child, Ruth's grandson, was named Nathan W. Buzby Junior, after his dead father. One of Ruth and Asher's two daughters, Beulah, married a carpenter, Charles Gaskill, and moved to Philadelphia. The other daughter, Mary, remained unmarried and "at home"; she would share the housework with Ruth and eventually take over management of the household when Ruth became elderly and frail.

Around 1836 or 1837 Asher and Ruth took in a three-month-old child from a neighboring family. The child, Martha Hancock, remained in Ruth's household for the rest of Ruth's life, for nearly fifty years, and was identified variously as an adopted daughter and as a household servant.[36] But Asher and Ruth wanted more. In 1849, when Beulah Gaskill's first child, Mary, named after Beulah's sister, was also three months old, Ruth and Asher took her away from her mother, their daughter. From then on, Mary Gaskill was raised as if she were the daughter of Asher and Ruth Buzby. She would stay in Ruth's household until some time in 1870, when she married George Waddington of Elsinboro.

Asher Buzby died in 1868. In his will, he left to his only grandson, Nathan Jr., a sum of $1,000, to be paid when Nathan Jr. turned twenty-one. Ruth was the executrix of his estate. However, when, in 1874 or 1875, payment of the legacy came due, Asher's estate had insufficient funds to pay Nathan Jr.'s legacy. Nathan Jr. consulted an attorney, and he may have threatened to sue his grandmother as responsible for distributions from his grandfather's estate. In any case, Ruth felt compelled to pay the legacy out of her own small assets.[37]

Around 1870, when she was about seventy years old, Ruth fell down a cellar. The fall permanently weakened her physically, and it may have affected her mentally. She was unable to see for some significant period of time. It was also unclear or contested whether she could read thereafter. However, according to her doctor she did eventually recover. She had always been a quiet woman; now she was still more so. Nevertheless, she continued to manage the money she had out at interest in the form of mortgages on farms in the area.[38]

Also in 1870, around the time that Mary Gaskill (Ruth's granddaughter and the daughter of Beulah Gaskill) had married George Waddington, the three remaining women in the household—Ruth Buzby, Martha Hancock, and Mary Buzby (Ruth's daughter)—moved together to the town of Salem, where the three women kept house. Granddaughter Mary and her husband, George Waddington, lived a few miles away, and George handled Ruth's investments, although he later insisted that he had done so while following Ruth's continuing instructions. Beulah Gaskill joined the women's household in 1881 or 1882, as her sister Mary became ill and after Beulah's own husband had died, leaving her without support.[39]

There was apparently a good deal of tension and conflict among the women in Ruth Buzby's life. Beulah resented Martha Hancock's place within her mother's family, and Martha reciprocated. According to Beulah, when she moved back in to her mother's house, Martha had told her that she had "no right there." There was also no love lost between Beulah and her own daughter, Mary Waddington. When Mary Waddington was asked at trial, "Who brought you up?" Mary answered laconically, "Mother [that is, Beulah], until I was three months old." Then she agreed with the attorney that her grandparents had really been "all the parents" she had "ever known." When Beulah was asked by her own attorney if her mother was "more fond" of Mary Waddington, that is, of Beulah's daughter, "than of any other [grand] daughters," she answered: "Her being there, and that is the only way." Then Beulah emphasized that one of her other daughters, Anna, had been her grandmother's true favorite. (However, Beulah continued, unlike favored Mary, Anna had to "support herself" by working in a store in Salem.) In cross-examination, Beulah was led to admit that Mary had lived with Ruth and Asher "as a daughter." "Was she not," the attorney continued, "regarded by your mother as her dearly beloved daughter?" "I have never heard her [that is, Ruth Buzby] express herself that way," Beulah answered. Toward the end of the trial, when Beulah was recalled to the witness stand, she was asked, "Is not Martha Hancock's character for truth and veracity beyond question?" Her answer: "I cannot say."[40]

All of Ruth Buzby's work to keep caregivers close to her had produced something less than a loving household. However, her work had also given her exactly what she needed and presumably had wanted: the attention and the presence of family in her old age. The trouble that became the case of *Waddington v. Buzby* burst out into the open only after Ruth's death in 1886, when she left an estate worth slightly more than $5,000.

Ruth Buzby's last will (there was at least one earlier one) had been drafted and executed in February 1882, about four years before her death. The night it had been witnessed and read was the night before Mary Buzby, Ruth's unmarried daughter and her closest companion, died. It must have been a terrible time for Ruth. Those who witnessed the will testified in the later trial that George Waddington had rushed them over to his house, where Ruth and the other women were staying, while Mary was dying upstairs. (One suspects that Waddington was afraid that Ruth would die quickly in the wake of her daughter's passing.)[41]

The will drafted that night gave to her surviving daughter, Beulah, some of Ruth's belongings and $1,500 (Beulah was also about to receive $1,500 from her sister Mary's will). Beulah's three children each received $100, and her two daughters each received an item of silver. Ruth's great-grandson, the child of granddaughter Mary and George Waddington, received a silver item and $600. Martha Hancock, identified first as Ruth's "adopted daughter," received half of Ruth's remaining "household goods," plus $600. This was then said to be "in lieu of any charge for services or otherwise she may make against my estate," indicating that she was also understood as a servant who might charge for her services. Everything else in the estate, including "the bed and bedstead formerly occupied by her aunt, Mary," went to granddaughter Mary. Assuming that the litigation did not, in the end, consume most of the estate, granddaughter Mary's share as the "residuary legatee" should have amounted to about $2,000. The will also specifically excluded grandson Nathan W. Buzby from any legacy.[42]

Beulah Gaskill and grandson Nathan Jr. brought suit to challenge Ruth Buzby's will. They characterized the will as the product of the "undue influence" of George Waddington and Martha Hancock. According to the "caveat" that the two of them filed with the Salem Orphans Court (a "caveat" is a protest or action to prevent probate of a will), George Waddington had not been a disinterested advisor to Ruth Buzby. The will unfairly and unnaturally benefited those in his own family, that is, his wife, Mary, and his son. Absent undue influence, Ruth would not have cut out Nathan Jr., the only son of her only son; she would not have preferred her granddaughter Mary Waddington over her daughter Beulah; she would not have given more to granddaughter Mary's son than she gave to Beulah's other children; and she certainly would not have given so much to Martha Hancock, who was no relation at all. According to Clement H. Sinnickson, the attorney for Beulah and Nathan Jr., Martha Hancock was only a "servant in the family" and "of no kin to the testatrix." Yet she was to receive "$600 and nearly half of the household goods, while the daughter, one of the two natural heirs of the testatrix, a poor dependent widow, advanced in years," received only $1,500. In addition, "the grandson, the only son of the only son of the testatrix, and the other natural heir," received nothing. If Ruth Buzby had been fully competent, she would never have made such choices. However, by the time that she signed the 1882 will, Ruth Buzby was old (about eighty-two), frail, and entirely dependent on Mary, her daughter, who had controlled her mother in the years after her 1870 fall. (As a witness put it in testimony, "I do not know that she was afraid of Mary, but she did not seem to have any will of her own in anything of the housekeeping affairs, or anything else; Mary was particularly kind to her, but she was treated like a child.") Then, after Mary Buzby's sickness and death, George Waddington and Martha Hancock had taken over.[43]

Sinnickson worked to demonstrate that George Waddington and Martha Hancock had conspired to write a will that benefited them and those near and dear to them. Much of the early testimony in the trial concerned what had taken place at the moment in February 1882 when the will was signed and executed. As mentioned earlier, everything had happened downstairs in George and Mary Waddington's house, where the women of Ruth Buzby's household had gathered as Mary Buzby, her daughter, lay dying upstairs. Sinnickson got witnesses to describe a scene in which witnesses and a scrivener were brought to Waddington's house. George and Martha sat with an unresponsive Ruth Buzby in the dining room of the house as the will was read. Meanwhile, Beulah sat unknowingly in the next room. At one moment, witnesses reported, Beulah had walked through the dining room on the way to the kitchen. The papers on the table may have been quickly removed and hidden, and no one apparently told her what was going on.[44]

According to Sinnickson, the terms of the will produced that night were "unnatural." That is to say, the document was "unreasonable, inconsistent with the duties of the testatrix to her property and family, and contrary to natural affection." Sinnickson also referred the court to the leading U.S. legal treatise on wills, which stated that anything in a will "contrary to natural affection, or what the civil law denominates an undutiful testament" always excites apprehension of undue influence.[45]

William Thomas Hilliard, the younger attorney who represented George Waddington and the estate and who had once been the law clerk of his opponent, Sinnickson, tried to reframe the scene of the signing of the will. However, he focused harder on Ruth Buzby's reasons for making the choices she did: her anger at Nathan Jr. for having pressured her to satisfy his grandfather's legacy (although all agreed that she remained civil to him when he visited) and the love, affection, and care she had received from Mary Waddington and Martha Hancock. He also minimized the work that George Waddington had done for Ruth. Beulah had not been excluded from the will, and it made sense to imagine that Ruth Buzby had incorporated into her moral accounting what Beulah was about to get as the primary beneficiary of her sister Mary's estate. There was, he argued, nothing unnatural about her decision to make Mary Waddington her principal beneficiary. Ruth Buzby "had brought [her] up as her own child." She had been "married from her house." She had been named after Ruth's "own daughter Mary," for whom Ruth "had always felt extraordinary affection and respect." In addition, the $600 legacy to Martha Hancock was "no more than a fair compensation to one who had served her faithfully for so many years, and whom she expected to be with her to the last."[46]

In attorney Hilliard's reconstruction, the choices Ruth Buzby had made were not "unnatural," and nothing about them should excite the suspicions of a court. Hilliard also referred the court to a variety of older cases in which courts had affirmed seemingly unkind, unconventional, or even immoral distributions on the principle of testator's freedom. Even if the choices could be construed as unnatural, they were still her choices to make.[47]

When the will went to the Salem County Orphan's Court to be probated, the court had accepted Sinnickson's arguments for the "caveators," that is, for Beulah Gaskill and Nathan Buzby Junior. The judge refused probate. The testatrix, that is, Ruth Buzby, was, according to the judge, "old, nearly blind, mentally sluggish and easily led in any direction by those about her." He also ruled that George Waddington and Martha Hancock were unreliable witnesses and that George Waddington had exercised undue influence over a clearly impaired Ruth Buzby. That local decision was appealed to the state Prerogative Court, where the Orphan's Court decision was affirmed. According to Chancellor McGill, sitting as the ordinary (which is what the judge in the Prerogative Court was called), there was overwhelming evidence of "undue influence." In McGill's view, Ruth Buzby was "an old woman, enfeebled in mind and body, nearly blind, and scarcely realizing her surroundings." Her daughter, that is, Beulah Gaskill, "her natural and recognized protector, and by law entitled to a large share of the residue of her estate," had been kept from "her side by a man," that is, by George Waddington, who had "prepared a will for her to execute." (The chancellor was clearly signaling the significance of Waddington as the only male present in the female household that Ruth Buzby had constructed for herself.) That "man" presented "to her for execution, a will, prepared by his own hand," in which he had "written for his son a substantial legacy, for himself the executorship, and for his wife more than one half of the estate." The document was not, therefore, a true expression of Ruth Buzby's last will. Rather, it was the product of a savvy and self-interested man who had unduly influenced her.[48]

However, when that second decision was appealed to New Jersey's Court for the Correction of Errors and Appeals, that court reversed the decision, allowing probate of the will. The lower courts had not, according to Justice Scudder, given sufficient weight to Ruth Buzby's right to decide what dispositions she wished to make. She was, of course, elderly. She was, the court acknowledged, "feeble and forgetful to the extent that persons ordinarily are at such an advanced age, and she was nearly blind." Nonetheless, she was still an intelligent and competent woman who managed her own affairs. Scudder also referred to a long series of decisions in which "persons who were aged, diseased, blind, and infirm" had executed valid wills. Had George Waddington exercised undue influence over Ruth Buzby? Scudder's first impression had been that he had, but "careful consideration" had changed his mind. It might have been "more delicate and prudent" if George Waddington had hired a stranger to prepare Ruth's will, but the choices made in the will were coherent with her life and with the care she had received. It all made sense. Therefore, the document appeared to be a valid exercise of her "last will." The choices expressed in her will were ones that gave effect to the way she had led her life and made use of the labors of others.[49]

So the case ended eventually to become an important precedent for New Jersey's law of "undue influence" and a case much reprinted in casebooks and guides to the law of wills.[50]

In all cultures before the second half of the twentieth century, the central strategic question of old age was "where or with whom" to live.[51] In many societies even today, that question would be answered clearly and relatively unproblematically. One child or another was clearly marked as being responsible for the aged parents' care and well-being. The old went to the child, or the child went to or never left the parents. Diverse cultures have had a variety of rules about how costs (psychic, economic, and moral) were to be allocated horizontally and vertically, that is, between siblings and between generations. However, in much of the world it was generally assumed that resources—labor and capital—flowed upward to the parents at least for a significant period of time.

In nineteenth-century America, by contrast, the law exerted only weak rhetorical pressures on the young to stay and to support their parents. American law sustained and continued a long-standing pattern distinctively characteristic of English law (one which goes back to later medieval times).[52] The standard phrase was that care of parents by an adult child was merely a "natural" or "moral" obligation. The "voice of nature" bade children care for their parents, but the machinery of state power regarded adult children as without enforceable obligations to parents. An early Massachusetts decision put it another way: "The law of society has left most of such obligations to the interior forum, as the tribunal of conscience has been aptly called." The court continued:

> Is there not a moral obligation upon every son who has become affluent by means of the education and advantages bestowed upon him by his father, to relieve that father from pecuniary embarrassment, to promote his comfort and happiness, and even to share with him his riches, if thereby he will be made happy? And yet such a son may, with impunity, leave such a father in any degree of penury above that which will expose the community in which he dwells, to the danger of being obliged to preserve him from absolute want.... Without doubt there are great interests of society which justify withholding the coercive arm of the law from these duties of imperfect obligation, as they are called; imperfect, not because they are less binding upon the conscience than those which are called perfect, but because the wisdom of the social law does not impose sanctions upon them.[53]

The law would not compel children to take in parents in need, nor did many parents wish to be taken in. If census records reveal anything about what most older people wanted and if the housing arrangements that actually existed reveal anything about how people wanted to live, they show that most older people worked hard to remain in charge of the households in which they lived.[54] Children should move to them; they should not move to the children. Throwing oneself on the charity of one's children was a bad idea. Far better to "keep the loaf under one's own arm" or "the reins" in one's "own hand," to use phrases that recur in the testimony.[55] Far better to keep control until death—or longer. To retain property was to retain power and to be able to demand love and care.

However, once again, retaining property might not get the older persons what they wanted, given the mobility, the distances, and the opportunities that shaped the economically explosive world of nineteenth-century America. Too strong a hold on the loaf or too tight a grip on the reins, and the children might just abandon the older persons, leaving them without care and isolated. Why would a child stay (or return) to wait for a parent to die at some indeterminate time in the future, after years of care and management and work? Why would the child stay for a share of an estate that was itself of uncertain and varying value, given the volatility of the land market? Why would the child give up life chances for a place at home? And if the child left, who would there be for the older person to turn to?

For older people with some property, the apparent solution (or at least the means to a solution) to the conundrum lay in that distinctive — and distinctively modern—set of Anglo-American practices identified with the term "testator's freedom" or "testamentary freedom." The common law, in fairly sharp contrast to civil law jurisdictions, confirmed landed older persons in their right to give by will to anyone or to no one. Children had no preemptive right. As any American law student who has taken first-year property law knows, no one is an heir until the testator (that is, the will writer) dies. In contrast to other legal cultures where children knew what they were going to get, American children could never know what inheritance (if any) awaited them. Elsewhere, children—male and female—bargained and made life plans in the shadow of relatively clear distributional systems. (Indeed, even English estate practice—law for the wealthy—had long been defined in terms of primogeniture and the "fee tail.") In the post-eighteenth-century Anglo-American world, by contrast, children remained at the mercy of their parents' "will" or willfulness.[56] As Chancellor Williamson of New Jersey wrote in a leading case of the 1850s, "The law permits a man to dispose of his own property at his pleasure. . . . It may be unwise for a man, in this way, to embarrass himself as to the final disposition of his property, but he is the disposer, by law, of his own fortune, and the sole and best judge as to the time and manner of disposing of it."[57] Alternatively, as was said in 1896 by the Court for the Correction of Errors to a woman who had relied on the promises that her adoptive father had made to her: Even if she "stood to him in the relation of his own child, still *he was not bound* to leave his property to her. He could have bequeathed and devised it away from his own natural children. And it is absurd to say that what he might neglect and decline to do for a *natural* child he is bound to do for an *adopted* child, *merely because of the relation between them created by the adoption.*" It was "the testator's right to weigh the claims upon his bounty and to deal with them as he thought they merited."[58]

Courts often described testator's freedom as a principle that existed to protect the old. As one New Jersey court put it, "The power of disposing of property is an estimable privilege of the old. It frequently commands attention and respect, when other motives have ceased to influence. How often, without it, would the hoary head be neglected, deserted and despised." For the old, according to a much-quoted Tennessee decision, "The power to dispose of their property is often the only means of securing that attention and care, for which they appeal in vain to humanity and natural affection. It then becomes the sole remaining staff of their declining years."[59]

More than a technical legal rule or practice, testator's freedom colored and shaped the tacit assumptions or background understandings of family conflicts, just as in other legal cultures different distributional expectations defined the negotiations and the behavior of parents, children, and others. Moreover, testator's freedom—or, rather, the strong and widely understood sense of its centrality to property ownership—helps to describe the comparative distinctiveness of the legal culture within which these New Jersey subjects lived.[60]

In the mid-nineteenth century, testator's freedom had many features (none of which will seem very surprising to those trained in modern Anglo-American law). Its core, of course, was the right to change one's mind or to reserve decision to the last possible moment. Doing so— waiting—meant that one ran the risk of running out of time. Many of the cases came into being because the old persons simply died before writing a will to accord with the understanding that they and their adult children had come to. In such cases, everything went by way of intestacy, according to a statutory distributional scheme that equalized the rights of everyone within a generation. However, until that apparent disaster, no child had a right to anything merely because of birth, birth order, or gender.[61] Nor did a child acquire a right to an inheritance merely because the child had worked or cared for the parents. Courts were careful to preserve older people's "sense of freedom to dispose of their property in recognition of kindness rendered" in a way that "was quite inconsistent with a consciousness that they were bound to convey or devise it" to anyone in particular.[62] Or, as a judge responded when a lawyer insisted that an old man had promised his dying wife that he would give one-third of his estate to her niece, who had stayed to care for the two of them:

> "Unfortunately, that does not show any agreement whatever." "But," the lawyer replied, "it shows the intention of the man." The judge was unmoved. "That is a different thing. What one may do out of the disposition of his heart, and what he may do as a legal obligation are entirely different things."[63]

No child could, merely by remaining and working, expect to earn property. Parents always retained the power to choose or to exclude or to change their minds. James Davison, the youngest son, who remained to care for his father and mother because of an agreement he had made with his father, could always be recharacterized as a child who was merely speculating on an inheritance. As his father said in his response to James's petition to the court of equity (I paraphrase slightly): I do not know why he stayed around and worked for me. Perhaps he thought that by doing so I would be moved to leave him land in my will. But that decision was always still mine to make.[64]

A will that gave everything to one child to the exclusion of all the other children or to a housekeeper or an informally adopted child, or a will that excluded all children and other blood relatives was, as such, an unproblematic act of legal freedom. Ruth Buzby was under no legal obligation to give Beulah Gaskill or Nathan Buzby Junior, her nearest blood relations, any particular share of her estate. What is more, if she had instead depleted or even emptied her estate by making a gift or conveyance of property prior to death, that also would have been her right. A will, to quote the recurrent phrase, could be "contrary to the principles of justice and humanity, its provisions may be shockingly unnatural and extremely unjust; nevertheless, if it appears to have been made by a person of sufficient age to be competent to make a will, and also to be the free and unconstrained product of a sound mind, the courts are bound to uphold it."[65]

Testator's freedom often seemed to produce injustice. Children like Beulah Gaskill believed—strongly—that property ought to go to them as rightful heirs. The notions of the "natural" that they and their lawyers mobilized connected to older understandings of land as owned by the family or by the lineage. Other excluded children often invoked notions of "equality." In the nature of things, all children—sometimes all sons—should get an equal share. This was also, as courts acknowledged, a principle "firmly rooted" in the "minds of men." Courts and treatise writers often suggested that there were strong presumptions in favor of giving to "next of kin" and in favor of equality. Plus, when will writers did otherwise, when they violated presumptions in favor of the next generation or in favor of equality of bequests, their doing so could be made to appear as acts of the less than competent or of the unduly influenced. Lawyers for disgruntled siblings and others who did not get what they expected had many tactics to discredit and challenge wills. Some tactics worked some of the time, especially if it was possible to portray a will as an expression of the power—the undue influence—of a younger caretaker or of an advisor like George Waddington. Young and old had reversed roles, lawyers argued; the child had become the parent. The will no longer described the competent "will" of a testator.[66]

Yet, as a leading New Jersey decision put it, a "plain intention" was "not to be disregarded" merely because it was unjust, unnatural, or unequal. Also, testators had a right to be whimsical in their choices.[67] "Inequality, or even what might be regarded by others as great injustice ... does not prove undue influence." New Jersey's Prerogative Court had no difficulty affirming the decision of an elderly Quaker woman who left a $15,000 legacy to a companion who had devoted herself to her for twenty-five years, from the time the companion was fifteen years of age, sharing the same bed and never leaving her "for even a single night." The woman was acting "in accordance with ... views long cherished and long previously acted upon, and in accordance, also ... with reasonable expectations, under the circumstances."[68] An 1889 decision confirmed a will-writer's gift to his mother-in-law, who had taken him to a medium and who had encouraged his belief in spiritualism. The judge who heard the case, Vice Ordinary Van Vleet, "strongly" suspected "that the testator was duped." Yet, that would not be enough to undo a particular disposition when the court could not definitively conclude that the testator was suffering from an "insane" delusion.[69]

In addition, one predictably unsuccessful move, yet one that lawyers repeatedly made throughout the nineteenth and early twentieth centuries, was to argue that older testators had lost the capacity to exercise their freedom merely because they were too old. Sinnickson, the attorney for Beulah Gaskill and Nathan Buzby Junior, tried that tactic repeatedly throughout the trial of Ruth Buzby's will. However, the New

Jersey Court for the Correction of Errors forcefully rejected the premise that age alone, even when accompanied by evidence of decline, offered proof of incapacity to make a will. Even when a good bit of testimonial evidence pointed to loss of memory or an inability to read and write, and even in the case of men and women who had reached their nineties, age itself was not a reason to conclude that the "will" necessary for testator's freedom had been lost.

Other New Jersey courts agreed: "The power of making a valid will is not impaired by the access of old age, nor is it denied to him who has attained the utmost verge of human life, on that ground alone." In more than one case, the New Jersey courts accepted a will after the will writer, the testator, had been formally declared a "lunatic." Nor was the "incapacity" of an eighty-two-year old man demonstrated "by the facts that he was miserly, squalid, dishonest, profane, and irascible." As treatise writer Isaac Redfield wrote, "Great age alone does not constitute testamentary disqualification; but, on the contrary, it calls for protection and aid to further its wishes, when a mind capable of acting rationally, and a memory sufficient in essentials, are shown to have existed." Redfield went on to quote Chancellor Reuben Walworth of New York: "The power and brilliancy of the mind in old age is an exception, but so is longevity itself." Then he quoted from Walworth's famous predecessor, Chancellor James Kent: "It is one of the painful consequences of extreme old age that it ceases to excite interest, and is apt to be left solitary and neglected. The control which the law still gives to a man over the disposal of his property is one of the most efficient means which he has, in protracted life, to command the attention due to his infirmities. The will of such an aged man ought to be regarded with great tenderness."[70]

What did competence, that is, being of "sound mind," mean for the old? An early New Jersey case had held that it signified a mind that was "whole, unbroken, unimpaired, unshattered by disease or otherwise." However, by 1831, the New Jersey Prerogative Court had decided that was too stringent a test. "If so, a will can only be made in the spring, or at the latest in the summer, and never in the autumn of life."[71]

In 1854 the same court was able to reinforce its views on competence and sound mind when it reviewed a lower-court decision denying probate to the will of Esther Horton. Her husband had promised their farm to their nephew Silas. However, when the husband died, he had instead left the farm to Esther, his wife, after she had promised to leave it to Silas in her will. Silas had continued to live with her until her death. However, in her will she had cut Silas off from any inheritance. According to the Prerogative Court, "That the mind of the decedent was broken, impaired, and shattered by disease, is beyond question. But with such a standard of capacity, very few who had reached the age of three score and ten years would be deemed competent to make a final disposition of their property." She was blind and sick. Yet, she continued to conduct her business. She made mistakes of memory, but she was still in entire control. She had very strong political and religious opinions. Some of them, the court acknowledged, may have been mistaken or foolish. That did not mean she lacked capacity. She and her nephew had had strong and open conflicts. "That there had been a change in the old lady's feelings towards her nephew, Silas Horton, was well understood in the whole neighborhood." Among other differences, she and Silas had fought over their pastor's decision to invite a "colored clergyman" to preach. He had supported the decision; she had denounced it and insisted that it was a misuse of money that her husband had left to the church. It was clear to the court that she was under a moral obligation to leave the farm to her nephew. Nonetheless, a moral obligation was not a contractual obligation. The fact that she had violated a moral duty did not reveal her incompetence as a will writer. Thus, Silas could be disinherited.[72]

Meanwhile, the New Jersey courts ruled repeatedly that if an older person gave a disproportionate share of an estate to someone who had stayed close to and cared for that person and had been "kind" and

attentive, doing so was not presumptive evidence of "undue influence." "A man enfeebled by age or disease," Chief Justice Kirkpatrick
had written in 1819, "must always be under the care, protection and
government of somebody; this somebody must generally be one of
his children who lives with him in his house, who administers to his
wants and his wishes, who has the direction of his affairs, who aids
him . . . and though there may exist the purest parental affection and
filial duty between him and his other children, this one will generally
be preferred in the distribution of his estate . . . upon the soundest
principles of equity and justice."[73]

Peter Cheesman had evidently repeatedly told witnesses that he intended to divide his estate equally among his ten children. Indeed, in
1853 he had written a will that gave effect to that intention. However,
three years later, shortly before dying, he wrote a codicil to that will,
giving his farm to his son John. The inconsistency was, according to
the majority on the court, no proof of "imbecility." So long as the court
was satisfied that the codicil expressed "the will of a sound and disposing mind," the court would look no further; it would not try to find
"reasons or . . . motives" to explain what he had done. "The right of
absolute dominion, which every man has over his own property, is sa-
cred and inviolable." Nor was his age, at least eighty-six, significant.
"Old age, failure of memory, and even drunkenness, do not, of themselves, necessarily take away a testator's capacity." Nor did the fact that
John had lived with his father demonstrate "undue influence." Undue
influence was presumptively present when "the subject of it" was "in
the power and at the mercy of another." It came into being when the
older person could no longer "say *no* to a mere request . . . made of him,
no matter how little the influence." In such situations, "free agency"
may have been "destroyed." Still, care and attention alone from a child
were not a demonstration of "undue influence," evidence that challenged the enforceability of a will by an elderly person.[74]

Or, as the court wrote in still another case, "A discrimination made
by a man of the testator's age [ninety-four], and in his condition, in

disposing of his estate by will, in favor of his only daughter, ... who has given him her whole time, and with assiduous attention ministered to his wants when he most needed care and sympathy, can neither be regarded as evidence of incapacity or of undue influence."[75]

Two potential boundaries were built into the concept of testator's freedom, boundaries that shaped legal doctrine and the practices of litigants (and potential litigants). One, a boundary that remains central to estate practice today, had to do with the competence of those who made an apparently irrational or culturally inappropriate choice with their property. Very large gifts to distant relations, informally adopted children, housekeepers, a mistress or lover, or one's daughter to the exclusion of one's sons always tested that boundary. The recipients of those gifts had to work hard to put into evidence the work and care they had undertaken to avoid the implication of "undue influence." Even so, judges could find reasons to rule against probate of such wills if that is what they wanted to do.[76] The second boundary had to do with how one understood the extent of testator's freedom in a political and legal culture committed to ubiquitous contracting. Could one contract to make a will? When, if ever, would a promise to make a will become an enforceable contract? Could one restrict one's freedom to change one's mind? In New Jersey, unlike some other jurisdictions, the courts had decided early on that a promise to make a will could under the right circumstances become an enforceable contract.[77] Yet the problem of what combination of language—promises— and behavior could undo the testator's freedom, could compel her or him to make a will, remained unresolved.

At one level this second boundary raised a difficult conceptual problem that ran through the moral life of a liberal capitalist society. That is, did the possession of freedom include the right to contract away one's capacity to exercise a present or future freedom?[78] At another level, one should not assume that older property owners were ordinarily anything but serious about the promises they made, including promises to remember a child or other caretaker in a will. Promise

making was as important a part of family relations as it was in the
broader economy and society. In addition, while the right to change
one's mind was certainly a cherished right, and it was always possible
later on in court to reframe an apparent promise as the articulation of
a mere intention to make a gift (understood as the opposite of a binding contractual obligation), still, the evidence of the trial transcripts
strongly suggests that many older people believed that they would be
bound by their promises, including their promises to make wills. To
return one last time to *Davison v. Davison*, remember the situation as
of the summer of 1859. Even as scandal swirled through his household,
James W. Davison never said anything to anyone about depriving his
son James of his expectancy. Presumably, he understood himself as
bound by his earlier promise. It was only when James Davison decided to charge his father with slander, which surely seemed to James
W. as a breach of contract on his son's part, that James W. came to
believe that he had regained his right to change his mind and to convey the land to Reuben and Joseph.[79]

Chapter Two

The Work of Promises

How did older people pursue the project of securing care for themselves using the tools of private law and testator's freedom? What strategies and legal tools did they employ?[1]

We can imagine that older people often incorporated into their life plans what demographers and economists who study the less-developed world label as the old-age security motive. That is, they would have worked to produce as many children as a wife's fertility (or sometimes several wives' fertility) permitted. Many children (many hands) may or may not make light work, but in a world in which infant mortality was still a common and predictable fact of life, many children might also mean that at least one would still be close to home at the end to take care of a parent.

That "motive" had certainly lessened by the mid-nineteenth century, at least in the northern United States. Over the previous half century, the number of children born during an average couple's fertile years had sharply declined. Why so many early nineteenth-century Americans began to limit their reproduction remains a matter of controversy and debate. However, there is broad agreement that the transition led older Americans to shift their investments from children toward other assets. Childbearing ceased to be understood as a form of asset accumulation, and children were no longer regarded as pension assets. A traditional strategy of old-age care apparently was falling out of use as part of a chain of events that historians label as the "market revolution."[2]

Yet James W. Davison, like others in the New Jersey case records, clung to an older pattern, and it is at least plausible to imagine that he still thought through the lens of the "old-age security motive." He had many children, at least nine, or at least his wife had given birth to at least that many, and he worked hard to keep them close to him. Like other older Americans, he concluded that he needed family to care for him. He knew, as historical demographers know, that having more children would produce a greater likelihood that one would be able to stay in one's own home when one became old.[3]

In particular, one may see the old-age security motive at work in the efforts of some older people to keep multiple relatives and pseudo-relatives in the household once it had become clear that there would be fewer, or not enough, birth children available. Consider once again Ruth Buzby. Why did she take both Martha Hancock and Mary Gaskill away from their "families" when each was only three months old? Why did she later take Beulah Gaskill back into her household after Beulah's husband had died? One could, of course, tell her story through the lens of love, sentiment, and kindness. It might be that Ruth Buzby acted selflessly, but surely Ruth was also working to protect herself. In the mid-1830s, when Ruth would have been in her mid-thirties, she knew that she had only three surviving children, all of whom might leave her home within a decade. A new child in the home, Martha Hancock, could be raised to serve and to stay. By 1849, when she took Mary Gaskill away from Beulah, Ruth was in her late forties. Her childbearing was completed. She had by then only one daughter left at home, plus loyal Martha Hancock. We can imagine that she felt she needed more insurance for her old age. (And, of course, she was right to worry since Mary Buzby, the daughter who would remain with her, would die before her in 1882.) Still later, after her own husband's death, Beulah Gaskill had not intended to move in with Ruth, her mother. She told her mother that she planned to take in sewing instead. This was a time, she had told Ruth, when she "ought to be doing something" for herself. Her mother, however, told her not to do that. She needed Beulah to stay and care for her. If she remained with Ruth, Beulah would eventually be "well provided" for; she "would not be dependent" after her mother's death. However, until then she ought to remain within Ruth's household. As the lawyer questioning Beulah put it, "It was a hobby of your mother not to be dependent on children." It was also Ruth's goal to keep as many women as possible working with or for her in her household.[4]

At the other end of formality from this rarely articulated and always unformalized "motive" stood a variety of formally drafted agreements between a parent and one or more children (almost always a son, occasionally a son-in-law). These agreements, known in the German-speaking world and in Scandinavia as bonds of maintenance agreements, have sometimes been identified as "retirement contracts." They can also be found in land and court records going back to the late Middle Ages. They typically involved an immediate transfer of title and possession, along with a covenant ensuring the care of the transferor (almost always the father), together with his wife, for the duration of their lives. Often such an agreement would guarantee the older person the private use of at least one room in the house. There might also be quite specific terms—about the quality and quantity of food to be provided, health care, quantity of firewood to be provided, specific family animals, and the continued care of a widow.

Such agreements have been found in early modern England and Ireland. Historians of early America have also found some use of such contracts by Anglophone landowners. In Scandinavia, Germany, and the Netherlands they were apparently quite common. That is to say, scholars have found many examples of written agreements for care in the archives. Still, even where the records are plentiful, it is difficult to know whether those that have been found are representative of a wider set of practices. In addition, what such documents indicate about the treatment of the elderly in the past is still more a matter of controversy. To some, they denote that children did not abandon their parents in spite of the lack of legal coercion. To others, they show that, without a formalized covenant, there would have been nothing to maintain caring relations between generations.[5]

Only a handful of formal bonds of maintenance agreements appear in the New Jersey case records even though numerous litigants (and their lawyers) were of Dutch or German ancestry. (The ones that appear are, not surprisingly, often in cases in which conflict arose after the agreement, in which the older person complained of mistreatment by the son and daughter-in-law and of their not abiding by the covenants in the agreement.)[6] What absence from the records means is, as always, unclear. It is possible that many such agreements existed but that few litigated them. On the other hand, there are indications that testator's freedom had a seductive effect on even property owners firmly located within German ethnic communities, leading them away from the use of such agreements.[7]

One can assert with some confidence that an immediate and formalized transfer of "possession" of one's land was exactly what an older person like James W. Davison or Ruth Buzby did not want to happen. A bond of maintenance agreement, which meant an immediate conveyance of property with a covenant or condition in the deed requiring the "purchaser" (the child in most cases) to offer care to the seller (the parent) for the rest of the seller's life, would have raised the King Lear problem. It meant a conveyance too soon. As was said to one old man, "I told him he knew how old folks got served generally, if he put his property out of his hands, that he must look out for that he did not get misused." The old man had answered that he knew "he must look out for that—he would keep it under his own thumb as long as his head was warm." No matter how strongly framed, the covenants in a deed that immediately transferred ownership to a child left the parent at the mercy of the child.[8] Few Americans trusted that courts had the institutional capacity to make children behave and care once the property had been conveyed. Moreover, there were good reasons for distrust. Power passed, along with the title. In addition, for technical reasons in the Anglo-American law of conveyancing, even a serious breach of a covenant for care within a deed that transferred possession of land to a child would ordinarily not lead to the return of the land.[9]

Like James W. Davison in 1849, older people for the most part avoided conveyances in advance of care and looked instead to the power of oral promises to produce care and attention. What they wanted was bait that was seductive and strong enough to keep one or more children close, attractive enough to equal or exceed the prospects that young men (or, in later years, young women) would find in the larger labor markets, and good enough to convince daughters to put off marriage or to persuade potential sons-in-law that it made sense to set up housekeeping with or near the parent or parents. Yet the bait should not constitute a formal transfer of possession. The commitment to convey had to be strongly and repeatedly expressed. As in *Davison,* everyone in the family and in the local community would have known of James W.'s intention to put his youngest son, James, in possession of the property. Everyone might have recognized that the son was effectively or practically in charge. Still, such knowledge was not the same as a formal transfer, which would come only with the property owner's death. What is more, men like James W. Davison understood the distinction and traded on it.

Such practices lived in a space between the apparently unconscious or semiconscious (like the old-age security motive) and the highly formalized (like formal bonds of maintenance property transfers). This was a space of promises expressed but not written, a space of commitments articulated but incompletely or not yet enacted. Men like James W. Davison talked contract constantly and often with a great deal of sophistication. Furthermore, the records are full of statements that could, once in court, be interpreted either as a mere intention to make a gift someday or as a recognition of a completed contract. Someone like James W. Davison might have said, regularly and loudly, to relatives, neighbors, and employees, "Look to James if you have any questions about the business. It's his now. He's in charge." Or he might say to James, when James questioned him about the uncertainty of his position, "Don't worry; it's yours; everyone knows that I'm committed to giving it to you." Nevertheless, he (and those like him) rarely said, "I gave it to him." Or, if questioned by others about a daughter like Ida, who gave up early marriage to stay and take care of the household of elderly parents and to do the personal care work that was needed, they might say, "Don't worry; she's been a good girl, and I know she has sacrificed for us. But I will take care of her. She will have property when I am done with it."

However, men like James W. Davison also rarely wrote down their promises or had lawyers reduce their assurances to formalized written commitments although they would often have lawyers prepare wills that appeared to give effect to them.[10] They did not want to make actual conveyances of property to the younger people who would live with and care for them. They kept their promises in a liminal space. After death, assuming that those promises were not kept, courts would have to sort out what was meant by looking to what had been said and done.

Van Horn v. Demarest (1910) illustrates such practices and strategies. As with most of the cases in the records, *Van Horn* comes to us after a relationship had fallen apart, although in this case, unlike *Davison*, the New Jersey courts ruled that the older person had retained his right to convey his property to third parties. Or, as the headnote to the decision of the Court for the Correction of Errors and Appeals put it,

"Equity cannot relieve against a testator's change in attitude toward a nephew, resulting in the nephew's expectant share being given to another."[11]

Vice Chancellor Stevenson summarized what had happened. In the fall of 1900 Garret Van Horn, elderly, childless, and unusually wealthy (his estate would be valued at more than $500,000), wrote to his nephew, John Van Horn, who lived and worked in Bayonne as a mason. Garret had been in the produce business in New York City, but now he had retired to a family farm across the river in Closter, New Jersey, in Bergen County, where he lived with his sister, Sarah Demarest. Would John and his wife, Louisa, move on to the farm to take care of Garret and Sarah? In exchange, the farm would be John's "when he [Garret] was through with the place." John visited, and Garret repeated his offer. They negotiated. Relying on the promises made in that meeting and in the letter, John quit a well-paying job, sold his boat, and moved on to the farm, where he and Louisa remained until 1905. However, in late 1904, Garret and his sister left the farm to move in with another nephew, Doctor Byron Van Horn, and Garret (or Byron acting as Garret's agent) soon began ejectment proceedings to evict John and his wife. After the eviction was completed, Garret sold the property at a price ($12,000) that John believed was well under its market value. Then Garret died—after writing a will that gave John nothing.

Over the previous five years, Garret Van Horn had had several wills drafted, all of which gave property to his nephew John Van Horn. He had also made the subject of his final will, and in particular how to structure a gift of the farm to John, a matter of continuing conversation with all of his relations and neighbors. Yet, to the vice chancellor, the complete history of their lives together, including the various wills and the language promising property to John, described an experiment that had failed. The various wills, in particular, indicated "the improbability that there ever was any definite contractual obligation." The fact that nephew John and Louisa were disappointed offered no reason to offer them equitable relief. In 1900 the two of them were still young (he was thirty-one) and poor. Therefore, they could "change" their "mode of life or ... place of residence without suffering any inconvenience or loss from such a change." There had, Vice Chancellor Stevenson recognized, been an agreement to split the profits from the farm while the four of them lived together. He also acknowledged that the old man had often expressed his intention to give the farm to John. Had they not quarreled, it would have been "strange" if he had not carried out that intention. Nonetheless, Garret's intention, according to the vice chancellor, always came accompanied with phrases like "if John behaves himself" or "if everything turned out satisfactory." Evidently things had not turned out satisfactorily. Stevenson understood that the "lure of a legacy" was "often held out to attract attention and service. Personal attention and service are often assiduously rendered in the hope of a legacy." In addition, "No doubt the relations of kinship and confidence existing between these men interpenetrated the legal contract which they made," but neither the work nor the relationship produced entitlement.[12]

What had led to the break? The New Jersey courts avoided resolving the conflicts in the testimony and portrayed the case as about nothing more than a deal gone bad. To John Van Horn and his wife, Louisa, the cause was the malevolent influence of their cousin Byron Van Horn, who had taken the two old people away when he realized that Garret was about to convey the property to John and who had convinced the old man to sell the property at an inadequate price. (According to Louisa, Byron had told her that he was having the two of them evicted because "it was costing too much to run the place; that he could get a nigger to go there and work the place a great deal cheaper than to have my husband and myself there.") John and Louisa acknowledged they had had small quarrels with the two old people. Garret, who seems to have been pretty notoriously tight (one witness, asked about Garret and his sister's manner of living, replied: "Well, from a casual glance of the table, I would say that neither Mrs. Demarest nor Mr. Van Horn would have ever suffered from the gout or indigestion"), had disapproved when John bought a new potato digger. Besides that, according to Louisa, Garret and Sarah, "like most old people," sometimes "got a little cranky." When asked to give an example of what she meant, she related that "one time" Garret "got it in his head that he wanted my hair off short, within an inch of my head . . . He said it took too much care every day. Then he wanted me to shorten my dresses to the shoe-tops, and got out of patience because I wouldn't do it." However, such quarrels never lasted long. "Just like a summer shower they would come and go."

Louisa and John and their witnesses emphasized how much work each had done, how the value of the farm had been improved, indeed, how beautiful it had become under John's care and how well Garret and Sarah were cared for. The whole farm was kept under cultivation, and they raised vegetables both for market and for their own use. Louisa did all the housework—washing, ironing, cooking, cleaning— without a servant. She made butter and sold milk and eggs. As the old man became more feeble, he needed attention. Louisa offered an example: "Well, when he was getting ready to go to the barber's I had to help him get ready. Sometimes I had to wash his neck and ears, and trim his eyebrows, and cut the hair in his ears and things like that." Then, as Sarah declined, Louisa took over the care of clothing and the mending. Occasionally Sarah was subject to attacks of diarrhea, and then she needed looking after. Meanwhile, Louisa also wrote letters for Garret and kept his accounts.[13]

Those on the other side, those who sided with Garret Van Horn's right to evict John and Louisa, told stories about how angry and abusive John had sometimes been. Garret, when asked why he had left, had explained: "Well, he [John] could not speak to me, nor would . . . [he] use good language; he was contrary and ugly to me, and it was impossible to live with him." John, according to Garret, was subject to "violent spells," and during those times, it appeared that he might "clean out and kill the whole family; and I found out he was a dangerous man and I could not live with him." Once John had "chucked" him "down in the cellar amongst a lot of vinegar barrels." Had he ever been afraid for his life? "Yes, sir; he had a pistol handy. That was one of the reasons I left, and being in poor health I needed care which I could not get there." (At that time, though not earlier, he also characterized John as just a workman.)[14]

Whether or not John had actually been threatening or violent, he had certainly been restive during the latter days of their time together on the farm. At one point he and Louisa had left to talk with some other relatives about the situation. An aunt, the mother of cousin Byron, had advised John to "Go back and live with them; don't notice any of their peculiarities, and be a good nephew to your uncle." John had replied, "I can't do it; I don't want the farm. My wife is all I have. I have no children to leave the farm to and I would rather have my freedom to go where I please and I can easily support my family by my trade and I would much rather do it." Another witness to the same conversation noted that John had added the following: "Nobody could live on that place. We have no time for any pleasure at all; it is work from early morn until late at night, and we have no time to ourselves at all. We have a worse time than the hired people on the farm."[15]

One might well suspect that the courts were correct to see this as a case about a plan that failed, about expectations that had never "ripened" into a contract. However, the nearly six-hundred-page trial record, produced through testimony and depositions gathered between December 1907 and June 1908, also offers a repository of the language of promise, as Garret worked to keep his nephew in tow while retaining control and possession. According to one witness, Garret had asked John to come to the farm with his wife "to take care of him [Garret] and he would take care of him [John], vice versa." What did that mean? the lawyer asked. The answer was that John was to have the farm and money. Then, on cross-examination, the agreement was restated: "John was to go upon the farm and work the farm and Mr. Van Horn was to pay all expenses, taxes and manure, and furnish all the seed, and they were to live as one family and John was to have half the profits. . . ." In addition, if John behaved himself, he was eventually to have the farm and enough money to run it. Another witness, who had come to the farm to buy some hay, was told by Garret, "I am going to give John this farm; he has built it up and made it a very nice home . . . and I am going to give him plenty of money to run it if he takes care of me and Aunt Sarah." Garret often mentioned both his desire to keep the farm in the family and that John was the only, or the best, farmer in the family. A man who worked on the farm insisted that he had heard Garret say the following at least a dozen times: "John, the farm will be yourn at my death if you only do as I ask you." Several witnesses heard Garret tell John that he was "doing it all" for his "own benefit; it is your place and not mine." A neighbor visited one day. While there, she "looked back on the beautiful landscape; I just stood aghast!" Garret, who was just coming out of the barn, was pleased. "A fine farm, isn't it?" She asked whether his nephew and niece, Byron Van Horn and Byron's sister Carrie Van Horn, both doctors, would turn the farm into a sanitarium after his death. He looked over the landscape, and then he looked at her: "They will never get this farm; I intend to give it to my nephew John; he is the only farmer in the family and I know he will keep it up" as his [Garret's] own father had. "I intend to give it to him with enough to keep it up." About six months before he left, according to Louisa, Garret announced that he would not take any more of the farm work "on his shoulders . . . [and] that he was going to take it easy, wasn't going to work any more, and that John had to run the house on his own hook." A month before he left, he told a man who supplied the farm with feed that he was going to give John the farm and enough money to run it." He was going to go to Hackensack the next week to meet with a lawyer to transfer the farm and he wanted to make the transfer before the beginning of spring work.[16]

But, of course, he did not. And he never would.[17]

Across the century between the mid-nineteenth and the mid-twentieth centuries, similar promises shaped litigation. In *Updike v. Ten Broeck* (1866), Ralph Van Dyke Ten Broeck, known in the family as Van Dyke, sued his father's estate for the value of his services, for work done on his father's Montgomery Township farm between 1831 and 1838. The core question in the appeal was whether the son retained the right to be compensated for the work he had done when the father had not fulfilled a promise to leave his property to his son in his will. In his final will, written in 1853, when he was well over ninety, John Ten Broeck, the father, had specifically excluded Van Dyke and another child from any inheritance, "they having been wanting in respect due to me as their father and showing by their unfilial conduct neither love gratitude nor honor." Van Dyke was "unworthy of any mark of affection or fraternal love from me in the disposal of my property."[18] In addition, it is clear from the record that there had been no contact between Van Dyke and his father for fifteen years before John had written his will.

John Ten Broeck had seven children: four sons and three daughters. Around 1831 his wife had died, two daughters had married and moved away, as had two sons, and he was already old, around seventy years of age. He was left with Van Dyke, who had just turned twenty-one, another son, Abraham, and a daughter, Mary. Abraham was no good as a worker on the farm, and he taught school until his death in 1842. Mary kept house for her father until she married in 1837. As John said to Van Dyke, "I can't spare you; you're the only boy who'll work." Van Dyke wanted to leave, believing that he should seek his fortune elsewhere, but the "old man" worked to keep him from doing so. According to Daniel Voorhees, a ward of the family, "the old man" regarded Van Dyke as the "only one he could put dependence on." Voorhees testified that he had "often heard the old man say he meant to satisfy Van Dyke in some way; he did not say how; he always said Van Dyke should have the farm after his death; this was his intention." So, relying on his father's promises, Van Dyke stayed and managed his father's farm for the next seven years—until 1838, when he was "ordered away" by his father for having accused his father of adultery.

Why had Van Dyke stayed during those years? One would guess, from the scattered records of the case, that he had stayed not to receive a salary but because he believed his aged father had promised him the land and the house (and perhaps because he thought his father would not live long). Still, his father's 1831 oral promises, as reported in the 1860s, were vague and susceptible to varying readings. One witness testified that he had "understood that the farm would be left to Van Dyke, charged with legacies to his other children." Another witness reported that the father had promised to satisfy Van Dyke for his labor and that he should have the farm "or that he intended him to have the farm after he was done with it." Van Dyke was to be satisfied, but no one knew exactly how. As a result, when the court looked back in 1866 to whatever had been said (or not said) in the 1830s, all that remained and that still had legal significance for the court was the crude conclusion that John and Van Dyke, father and son, had dealt with each other as contractual actors. That meant that Van Dyke should be paid for his time as an adult who worked on his father's farm.[19]

The seemingly endless litigation between the brothers Beach and Pierson Vreeland told a very different story.[20] More than two years before his death in 1890, their father, Cornelius Vreeland, had deeds prepared that conveyed his lands to his children. Fourteen of the deeds were found in a locked trunk in his house after his death. One was found in a lawyer's office. One day in January 1888, according to Pierson, his father had visited his store in Patterson. "I will give you your deeds," Cornelius had supposedly said, "and also the deeds for the other heirs. I am an old man, and it is absolutely necessary that I should deliver those deeds in person while living." Later that night, when they were back at Cornelius's home at the family farm in Wayne, a few miles outside of Patterson, Cornelius had unlocked the trunk and handed Pierson seven deeds. He told him what property each conveyed, and then he handed him the tin box, saying that it contained eight more deeds of property for his siblings Beach, Adelia, and Lizzie. "You take them, and deliver them, after my death. I do not wish you to record them until after my death." According to Pierson, his father did not want the deeds recorded because he feared that putting them on record might injure his credit. Cornelius, the father, supposedly added, "I have made no will: I have divided my property" by means of these deeds "so that there can be no question; I do not know that you will have any trouble, but I am afraid that Beach will make trouble for you. I think Lizzie will stand by you—she will give no trouble—but now that she is married her husband may influence her." As Pierson Vreeland remembered that night, he then promised "to obey his father's command" not to record the deeds. He remembered saying, "All right." Then Pierson put his deeds back into a box with the others, put the box back into the trunk, locked it, put it away in a closet in his father's room, and laid the key on a shelf of his father's bookcase. The reason he gave for putting the deeds back into his father's possession was that he wanted his father to see that he would not record them without his father's knowledge.[21]

The legal question all this raised, when litigation followed Cornelius's death, was whether Cornelius had "delivered" deeds to Pierson, thereby completing the transaction and giving Pierson legal title to all of the property that the first seven deeds described. According to Pierson and his lawyers, that is exactly what had happened. However, to the various New Jersey courts that heard the case, what Cornelius had done was to show Pierson deeds that he had drafted but not yet delivered. As Vice Chancellor Van Vleet emphasized, up to the day he died, Cornelius continued to exercise full and complete dominion over his lands. The undelivered deeds were just that—undelivered. They were markers of a promise not yet completed, still mere pieces of paper. Cornelius had never limited his continuing freedom as a testator. The judges also believed that Pierson's testimony in 1893 about what had happened in January 1888 had been a fabrication, a reconstruction to fit his desires; otherwise, Pierson would not have been so stupid as not to have recorded his new possessions. In other words, they found his testimony—his description of what his father had supposedly done—implausible and inconsistent both with what an older person would have done and with what a legally knowing son to whom a father had just conveyed property would have done. They challenged his description of his obedience to his father's wishes—his dutifulness. "The conduct which he ascribes to himself stands in such sharp conflict with what a man of ordinary selfishness and caution would have done under like circumstances as to put the mind in a state of painful doubt whether any such occurrence as he describes ever took place—whether the whole affair is not a fiction, having no foundation in fact." It all seemed too convenient.

On the other hand, the judges found it entirely plausible that a father might have shown his son drafted deeds, prepared in advance, to be given at just the right moment (presumably just before death), ready but not yet given effect. It was a way of making or ratifying a promise. It was also a way to secure continuing care. The judges saw nothing odd in holding that the deeds were in the end worthless paper because they had never been delivered.[22]

Yet *Vreeland v. Vreeland* had a second act, one that ended with an 1895 decision that required the administrators of Cornelius Vreeland's estate to convey Cornelius's farm to Pierson Vreeland. Having lost one battle, Pierson and his lawyers moved on and began again. They retold the story of the old man and his son. As of April 1883, according to this version, Cornelius was living on the family farm with his wife, Rachel, and two daughters, Elizabeth and Adelia. Cornelius was about seventy; Rachel was sixty-five, feeble, and nearly blind from cataracts. Elizabeth was about to marry and move away, and Adelia was subject to epileptic fits and fainting spells and therefore incapable of "domestic responsibility." Meanwhile, Pierson Vreeland, Cornelius's older son, lived in Little Falls, a few miles away, with his wife and son (also named Cornelius, in honor of his grandfather). Beach, Pierson's younger brother, worked for Pierson and lived with him. Pierson Vreeland was a successful "flour and feed dealer," and he was an elder of the Reformed Church of Little Falls and a respected member of the Holland Society of New York.[23]

Cornelius needed help, and for that help he turned to his older son, Pierson. Cornelius and Pierson struck a bargain. They agreed that Pierson would move his family to the farm to care for the old couple. Pierson's wife would "superintend" the household, while Pierson would "advise and assist the father, as the father grew older, in the management of the farm." In exchange, his father would deed him the farm. According to his petition, Pierson had fully performed that agreement "at personal inconvenience to himself and his wife, and in detriment to his business." Beginning in 1883, Pierson and his wife spent much of their time caring for his father, his mother, and his sister. He could no longer give his undivided attention to his "flour and feed" business a few miles away, and it consequently lost value.

After he had moved on to the farm, he had "demanded" that his father prepare a deed that would formalize his right to the farm after his father's death, and he had threatened to leave if he did not get one. One day in June 1884, at his Patterson store, his father handed him a simple quitclaim deed. Pierson gave it back to his father as it was not good enough. He obviously wanted a more formal transfer of title to the property. Then, in 1888, Cornelius had a more formal deed drafted, one that gave Pierson what he wanted: a life estate in the property with the remainder going to his son, Cornelius, if the son survived him, and the fee (that is, full title) to the farm if Pierson should outlive his son. According to Pierson Vreeland's new petition to the court of equity, this deed was produced at the same time as and "together with other papers." Presumably the petition was here referring to the collection of deeds that the courts in the earlier litigation had ruled were not delivered and therefore not legally effective to convey title. As the court knew, this formal deed was at most evidence of an unconsummated intention.

So, after having lost the first time around, Pierson Vreeland petitioned the court of equity for a decree ordering Cornelius Vreeland's estate to follow through on Cornelius's promises to convey the farm to his older son. The deed Cornelius had drafted and had shown Pierson may have been declared invalid by the earlier decision. However, he had earned the property that his father had promised. Pierson argued that it would "work a fraud" on him if he were not given immediate possession of the family home.

Pierson Vreeland was not, as Chancellor Alexander McGill emphasized in his 1895 opinion, a particularly sympathetic or believable petitioner. Who was he to complain that a fraud had been worked on him? "Unfortunately for the complainant's credit," the chancellor opined, Pierson's contention that the deed had been delivered to him had already been the subject of much litigation. The conclusion of that litigation—that he had perjured himself in testifying that his father had delivered deeds to him in 1888 (including the deed now at issue)—threw serious doubt on his veracity and stigmatized his attitude toward his brother and sisters as "rapacious and unjust." Thus, very strong proofs were needed to counter these conclusions. However, fortunately for Pierson, his cousins, a pastor, his neighbors, a hired man, and a tax collector all corroborated his description of the promises his father had made to him. In the end, the chancellor was "satisfied" that the father had, in fact, secured "the watchful care of his son and daughter-in-law for the price suggested in the agreement." Pierson may have lied about the delivery of the deeds, but he had in fact changed his life, moved on to his father's farm with his wife and son, and cared for his father's family for the rest of his father's life. He had "performed"; he had earned the farm. The price was high but not "unconscionable," particularly if one factored in "the depreciation in the value of the complainant's business, the complainant's attention to his father's affairs, and his wife's unremitting care of the household matters . . . [I]t did not exceed that which was just." Consequently, as in *Davison v. Davison,* a father's estate would be compelled to convey land to a son whose life had been fundamentally altered as a result of an oral agreement made with his father to provide care in the father's old age.[24]

Other cases involved promises made to informally adopted children (and sometimes to the birth parents of children about to be adopted) or to stepchildren. The leading New Jersey adoption case, at least until the passage of modern adoption legislation in the twentieth century, was the 1857 case of *Van Duyne v. Vreeland.* John Van Duyne's birth mother testified that thirty years earlier she had given up John to John and Rachel Vreeland, her older relatives, after the Vreelands promised to make the baby their heir. What had induced her to give up her baby? "Nothing, only the promise they made." In John Vreeland's rendition of the same transaction, he and his wife had promised to treat Van Duyne as a son "as long as he treated and behaved to them as a dutiful child should do." Why had he done so? "By adopt[ing]" John Van Duyne "and bringing him up in his own family," he had hoped "to secure some one who would from ties of affection as well as the hope of reward look after him in his old age and not reproach him for his infirmities." When young John was about sixteen, his birth father came to Vreeland to ask whether his son was going to learn a trade. Vreeland told him the son did not need a trade and that if he worked and stayed and cared for Vreeland and his wife, he would always be taken care of. Throughout all of the years that John Van Duyne worked for Vreeland, he received no pay for his labor.

"I pay him nothing," Vreeland was reported as having said. "When I pass over it belongs to John."

John Vreeland, like John W. Davison, would eventually find that those words, those promises, would constitute an enforceable contract to make John Van Duyne his heir. However, the question of when promises to young people taken into a household became rights to property was a difficult one. John Van Duyne inherited his adopted father's property, but more often the "adoptee" lost.[25]

The petition brought by Anna V. Ibach Dusenberry, née Schneppendahl, told a similar story eighty years later. Unlike John Van Duyne, however, she would eventually lose her claim. She was born in 1889. Between 1892 and 1897 the Ibachs, an elderly childless couple, had repeatedly asked her father to give her to them and had stated that they would legally adopt her and make her their heir. Her father had refused, but then, when he was near death, with three other children to see to, her father and the Ibachs "mutually agreed" that he would "surrender the care, custody and control" of his daughter to them. In return, the Ibachs would give her "full parental care and affection, . . . legally adopt" her, and "take her into their home," where they would treat her as their own child. They promised that when they died, they would leave her "all the property of which they or the survivor of them should die possessed."

From then on she was known as Anna Ibach, and she spent her childhood as their dutiful daughter, although she was never legally adopted. According to her later petition, she had relied on their promises. She left high school even though that left her unprepared for a career of her own, and devoted herself fully to their "care, comfort, and assistance." Until she was well over thirty, "She did the things that a daughter would do," including household work, washing dishes, cleaning up the rooms, and getting meals. When they were sick, she took care of them. She "bathed them and gave them their medicine—changed dressings in a surgical case." While they were sick, she would also run the household. She did much, and they had promised much, but in the end she lost. According to the New Jersey courts, "No fraud was practiced on the complainant, but her condition in life was improved by her transfer to the Ibach home."[26]

In another case, decided in 1928, Sadie Hirschberg and her husband, Arthur, were convinced by promises to move in with her elderly uncle and aunt, the Horowitzes, who had raised her. "Sadie, we miss you. We miss the children. We miss Arthur, and we want you to come back, and if you do come back . . . I will give you everything that I own when I die." Over the next two years, the health of the Horowitzes was never good. "They were both sickly people." What did Sadie do to care for them? "In regards to taking care of their special diets, washing of their personal clothing, keeping house, cooking, and taking care of the table." There was no housemaid, and both were bedridden toward the end. Meanwhile, the uncle would tell Arthur not to worry. "There is no question that I will give her everything that I own." One neighbor reported on a conversation held "under the clotheslines" with old Mr. Horowitz. According to her he twice declared, "Oh, my Sadie! Oh, my Sadie! She is all what I have got. I promised her if she came back I [would] give her what I have got." However, as in so many of these cases, in the end Sadie got nothing because promises to write a will were never carried out.[27]

Similarly, in *Epstein v. Fleck* (1948), the New Jersey courts had to decide whether Ruby Prenowitz, the illiterate owner of the Asbury Inn in Asbury Park, had made an enforceable promise to make his three stepsons his heirs. The vice chancellor decided in favor of the stepsons, but on appeal the Court for the Correction of Errors and Appeals reversed that decision after a full review and reanalysis of the evidence. "To doubt," the high court declared, "is to deny." According to the stepsons, Abraham, Joseph, and Leo Fleck, Prenowitz had promised to make them his heirs many years before, in 1915, 1916, or 1917, soon after he had married their mother (one might suspect that their uncertainty about the date was fatal to their case). What was not at issue, though, was that from 1928 until Prenowitz's death in 1943, they had worked for him, managing his properties and keeping his books. Prenowitz told one friend why he had turned over the business to them. "When I was younger, my memory was good, and I used to conduct some business by memory. However, now I am sick, the boys take care of everything now." One of the stepsons was asked at trial whether Prenowitz had ever repeated any promises during the years they had worked for him:

> "Yes, he did; every time he tried to get us to do something that was extra arduous or we thought there was bugs in his idea and objected to it, then he would go into all sorts of tantrums and tell us again all those details."
>
> What did he say, then?
>
> "He told us it was all ours, we were not working for him, we should not be so obstinate and do as he directed us."
>
> "And would you do it?" the lawyer asked.
>
> "We never could resist him because he was a very emotional man, and rather than create a scene we went along with him. And besides that, he was right; we always felt we were doing it for ourselves."[28]

For the courts who decided such cases, the problem was to understand what had convinced the young people to stay or whether they had actually needed convincing. In addition, it was necessary to ascertain what work they had done to earn the land or other property at issue. Was it possible to understand their actions as reliant on promises made by the older property owners? (Or, more precisely, was it impossible to understand their actions except through the lens of such promises?)

Around these questions swirled the gendered premises of the culture. Young men would not, so the courts often presumed, have stayed or returned to work for parents or others without an agreement, something close to a contract. The promises they had heard had to have "ripened" into contracts. Young men were presumptively restive and mobile. They needed to learn trades away from home, or they had already established careers or jobs elsewhere that they would have given up in coming back home. Furthermore, the work they did was work for which pay was presumed. So, when there was no pay, or only inadequate pay, the notion that they were working on the basis of an enforceable understanding—promises that had become a contract—could become a compelling one.

By contrast, the characteristic work of young women, particularly those who stayed to do care and household work, was ordinarily understood as noncompensable.[29] The work they typically did within families—intimate, personal, household care, cleaning, and cooking—often became, in judicial scrutiny, just what daughters did. It lacked the ability to reveal either a contract or presumptive ownership. Such work also did not seem to come into being as a response to promises. Promises heard (and reported on in later testimony) became nothing more than expressions of intentions to make gifts. In a few cases, a daughter or other female relative would be able to show a clear promise by a parent or an older relative that was made before work began. Also, in cases where a daughter took on an "exceptional task," such as the continuing care of violent persons or persons with dementia, courts came eventually to see such work as a job that one took on or continued at only because of an expectation of pay. However, a daughter who remained at home until marriage, where she "helped out," was simply doing what daughters did. In staying on, she might have remained legally "a child unemancipated in fact" even though her chronological age made her an adult. Or, as the brief opposing Anna Ibach's claims put it, the result of her life as a dutiful daughter had caused her no suffering. She had not given up any "prospects in life"; she had not suffered any detriment, and no fraud had been practiced upon her.[30]

In *Ridgway v. English* (1850), a case that set the New Jersey baseline for the treatment of daughters who asked for compensation for work done, a father had asked his older daughter to stay on and help after his wife, the daughter's mother, had died, leaving him with other children to raise. The father had told witnesses that he meant to pay her. When, four years later, she married and built a house, he promised to furnish her with a parlor. Another witness reported that the father had once intended to give her "an outfit; but things had turned out differently, and now he intended she should be well paid." She had been a good housekeeper, he had said, and although she had never been paid for that work, he meant to do so. Still, when he died in 1849, he left her nothing. To the New Jersey Supreme Court, all she had done from 1836 to 1840 in staying on to take care of the household merely constituted the acts of a "dutiful child." While her services were "doubtless useful and meritorious," they remained of the "usual character between persons so related and of such condition in life." All of the services she had rendered could be understood and explained as offered "upon considerations of mutual kindness and mutual comfort and convenience, without presuming that there was any understanding or expectation of pecuniary compensation." The father's promises then became gift talk, which was, by definition, unenforceable.[31]

Such decisions, and there were many of them, can be read as simplifications of a much more complex reality and as decisions that rhetorically squeezed all the various kinds of work that the old drew from the young into a gender binary. In these decisions, inside work was contrasted with outside work, care work contrasted with economically productive work, the ordinary work of a household contrasted with "exceptional" tasks that were explicable and undertaken only because of a contractual understanding, the prospect of marriage contrasted with the prospect of a career, and voluntary gifts contrasted with enforceable contracts.[32] That binary obscures the actual work that both men and women did, which crossed boundaries on both sides. It also probably obscures the seriousness and the intensity—often desperation—with which many parents and other older people negotiated (that is, made promises) for the work of daughters,

daughters-in-law, and other young women. As in *Davison,* the work of a daughter-in-law was at least as crucial to the success of a retirement as that of the son to whom the promise was made. The cases may also hide some of the ways that young women were in fact compensated for remaining and for responding to their parents' promises. Remember Ida in *Davison,* who married later than her sisters and who received a $1,200 marriage portion, as contrasted with the $700 and $900 portions her sisters received.

Furthermore, consider *Hattersley v. Bissett* (1892–1893), in which a daughter postponed marriage until she was well into her forties to care for her father, who had owned a piano factory in Trenton. At trial after her father's death, she was asked how long her husband-to-be had been calling on her. Ten or twelve years, she answered. "Q. Had you a reason for not marrying him sooner than you did? A. My only reason was to stay with my father," who had said to her that "he should remunerate me well for all that I had done, or was doing for him. . . . [H]e felt that he owed it to me." She was her father's housekeeper. They kept no servants. Then, when his health deteriorated in his later years (he died at eighty-four), she served as his nurse. She was never paid. However, shortly before her father's death, he gave her deeds to several pieces of property. Apparently, he did that both to make her equal to her brothers, who had already been given valuable properties, and to pay her for her services. The brothers apparently resented their father's disposition "to prefer her" and fought his decision after his death. They were unsuccessful because, as Vice Chancellor Bird stated, "testators have a right to dispose of their own property according to their own pleasure."[33]

If we imagine the older people as rational economic calculators, we might presume that who got the property in the end was a secondary concern. Of course, they wanted to be able to specify who inherited their property, and they would usually not have wanted conflict between their children or other relatives to result from the dispositional choices they had made. They might also have wished to keep property within the family. However, what was most important was the care, and they would make whatever promises they needed to secure care and attention. All the rest would happen after they were dead.

While they were alive, they did not want to have to pay for the care they received. Why not? Perhaps they lacked cash or were unwilling to convert capital resources into cash, and they did not know that they could borrow against capital. These were not people working within a subsistence economy, yet they were still people for whom paying for domestic services seemed odd, perhaps even "unnatural." They did not want to see themselves as employers. They particularly did not want to "employ" their daughters and sons (including adopted daughters and sons) in tasks that intertwined with a household economy. They wanted to act as if those tasks—that work—belonged to an unmonetized or relatively unmonetized economy, to what the economic historian Avner Offer calls "an economy of regard."[34]

The avoidance of direct pay appears even in many cases that involved unrelated employees—housekeepers, seamstresses, people hired to read to the old, nurses—who sued because they had been promised a legacy in lieu of wages. In *Mulrooney v. O'Keefe* (1923), a middle-aged nurse sued for the work she had done between 1896 and 1906 for Mary Prendergast, an elderly dressmaker. The two of them worked together as seamstresses. In addition, because Prendergast was illiterate, she also needed help with her accounts. "Margaret, dear," she would say, "I have these letters to answer and I have these books I want you to look over and take care of for me." Margaret Mulrooney would work until late at night to get them finished, some nights from seven p.m. until midnight. That happened, she testified, about three times a week throughout that period. When she asked for pay, Prendergast would reply that "She didn't have the money . . . and couldn't pay her; her money was all tied up; but she said, God bless her; she would remember her in her will." Mulrooney described making about twelve dresses a year over a ten-year period for Prendergast and also continued to keep Prendergast's books and to write her letters for her. Then, when Mulrooney decided to leave to go to nursing school, she told Prendergast that she needed money to cover her expenses. Prendergast replied: "God bless you, Margaret. My money is all out on mortgages, but I will remember you in my will."[35]

Other cases revolved around the lives and the work of housekeepers, who often stayed and cared for older men and couples on the promise of an inheritance. In *Cooper v. Colson* (1904), an important case I return to later, a housekeeper stayed with and took care of an old man from 1876 until 1901, when he had to be placed in the Trenton Asylum, probably suffering from the final stages of Alzheimer's. She had worked for him for a year or two and was paid two dollars a week. Then she had made up her mind to go to Montana, but her employer would not let her go. "And then he made a promise that if I staid with him and took care of him as long as he lived, he would give me a farm." So she stayed, and for the rest of her time with him what money she earned came from the chickens she raised. She relied on his promise to give her one of his three farms, a promise repeated endlessly. In the end, however, that promise would not be fulfilled.

What services had she "performed" for the old man? "I did all the work around the place, around the house, I cooked for him, and I cooked for his men—not all the time, but at times I used to milk and I went out into the fields to work, I dropped corn, and husked corn, and I carried the sheaves of wheat and tied them together and carried hay to the mow, and I pitched sheaves of wheat and I did all that one day, and I used to separate the corn . . ." What did she do for him personally? "I used to cut his hair, I had to give him his bath and attend to his clothes, and waited on him every way I could." For how long? "Ever since I lived with him, until about a year before he died, I would cut his hair every time it wanted it. . . . But the last summer we were there I had to give him his bath just like a trained nurse would have to do; he could not do it himself." She never received any extra compensation. Not even toward the end, when she rented a small house in town, where she cared for him. "How long had he been queer and troublesome on account of the softening of the brain . . . ?" "When he got to be real funny, I suppose about six months." Before that time was he any more trouble than an ordinary person? Only at times. "There would be other times before that that he got so he didn't know how to get his clothes on and I would have to help him." Many witnesses confirmed her narrative, both about the work she did and the promises he had made. One witness reported that the old man had frequently said "that all he was giving her was the privilege of raising the poultry for her services." However, "if she remained with him . . . she shall be well repaid for her services." He expected "to deed her the little farm." Another testified that "he wanted her to have a farm . . . [f]or being good to him, and working for him, and he didn't think anyone could do like Maggie did for him. . . . [N]o ordinary hired girl would ever do for Mr. Colson what Maggie Sayres did for Mr. Colson, as their ain't one-half of them cares, and she did care." Over games of checkers and while husking corn, he was always telling listeners that a farm or "the" farm was going to be hers. Another witness described how he had once asked the old man whether he could take some apples lying on the ground, "and he says: 'I have plenty of apples there on Maggie's farm; if you want any, go over there and get them.' . . . and when I was there he came up and said to me that that is Maggie's farm."[36]

Why not just pay for the work needed? Promisors gave many different reasons to avoid pay. Some of the time, an employer/property owner was simply cheating or fooling a naïve younger employee. (Perhaps that is what Mary Mulrooney was doing.) Many women were not used to being paid for their work; perhaps they did not fully expect to be paid and probably found it difficult to ask parents or older authority figures for wages. Some employers then traded on their employees' ambivalence. Often, obviously not in the *Mulrooney* case, the things that people did for one another were not the sorts of services for which pay was expected, or at least those services and activities were at the boundary of what would and would not be paid for. Some of the time there really was little cash available. Many families had little cash, and what they had should not, they believed, go for care. Even small business people often operated with little liquid capital. Thus, it was often easier to use the promise of an inheritance as an alternative. In a few cases, there was testimony that an older person near death had asked a lawyer to figure out how best to compensate a dutiful and long-standing caretaker, and the lawyer had answered that the older person need not worry because that compensation could be worked out after death.[37]

Of course, most of the time wages had not been paid because the "employers" did not want to pay. They did not understand themselves as employers. Even when they did, they often found it convenient to leave the matter to be dealt with after their death—when others could sort out what was owed. Meanwhile, they and their employees could live out the partial fantasy that everything that was going on was being done out of love.

Yet, as always, not paying also carried risks for older people living in a free economy and a mobile society. Many surely felt that it was inappropriate and wrong to have to pay for intimate care or for household work. Many daughters, granddaughters, and adopted children probably did not expect pay or felt uncomfortable asking for it. Nonetheless, when "better" opportunities appeared, those daughters, granddaughters, and adopted children also might leave unless they received something more. Without pay there was little to keep them once they had become adults. Consequently, parents and other older people, like the father in *Ridgway* or the employer in *Colson,* talked about the things they would eventually do for those who worked for them.

Both for older people and for younger family members, legacies and deeds were a way to pay for family work generally and for care work in particular. The point may be less the avoidance of cash payments and more that the legacy—inheritance—was what was in trade within a family. It was what families negotiated over and contracted over, and it was the foundation for the power that property holders and the old in particular retained over younger people. A promise to remember someone in a will, a promise to convey a legacy, the writing of the will, the talk about how to distribute legacies—all of these were ways to mark work as belonging to family space. The promise of an inheritance mediated, created a fuzzy middle ground, between a contractually defined relationship—a labor contract—and freely given familial care. It may have been easy for the courts to imagine that women—daughters and others—usually fell on one side, while sons and other men fell on the other side. Nonetheless, one should not make too much of that. The important thing was the middle ground, where care was still lovingly provided even though everyone knew that there might have been no one available to provide the care had there not been a promise of a legacy.[38]

It may be that many parents resented having to make any promise at all and wanted to be cared for out of love. However, promises to remember someone in a will were easily reconstructed as something different from bargains for care and appeared to construct the relationships as something other than employment. Even when the relationship was unquestionably founded on a labor contract, in a case like *Cooper v. Colson,* for example, the promise of a farm in lieu of adequate wages was both a way of marking how valuable and important a housekeeper's work was and a way of making her into something like family. Throughout much of their lives together, the housekeeper in that case had called her employer "uncle," although they were not kin.[39]

Older men would ostentatiously show children and others a will (or several wills) they had written that accomplished what they had promised. As we have seen, there was such a will in the *Davison* case and several in the *Van Horn* case. Additionally, some of the cases put many wills into evidence, along with much testimony about the brandishing of these documents. We can imagine that showing the will was a way of demonstrating appreciation for and approval of what one had received in care.[40]

Of course, no will meant anything if it was not the final will, formally expressed and witnessed and not revoked. Otherwise, it was just one more expression of an intention to convey and of what had been promised. As in *Davison*, all it took was a quarrel (or a new love), and the will became an old will, superseded either by a new will or by an immediate conveyance to someone other than the child who had been promised the legacy—or by nothing. Whatever happened, once a will was undone by the testator, it became a nullity; the old will became nothing more than evidence of an intention that had not come to fruition.[41]

Sometimes, as in *Davison*, the testator destroyed the will, or it was superseded by a later will, or it disappeared. In a few cases, a technical error (e.g., too few witnesses) voided an otherwise valid will.[42] Others put off writing a will. This could lead to a deathbed will, a situation ripe for an "undue influence" case if the will ended up giving the caretaker at bedside all or most of the property.[43] Other older people waited until it was too late. In *Cooper v. Colson*, for example, dementia intervened, preventing the fulfillment of a promise. In *Scott v. Beola* (1932), Catherine Simms had taken several boys out of orphanages. She had been paid for taking care of some of them (we might call it foster care). She ran a small penny candy shop. Two of the boys stayed with her after they became adults and continued to give her a portion of their wages. She was fond of them, and they were dutiful, for, according to the court, "they knew no other mother." There was no question, the court concluded, that she had promised that they should inherit what she had, including her home. One week before she died, she had asked a neighbor to find a lawyer to write a will for her. She gave one of the boys (now an adult man) the deed to her house and her bankbook to take along to the meeting. However, "she delayed too long." She died before signing a will. In the end that meant, the court concluded, that the testimony showed nothing other than intention. "Mrs. Simms promised bounty, which misfortune thwarted. Intention to will and a contract to will are far different things."[44]

Some persons said that they were superstitious and that writing a will invited death.[45] Others said that they were too busy or were trying to get the will just right. In the case of Bertha Kulat, it was all of the three. She feared that "if she would do so, she was going to die." "I just feel," she told one witness, "if I put my name on that line, I am finished." Bertha, the elderly owner of a butcher shop in Jersey City, had promised to leave the shop to Frank Ehling, a former butcher boy who had over a twenty-six-year period become her informally adopted child. According to Ehling's wife, Grace, and other witnesses, the demands that Bertha constantly made on him drove Frank to drink and threatened their marriage. Still, Bertha also often reminded them that Frank would be her heir. In 1937, while Frank was fixing up the cemetery plot of Bertha's dead husband, the two women talked. Bertha greatly appreciated Frank's care. "There isn't any of my relations would ever think of coming . . . [t]o look at the grave, take care of anything. . . . I could lay and die. That is the only time they would ever attend it." However, "don't worry, Grace. He has been a good boy to me, and I will well take care of him to the rest of his days." Meanwhile, Bertha Kulat consulted regularly with lawyers on various matters. In 1932 she had met with one about an accident. Along the way she told the lawyer, "You know my relationship with Frank Ehling. You know how he has been with me for all of these years, and I promised to make a will whereby I would leave everything to him directly after or immediately after my husband died." The two of them made a second appointment to write the will, but Bertha missed that appointment. In 1938 she met with a different lawyer, who drafted a will for her. She was dissatisfied with some of its terms, although not apparently with making Frank Ehling her residual legatee, who would receive the bulk of her estate. She sent Frank back to the lawyer several times with instructions that detailed how she wanted the will changed. (The lawyer noted that he knew she was waiting in the car, while Frank came upstairs to deliver the instructions.) A new will was prepared. Bertha was still dissatisfied. According to the lawyer, when he got no response to the second draft, he went over to her store and spoke to her about the will. Nevertheless, she still did not sign the will "Because of the fear, as an evil omen in signing the Will." And then she died. That meant that Frank would get nothing.[46]

Chapter Three

Keeping Them Close

I n 1895, when Frances Suchy was not yet ten, her mother died. Antonia and Albert Gedicks, her aunt and uncle, took her in, and from then on, she lived with them, at first in a house in Brooklyn. When Frances moved in with them, the Gedickses were childless German speaking immigrants in their late thirties. Albert was a wigmaker at the firm of A. H. Simonson in New York City. Until 1902 or so, Antonia was a supervisor at J. C. Stratton's cloak and suit factory.

More than a quarter century later, Frances's lawyer described her childhood in a petition to the New Jersey chancellor: "She was treated by them in every respect as though she had been their own daughter; and . . . she grew to womanhood entertaining the same feelings of trust and confidence in her foster parents as though she had been of their own flesh and blood; . . . on her part she rendered and accorded to them the love, duty, service and obedience incumbent upon her and such as would naturally flow from a daughter to her own parents."[1]

When Frances was little, her aunt took care of her and hired help during the hours she had to be at work. Frances went to school until she was sixteen and then worked for three years as a "stenographer and typewriter." Throughout her childhood, Frances did the ordinary chores of a daughter in the home of working parents. As she testified in 1922, "I used to look after the house while Auntie and Uncle went to business; I prepared meals and took care of the chickens—fed them when I got home from school; make beds and dusted; did little things around as I say, every day, until they came home in the evening; and I always had their dinner prepared for them." She also helped her aunt with her business affairs. She was the "custodian" of her papers and wrote out checks for her.

Her aunt was often ill. As Albert testified, Antonia was "troubled with headaches all the time—she was always sick. When she was married, she was always sick," but that did not stop Antonia from doing the family work. "She no was so sick that she laid [sic] down for a long time. She was sick for a couple of days or so, like that, but she always done the house work." Even when she was dying of stomach cancer, Antonia did her own work. At least in Albert's memory, "We had nobody in the house. She done all her own work to the last day. . . . She had a great lot of stew made for me—that means cooking something."

Meanwhile, Frances did not do that much work; instead, according to Albert, she "went out shopping; had the horse and carriage," although he added that he did not really know since he "never was home in the daytime." Other accounts differed. Yet, no one suggested that Frances ever became her aunt's caretaker or the family housekeeper. But Antonia loved Frances and wanted her company.[2]

In 1904 Frances married William Roberts-Horsfield with the permission of her uncle and aunt. William, a salesman and an English immigrant, moved in with the Gedickses. For the next five years or so, the young couple shared housekeeping with the older couple and paid ten dollars a month to Mrs. Gedicks. In 1909 the Gedickses decided to move to New Jersey. There they would build a house on Johnston Drive in North Plainfield. Antonia Gedicks put up most, perhaps all, of the purchase price, but title to the property was held by Albert and Antonia Gedicks as marital property. That is, to talk the language of lawyers, they held it as a tenancy by the entireties, and the whole would automatically go to the spouse that survived after the death of the other. The Roberts-Horsfields, who by then had a small child (they would soon have two more), moved with them and shared the North Plainfield house until 1912, while the Roberts-Horsfield family continued to grow. Frances and Antonia divided the expenses. Throughout those years, according to Frances's petition to the chancellor, "the relations . . . between all parties was of the most pleasant character."[3]

In 1912 Frances and William decided to move out because they wanted to live in their own house. What had led them to that decision? According to the petition drafted with their lawyer, "their desire to take this step was not the result of any break in the old home, or in any change in the pleasant relations existing there." Rather, they made that decision because setting up housekeeping on their own in their own place was what a married couple with children did. It was their "natural wish and desire . . . to have a home of their own where they might rear their children in their own way and entirely removed from any influence or interference from others." They advertised in the local paper for a place they could rent with a purchase option.[4]

Then, however, at least as Frances remembered it, Antonia and Albert Gedicks made the young couple an offer. There was no reason for them to move away, they told them. In fact, the property the Gedickses had bought had plenty of unused land, so the young couple could build a house on one corner of the lot. "We will give you that corner there for yourself." They would also have a deed drawn up; "it would be ours," according to Frances. In addition, Antonia would help with the costs of the construction of the house. She had money of her own from the sale of property in Brooklyn, and she wanted to spend it on them.[5]

Why had Antonia and Albert made the offer? Mary Groszmann, a neighbor and the wife of the head of a pioneering school for "nervous and atypical children" located in North Plainfield, had an answer. She talked with Antonia regularly when she walked by the Gedickses' property on her way to and from the grocery store. Both Antonia and

Albert were very fond of Frances and of the Roberts-Horsfield children. It was "perfectly natural," Antonia had told Mary Groszmann, for young people to look for a place for themselves. For that reason, if one wanted to keep them near—in what was, Antonia conceded, a "lonely country"—it was important to offer "some inducement." That was why they had decided to give them a piece of ground where they could build a home. "Of course, I will try to help them with the home, [help in the] building of it." However, her son-in-law was "a very independent self-reliant young man and I cannot help him as much as I would like to, and I am [a] very lonely, unhappy woman, I am very much alone here." She dearly wanted "to keep Mrs. Horsfield near me, and the children."[6]

The Roberts-Horsfields accepted the offer, and Antonia Gedicks drew up a contract with a builder. The builder asked why the land was not in the name of Mr. and Mrs. Roberts-Horsfield. Antonia answered, "No, it hasn't been transferred yet." The contract had to be with Antonia Gedicks alone, but the building expenses were shared between them. According to Frances, she and her husband paid for the heating, the kitchen range, and all of the piping, plumbing, electric fixtures, and wiring. They also painted the house inside and out. William's father gave the plumbing fixtures as a gift. William, who was "handy," did much of the work himself.

Once they were in the house, the Roberts-Horsfields paid no rent, and they did not pay the property taxes, although they offered to do so repeatedly. While Antonia was alive, she continued to pay the insurance as well.[7]

There are glimmers of another, less idyllic story behind the words that Frances Roberts-Horsfield's lawyers crafted with her in a 1921 petition to the chancellor. When William and Frances testified at chancery chambers in Newark on April 26, 1922, about why they had decided to move out in 1912, the story became less about a natural evolution toward a predictable nuclear family. There was a push, as well as a pull.

According to Frances, "Uncle would come home night after night and we never knew just when he would be in good humor and he wouldn't think anything of coming in and firing around the furniture and using vile language." The Gedickses' home "was not the place for us to raise our children—they were just at that age to know and understand those things—we thought it would be the best thing to have a home for ourselves."

William was more discreet in his direct testimony: "I wanted a home of my own. I was dissatisfied with conditions with respect—that existed in the home. I wanted to bring up my son and my daughter in a homelike atmosphere the same as I had been used to." However, then under cross-examination, he expanded. Had they left, as Albert had claimed, because Antonia Gedicks was in so "nervous" a state that she suggested they leave? Had the young children "made too much noise" and thereby prevented her from sleeping during the day? No, that was not correct.

What, then, had William not liked about the Gedickses' home? "There was constant bickering and squabbling between them [Albert and Antonia] over various things and money matters—lots of other things that were unreasonable. Uncle would come home in a very excited state and things—sometimes he would come home under the influence of liquor—he would get up in the morning at one o'clock and stalk around the household making a general racket and a general noise. He sometimes got his wife so excited that she screamed. I remember once she lay on the floor and screamed because he was constantly bickering with her and bickering at her and picking at her." Their fights, William insisted, were about "money matters and other things," not about the presence of the younger family in the home.[8]

The trial testimony dredged up more. When Antonia died, which happened in 1916, she did so in Brooklyn, not in New Jersey with her husband. She went to die with other relatives, not with her husband. Throughout their lives together, Antonia and Albert kept separate accounts. At some point after the move to North Plainfield, Antonia brought a lawyer to the house to threaten Albert and tell him that he had to provide more for the house maintenance. Antonia had told Frances to listen in on the conversation, and Frances did so sitting upstairs. She heard her aunt say that she could not "get along on $10 a week, to pay the insurance on the house, and buy the coal and clothe her, pay her doctor's bill and everything." The lawyer told Albert that he had better give her more money and treat her better. If he did not, "he would put Uncle under bonds of peace." The meeting concluded when Albert agreed to give Antonia fifteen dollars a week and promised to try to treat her better.[9]

Albert Gedicks, not surprisingly, told a very different story. According to him, he was always the main breadwinner and always handed over most of his paycheck to his wife. When he was earning fifteen dollars a week, he gave it all to her (except for a couple of dollars). When he was earning thirty dollars and more, he would give her twenty to thirty dollars a week. He did not know what became of the money she earned at her job. Antonia may have cared for Frances when she was little, but he had paid the expenses of her care. "Yes, sir; I got to pay the money." Why had they moved to New Jersey in 1909? His wife was sick, and she wanted to live in the country. "It was a little far for me, but I wanted to suit the women, and I went out and lived there too." Why had they asked the Roberts-Horsfields to come along with them? "We were getting used to them." The argument that brought the lawyer to their house was pure "imagination." "They . . . had an argument about I no give her money and right away the next day was the lawyer there." He always paid her regularly (though this time he marked it at fifteen to twenty dollars a week), "and I got to pay the coachman. . . . Had a coachman? Yes, sir. Mrs. Gedicks wanted . . . a horse and carriage."

Albert insisted that large sections of the narrative contained in the 1921 petition to the chancellor were false. It was not true that in 1912

Frances and William were moved "by a natural desire to have a home of their own where they might rear their children." The truth was rather that Antonia was by then an invalid and "of a nervous disposition." The children were "a continual source of irritation and annoyance" because of the noise they made. "You know a woman that is sick is cranky." Albert suggested that it was time to make a change. Moreover, it was he, he claimed, who came up with the idea of building a house in the corner of their property where the Roberts-Horsfields could live—near but apart. As a result, his wife, "under my instructions," entered into a contract with the builder. The only contribution made by the Roberts-Horsfields was for the plumbing and plumbing supplies, which William said he could obtain at wholesale and which amounted to $150, and the painting, which was worth $100. There was no promise ever that this property would be deeded to them.

That said, Albert, like his wife, wanted the Roberts-Horsfields to stay close in order to keep them company. At the time they had moved to North Plainfield, it was still a very rural place. Their nearest neighbor on Johnston Drive lived about a half mile away. Neither he nor his wife had any friends nearby, and he did not want his wife to be lonely. He knew his wife needed the company of Frances and her children. "We feel lonesome in the house, you know. I was all day out, leave in the morning at half past six and come home half past seven in the evening, and she was all alone in the house." Besides, he loved the children. "I got them presents every night" both before and after they lived in the same house.[10]

When William Roberts-Horsfield was pressed in cross-examination to explain why he had not insisted on a deed at the time the second house was constructed, he could "only explain it this way ... Mr. Gedicks and Mrs. Gedicks with us were as good as gold. Uncle to us was the finest fellow that walked. He really was. No question about it. He was good to me, good to my children and good to all of us in every respect, and I am not mercenary enough to take people like that, who are doing the right thing, and I say they were doing the right thing, and hold them by the throat, under the circumstances."[11]

Antonia Gedicks became sicker in the three years after they built the second house on the property. One day, while they all sat in the front parlor of the larger house, the question of a deed came up. Frances asked that it be "attended to." And her uncle agreed. However, her aunt "got another spell," and nothing happened before Antonia's death in June 1916.[12]

Antonia's will, prepared in 1903, thirteen years earlier, gave Frances Suchy (not yet Frances Roberts-Horsfield) half of her estate, while the rest went to Antonia's sister and brother. Albert was excluded. He felt unjustly treated by his wife, especially as her "accumulations" were, he felt, the result of his thirty years of work. The land in North Plainfield, though, became his because it had been conveyed to them as a tenancy by the entireties.[13]

Shortly after her aunt's death, Frances again asked her uncle to make a deed for the property that she was living on. "If anything happens to you you know how we would stand in reference to your relations." According to her, he agreed that it ought to be "fixed" and said that it would be "attended to."

A few days later, in mid-July 1916, they went to a lawyer's office to have Antonia's will read and explained. After the lawyer had completed that task, Albert said, "Now, Mr. Blatt, . . . I want to protect my niece; she has that ground down there." He continued, "I want to protect her in every way—the best way I thought was to adopt her." However, Blatt discouraged Albert from adoption. "That is not necessary," he said. Instead, the lawyer recommended that he draw up a will that left everything to Frances. Right "then and there" Albert told the lawyer to prepare such a will. Frances would get everything, including the property on which the Roberts-Horsfield home stood.[14]

Then, in November 1917, Albert remarried—to Cecilia, a twenty-seven-year-old Irish woman (he was by then in his late fifties). Frances again asked him for a deed. "I could see that his present wife didn't want to have anything to do with us[,] and I could just see what sort of person she was, and I thought to myself, well, if anything should happen to Uncle, I would know just how we would be placed." The attorney cross-examining her wanted to know why she was not satisfied to rely on the will that Albert had made. She answered: "Because I knew that he was married and that his wife . . . would come in for the property—all the property." They would lose "that ground" on which they lived because they did not have "proper deeds."[15]

What Frances suspected would happen did indeed happen. Albert soon wrote a new will that gave all of his property to his new wife. Then, on July 8, 1920, after the birth of Cecilia's first child (by the time of the litigation there would be two), he conveyed the property on Johnston Drive to Cecilia. When asked why he had done so, Albert described it as a natural husbandly and fatherly act: "I got a wife and got two children now, I got to protect my family and myself; before I had no children." Earlier, in his "Response" to the Petition of Frances and William, he had explained it somewhat differently. He was tired of their "disposition" to "take all they could lay their hands on:

> Ever since the marriage between the complainants there has been a constant desire upon the part of both of the complainants to acquire all of the property belonging to my wife and myself at the expense of any member of my family who is closely related to me. They always used and considered what I owned as theirs, and when I had an automobile continued to use it to such an extent that I finally got tired of paying repair bills and cost of operation, and made them a present of the automobile; and by reason of their disposition, they never looked with favor upon my marriage and my efforts to perform my duty and protect my wife and child.

From Frances's perspective, of course, the story was rather about an old man who had fallen into the hands of a designing woman who had "conceived the design of stripping" Frances and William of their home and who had poisoned Albert's relations with his niece's family: "Almost immediately after the said marriage the conduct of her . . . uncle changed in a great degree toward her; his former daily visits almost entirely ceased; he avoided in every way meeting or being with . . . [her] and her husband; he even refrained from calling at their home when her child lay dangerously ill, although theretofore the child had been a pet with him and had received many gifts as tokens of his love and affection."[16]

Cecilia speculated that Frances and William probably did not like the idea of Albert remarrying, but she also acknowledged that she "didn't really care to mix in with them, that is all. I kept by myself." At a certain point she became tired of being treated "as an interloper." In December 1920 she told Frances that thereafter they had to pay twenty-five dollars a month rent if the Roberts-Horsfields intended to stay on her land. When Frances replied that she would see her uncle about that, Cecelia replied, "He has nothing to do with it; it is in *my* name." Frances protested: "This is my place; it was given to me by my aunt and uncle." "*Your* ground?" Cecilia replied. "Have you papers to show for it?" Frances also remembered that when Cecilia asked for rent, she also said that "we could take our house on our backs and walk off with it if we refused to pay the rent."[17]

In January, when no rent was forthcoming, Cecilia began an action to evict them. Frances and William called movers to see about moving the house they had built from the land they thought had been given them. However, after giving up on this idea, they went instead to a lawyer and soon thereafter brought an action in equity. Their petition claimed either that they had made a binding contract with Albert and Antonia Gedicks for the parcel of land on which their house stood, a contract that Albert was bound to fulfill, and a contract that Cecilia was fully aware of when she was deeded the property or, in the alternative, that Albert and Antonia had already given the parcel to them as a gift.

In 1922 Vice Chancellor Backes decided that Frances Roberts-Horsfields had received her land as a gift "pure and simple" from her aunt and that, "under the circumstances . . . shown," that gift was enforceable in equity. Two years later, after the death of Albert Gedicks, the New Jersey Court for the Correction of Errors and Appeals unanimously affirmed the vice chancellor's decision. A "parol" gift of land was ordinarily invalid, but when the gift was accompanied by possession and when the recipient had been induced by the promise of the gift to make improvements to the property, to mark it as belonging to the recipient, then an equity court could enforce the gift and could compel a conveyance by the legal owner to the recipient so that the recipient would have full title to the property. In this case, the fact that Antonia Gedicks paid for many of the improvements—the construction of the house—should be understood, according to the vice chancellor, as not undercutting Frances's claim. The evidence revealed that Antonia intended that her payments and purchases be understood as a separate gift to her niece. Albert clearly knew of his wife's intentions, and whether his new wife, Cecilia, knew all the circumstances or not, she was put on notice by the "open and notorious possession" of the Roberts-Horsfield family. Thus, she could not claim to have been an innocent purchaser, a "bona fide purchaser for value without notice." She, like Albert, would be bound by Antonia's acts. She would also have to convey to Frances a deed to the land.[18]

When aging people thought about what they needed for their old age, when they thought about the project of preparing for old age, they did not only think about direct physical care. Surely, keeping the young close was often intended as a form of insurance for future care. Yet that was not all the older people assumed they needed from the young. Indeed, we might imagine that at a time of life when they were still mostly hale and healthy, most of them avoided thinking much about direct physical care. Rather, they might have focused on securing presence, about making sure that those one loved remained present. Obediently present was important, as was caringly and lovingly present. But it may well be that presence itself was most important.

We might imagine that an unwell Antonia Gedicks was thinking at least some of the time of her own physical care in some imagined but not to be realized future, of a time when Frances, her niece and adopted daughter, would have been needed and used. Yet the care that Frances might have offered Antonia never appeared in the trial testimony. Instead, what witnesses emphasized was that Antonia wanted Frances close at hand. The New Jersey she was moving to was lonely and isolated, and quite different from the thicker community in Brooklyn she had left behind. If she wanted Frances's presence, the culturally approved (and usually economically rational) desires of younger people to move away had to be countered.

Indeed, to survey nineteenth- and early twentieth-century advice for the elderly is to be overwhelmed by the anxieties of solitude. There was no imagined escape from abandonment. Children and grandchildren would always depart. One would always confront old age, in the end, as a solitary individual or, at best, as part of a temporary couple. Those you loved had left you. And in America that probably meant that they were far, far away. Without them life was hard to bear.

In Lydia Sigourney's 1854 advice book for the old, *Past Meridian*, she imagined herself talking with an elderly couple who ought to be happy with their situation but who complained of their loneliness. In the hectoring voice typical of such literature, Sigourney told her imagined subjects, as well as her readers, to get over it and to be reconciled to their situation. "Age should clothe itself with love, to resist the loneliness of its lot." However, moaned the old people, "Our children are married and gone. . . . We cannot be expected to have much enjoyment." She pounced. Would they have it otherwise? Would it be better if those children remained "all at home," disconnected from the growing economy, "pining with disappointed hope, or in solitude of the heart?" Instead they were elsewhere, implanting virtues they had learned from their parents. They were diffusing "the energy of right habits and the high influence of pure principles" "in newer settlements." They were "Gone!" The old couple ought to "Praise God that it is so."[19]

At least in the advice givers' imaginations, to be old was to be confronted with the death or the absence of everyone one had loved or cared for. To be old was to be lonely as one became decrepit while awaiting death. "Your afflictions may have been many and sore, and your present circumstances may be embarrassing, and your prospects for the future gloomy" was how Archibald Alexander of Princeton Seminary described the situation. "Providence may seem to have set you up as a mark for the arrows of adversity. Stroke upon stroke has been experienced. Billow after billow has gone over you and almost overwhelmed you. Truly the time has come when you can say, 'My joys are gone.'" William S. Plumer described the many reasons the old had for feeling depressed. Most of them were about absences and the deaths of others, loneliness, and isolation, although he also mentioned the potential pain of having ungrateful children nearby.

In mainstream Protestant texts, absence and loss were reformulated as opportunities for individual salvation. According to Archibald Alexander, only God remained true and present for the old, as all others either disappointed or disappeared: "But though friends have been snatched from you or have proved unfaithful; though children, once your hope and joy, are numbered with the dead, or what is far worse, profligate or ungrateful; though your property has wasted away, or your riches suddenly taken wings and flown like the eagle to heaven; though bodily diseases and pain distress you, still trust in the divine promise, 'I will never leave thee, nor forsake thee.'" In a "Sketch from Life" in the Reverend S. G. Lathrop's *Fifty Years and Beyond, or Gathered Gems for the Aged*, an elderly wife says to her husband, "What are we going to do? Children gone (dead). We will have to go to the poor-house." The wise husband answers, "We are poor but not yet forsaken. Heaven will help us." The wife: "I know God is our friend; but we should have friends here." But they do not, so they pack up to go to the poorhouse. Then, at the last moment, God saves them by the fortunate arrival of a young man the husband had once saved from the house of correction.

Such works advised old people that if they were lucky, they would "be cheered by frequent contact with the buoyant cheerfulness of chil-dren, and the kindly deference and sympathy of all in the family and social circle." Yet, there were constant reminders that old people had no way to ensure or rely on the presence of others. Indeed, the only real salvation came not from company but from contemplating one's fast-approaching death. The old ought to investigate "How to die safely," as Alexander titled one of his sermons. What is more, death would be experienced alone, not with others. After death, one might, if saved, be rejoined with loved ones gone before, but until then one ought to be reconciled to the reality that one's remaining life would be lived alone.[20]

More liberal works, often authored by women, reformulated the "extreme loneliness" that was identified with old age as instead a tran-sition toward something better. It may, wrote Lydia Maria Child, "prove to be but as the quiet dreamy hour, 'between the lights,' when the day's work is done, and we lean back, closing our eyes, to think it all over before we finally go to rest, or to look forward, with faith and hope, unto the coming Morning." Henry Ward Beecher believed "you should so live that when you come into old age you will not have to begin in a new and untried way." By then piety should be "measured to your form." Such works also challenged readers with examples of service and generosity to others that might counter isolation.[21]

Lydia Maria Child began *Looking toward Sunset,* her 1865 compila-tion of advice, poetry, potted biographies, and short stories for the old, with a story she had written, called "The Friends." Here she contrasted the lives of two childhood playmates, Harriet and Jane. Harriet spent her life being served rather than serving. She married a wealthy man, and she would die lonely and alone except for the convenient and saving nearby presence at the last of her old friend Jane. Jane, by contrast, had a happy life of service and was nearly always in the company of others.

Some highlights of Jane's happy life, one that epitomized for Child the selfless female life of service: She married a storekeeper and had two children. After her husband developed a disability, she went to work as a mantua maker to support the family. Neighbors sympathized with her "hard row to hoc." However, Jane regarded it as a "mingled cup," one that she would not exchange for another. Then her duties expanded. Her husband's parents became feeble. "They needed the presence of children and could also assist their invalid son by receiving him into their house." So, all of them moved to his parents' home in Massachusetts. Her parents moved with them because they were "unwilling to relinquish the light of her presence." Now she was taking care of two sets of older people, a "great increase of care, to which was added the necessity for vigilant economy. Yet, Child added, "the energy of the young matron grew with the demands upon it." Again, others commented on what a hard life she had. She replied: "Nobody can tell, until they try it, what a satisfaction there is in making old folks comfortable. They cling so to those that take good care of them that . . . I find it does me about as much good as it did to tend upon my babies."

As the years passed, her husband, her parents, and her son all died. Still she smiled through her tears. "God has been very merciful to me. It was *such* a comfort to tend upon them to the last, and to have them die blessing me!" Her daughter married and moved to Illinois. Jane would have liked to follow, but she needed to stay in order to take care of her parents-in-law. Eventually they died, too, and left her a small house, an acre of land, and $1,000. Now that she was all alone, she wrote to her daughter that she was coming to join her in Illinois. However, at that moment a stranger arrived with two young children, a boy and a girl. Her daughter and her daughter's husband, it seems, had both died in an epidemic, leaving their children orphans. It was those children who had just then been brought to her door for her to raise and, Child emphasized to the reader, to lighten her old age. Once again she responded to a neighbor who wondered why she did not seem burdened by her troubles: "The troubles of this life come so mixed up with blessings that we are well to endure one for the sake of having the other; and then our afflictions do us so much good that I reckon *they* are blessings, too." Eventually the grandson grew up and moved west to teach school. The granddaughter in this fantasy "never did desert" her but declined marriage during her grandmother's lifetime and cared for her grandmother "tenderly to the last." Jane would never be lonely.[22]

Service was supposed to make a difference and was thus one of the mantras of the advice genre.[23] Besides, service, at least in Child's happy ending, would keep an old person from dying alone. However, within the confines of the old age advice literature, whether liberal or orthodox, there was no easy escape from solitude and loneliness. To return to Lydia Sigourney's peroration, would you want your children to be constrained and limited in their ambitions and life chances by the need to stay near you? Would you want them stuck in or near the family home?

For many older people, the answer to such questions must have been yes. It might have been good for the soul to experience old age as abandonment and isolation and as the absence of all relationships aside from that with God or Christ. However, that is not how many older people wanted to live their later lives. They wanted family close at hand.

How, though, could they keep their children close in an explosive and mobile economy? Love and service provided often inadequate answers. Punishing or threatening to punish those who ignored or abandoned their parents offered perhaps a better way, and the New Jersey courts repeatedly made it clear that cutting out those who neglected to visit or stay, while rewarding those who did, was an entirely legitimate use of testamentary power. The New Jersey Prerogative so ruled in an 1875 challenge to the codicil to the will of a ninety-four-year-old man, an early doctor of homeopathy, who undid the legacies in his will to several children and grandchildren. It was fine to discriminate in favor of a daughter who had devoted herself to him and had "ministered" to his care and sympathy. Furthermore, that conclusion was reinforced by the fact that he had been neglected by others who had earlier been mentioned in the will, most of whom did not live that far away. If they had "felt an interest" in his "welfare, some of them, at least, would have visited him." Since they had not, it was entirely rational for him to take their absence into account when he added a codicil and decided on the disposition of his estate.[24]

Another possible solution to the problem of how to prevent loneliness and abandonment was one that *Gedicks v. Roberts-Horsfield* illustrates. The trick was to give but not to give: "keeping while giving."[25] The trick was to find a balance. Children had to feel secure enough that they would sink roots, invest, stay. They also had to feel that the land or the business had become theirs. At the same time, older property owners knew that it was important not to transfer title, at least not until after death.

We can assume that most such later transactions occurred relatively unproblematically. Had Albert Gedicks not remarried, he would surely have transferred land to Frances Roberts-Horsfield. One can also imagine that he would have had the continuing company of her family for the rest of his life. In fact, something like that must have happened routinely. Before or after death, by deed, or in a will, a father or mother would have completed the transaction, given the son or daughter the land or business the child had worked, leaving a warm glow of remembered generosity.

However, often—indeed regularly from the vantage point of the courts—the routine became the exceptional. Families quarreled, or sons died untimely, fathers remarried, creditors interfered or prevented an expected transaction, or property owners changed their minds about bargains previously made. When something like that occurred, then family members confronted the complex question of whether the younger person's "possession"—that person's demonstrations and markings of ownership—of the land or business was of such a form that the court (usually an equity court) should recognize that an effective transfer of possession had already been carried out and that the older person had already given what that person thought had been kept.

The common and conventional legal answer to that question was that, without a deed, without a completed conveyance, the younger person was there on sufferance or as a tenant and thus was without rights or powers. The adult child, as an adult, was imagined as a competent individual who could have negotiated a sale with another competent adult, that person's parent. If no sale, no deed, and no conveyance had occurred, then no transfer of ownership had taken place. What had occurred was at most an uncompleted gift. What is more, if the adult child had stayed on land owned by a parent without a full transfer of ownership, the adult child assumed the risk of being evicted or of discovering that someone else had become the new owner. That was what testator's freedom meant in such situations.

However, from the 1850s on, New Jersey's equity courts applied a variety of doctrinal tools—exceptions to the common and conventional legal answer—to find ways to confirm the rights and the possession of some children who had been put on land by parents or other older relatives. Younger people, through their lawyers, could look to a line of appellate decisions—*Davison v. Davison* would have been one common precedent; *Van Duyne v. Vreeland* would have been another—that enforced the older people's promises to younger people about land. Such decisions depended on the weight that particular judges and chancellors gave to the strictures of the Statute of Frauds against oral promises to convey land, to their varying understandings of the role of equity in moderating or countering rigid common-law rules about property, and most of all to the evidence—the stories—the litigants and their lawyers presented. Much of the time the testimony would have failed to convince the court that there had been enough reliance, enough evidence of a life fundamentally shaped—warped—by the older person's undertaking, enough "performance" that could be understood only as responding to commitments made. Still, numbers of younger people and their lawyers did manage to meet those standards.

What chancellors and vice chancellors looked for from the testimony in cases like *Gedicks v. Roberts-Horsfield* was whether older people had put children on land because they wanted them to stay. Staying became a core consideration: the burden the younger people had assumed when they had accepted the offer to live on the land. The courts also looked to the investments made or the "help" provided by the old in getting the young settled, as well as the ways that the young worked to make the property their own. The point was not care as such. Rather, it was settling in and staying close by in response to one's parents' wishes (or those of another older person).[26]

In 1852, in the first such New Jersey decision to appear in the published records, Chancellor Williamson ruled that Jacob France Junior had the right to compel Jacob France Senior to convey to him the tract of land in Blairstown, New Jersey, that he had lived on for the previous eighteen years. According to his petition, Jacob Junior had been about to purchase land in 1834 "for the purpose of clearing it up & cultivating it." At that time, as Jacob Junior remembered it, his father told him that "it was unnecessary . . . to buy land and that too of a stranger" when he had "so much uncultivated land." The land would be his if he would "only clear it up." His father promised that if his son would improve and clear that land, making it "proper for tilling and meadow," he, Jacob Senior, would give Jacob Junior "a good and sufficient deed of conveyance." Jacob Junior accepted his father's offer and spent the next years clearing most of the heavily wooded twenty-five acres, putting in an orchard, cultivating a garden, and building a "neat" log home and barn. Along the way the land grew in value from five dollars an acre to fifteen dollars an acre. All of his labor was carried out "in the confident expectation" that his father would honor his good-faith agreement.

However, in September 1847, thirteen years after Jacob Junior had moved onto the land, his father served notice on his son that he "demanded" possession of the premises. In May 1848 Jacob Senior proposed that Jacob Junior and he make a lease and that Jacob Junior start paying him rent. Jacob Junior refused, and in 1850 Jacob Senior began an action of ejectment.[27]

Jacob Senior may have wanted the land back because Jacob Junior's improvements to it had increased its value. There had evidently been earlier litigation between father and son in 1837. In any event, the relationship between them had soured. According to Jacob Senior, he had never promised to "set off" land to Jacob Junior. Rather, back in 1834 he had noticed that Jacob Junior was "not doing very well, living upon property for which he had to pay rent." Jacob Junior was "in debt," but he was "desirous of bettering his condition." It had therefore been an act of simple fatherly kindness on Jacob Senior's part to give him "permission to go upon" the twenty-five-acre lot "upon condition that he would improve it some and that he might remain there a few years without paying rent."

Most of the testimony confirmed Jacob Junior's version of how he came to "possess" the land in question. Isaac Blackford, a neighbor, had been present when Jacob Junior's house was raised. At that time, Jacob Senior told him "he was going to set off" land to Jacob Junior and that "as soon as he got a deed wrote for it he would sign it." Jacob Junior "had talked about buying land of somebody else," but Jacob Senior "said he told him that he had land enough and he would give him a piece there and there was no use of his buying land. . . . Jacob [Junior] might as well be working for himself as working on other people[']s land." He and several other witnesses described how much work Jacob Junior had had to do in order to bring order to the farm. All of them suggested or said that no one would do such work without an expectation of ownership. George France, Jacob Junior's son and Jacob Senior's grandson, described what had happened when his father went to his grandfather to ask for a deed. He remembered that his grandfather had denied ever having promised to give his father a deed, but then his grandmother had entered the conversation. She had told her husband that there was no use in his denying it for she had heard him. Jacob Senior then told his wife, George's grandmother, "to be still."[28]

In the small town of Harmony, a short distance away from the tract that Jacob Junior and Jacob Senior fought over, lived a farmer, Henry Young, with three sons.[29] About the time that Jacob France Senior demanded rent from Jacob France Junior, Henry Young's oldest son, another Jacob, brought home a wife, Huldah Miller, from New York City.[30] Soon thereafter Henry Young took Jacob aside and said that he had bought a neighboring farm for him. Then, according to Huldah, testifying many years later, Henry said that if Jacob "would move on said farm and keep it up and repair and improve and cultivate it and bear his own expense in so doing he [Henry] would give him the farm when he was done with it." The 110-acre parcel would be conveyed to Jacob either by will or by deed.[31]

Jacob Young and Huldah, his bride, moved onto the land and, with his father's help, built a house and several outbuildings, put in an orchard, fenced the property (perhaps using lumber from his father's land), paid taxes on the land, and painted the name "Jacob Young" in bright bold letters on the barn. Around 1850 Huldah received an inheritance of $1,872, which was invested in "improvements" to the property. Jacob and Huldah worked this land for the next twenty-seven years. They had a daughter, Dorothea, who grew up there, and all their neighbors knew the farm as Jacob Young's property. Moreover, father Henry Young repeated his promise often, and for nearly thirty years he did nothing inconsistent with the understanding he and Jacob had apparently come to in 1848.

Meanwhile, Jacob Young was also investing in other real estate with a notable lack of success, and by 1876 he was indebted to several creditors, including his brother, William. William later testified that he was owed either $900 or $1,400 and that Jacob had not paid any of the interest he had promised to pay.

In mid-March 1876, Jacob and Huldah's daughter, Dorothea, married Benjamin McCord in New York City. Huldah went there to help her set up housekeeping, while Jacob stayed behind in Harmony. On March 30, a Sunday, Jacob went to his father's house for a midday dinner, and while there he got into an argument with brother William. Two days later, early in the morning, he was found, dying, in a smokehouse or summer kitchen on "his" property. His skull had been fractured, and he had been beaten with a stick.

No one was ever arrested for the murder of Jacob Young. The murder would remain unsolved, a continuing Warren County mystery. However, folded in with a published transcript of testimony taken before the Warren County Orphans' Court were three handwritten sheets that included the following list of suspects:

1 "Pompey" Garren, a neighbor and an auctioneer who had quarreled with Jacob Young before the murder; when Jacob Young was found dead, Garren became nervous and hanged himself in a barn a few days after. (The unknown writer added: "He was thought to be innocent.")

2 Charlie Hunter (referred to in later testimony as "filthy Charlie Hunter"). He and his family "stole all they could get their hands on and were of bad repute among the neighbors."

3 "Hank" Merrill.

4 "Brother," William Young, "who Jacob owed 3 notes on April 1st (was due day of murder)"

[In the margin of the first page someone else had added "5 Benny McCord," who was Jacob Young's new son-in-law.][32]

Brother William Young was one of the first to find the dying or already dead Jacob, and evidently his thoughts ran to his debt and his lack of a piece of paper—a note—that acknowledged the debt he was owed, or at least so reported a number of witnesses. William was said to have climbed into the window of Jacob's locked study, looking for a tin box. Many witnesses were asked whether they had seen anyone take a key that would unlock a box of that sort.

However, for our purposes William's most important act was to call on his cousin William Mackey, an attorney. He wanted the attorney to go to his father's house and change Henry's will, which, as drafted, did give the land on which Jacob and Huldah had farmed to Jacob on Henry's death. Mackey did so on Wednesday or Thursday, and Henry Young's will was changed to give the land to William and to his brother Peter on their father's death. According to Mackey, William also took him aside at that time and asked him whether, if no note for the debt could be found, he and Mackey could write a new note and put Jacob's name on it. Mackey answered that he did not think "that would do."[33]

The next day Jacob's wife and daughter, Huldah and Dorothea, returned to Harmony from New York City. That weekend, while Dorothea was visiting at her grandfather's house, William took her aside. He planned, he told her, "to file in" to her father's estate in order "to beat" her mother. If she would go along with that, "he would divide the money" with her. Her mother "need not know anything about . . . how things were fixed." Dorothea refused.

Henry Young, Jacob's father and Dorothea's grandfather, was old, and apparently his sons William and Peter worried that he might weaken and write a third will, one that would have either allowed

Huldah to stay on the land or have given it entirely to Dorothea. So, a few days later, they brought their attorney cousin, William Mackey, back to the house. There he drafted and formalized an immediate transfer of the property on which Huldah was living from their father to his surviving sons, William and Peter. Now the two surviving sons would not need to wait for Henry's death. The land was theirs.

In June 1876, William and Peter Young sued Huldah Young and Dorothea McCord as trespassers. Henry Young, the father, died in January 1877. Then, in March 1877, the two brothers began a second action for trespass against Huldah, Dorothea, and Dorothea's husband. That same month William and Peter also brought an action of ejectment against Huldah and Dorothea. Trial on the latter was held in September 1877, and judgment was entered in William and Peter's favor. Huldah and Dorothea "submitted to judgment," that is, agreed to be evicted, in exchange for having the trespass suits dropped.

Huldah was then evicted from the farm that she and her husband, Jacob, had worked and lived on since 1849. Litigation between the Young brothers and their widowed sister-in-law continued for the next six years: Their legal actions concerned the debts owed to William, as well as Huldah's desire for compensation for the improvements to the land that she had paid for with her inheritance. However, in those suits one can read Huldah's claims as implicitly acknowledging that the land now belonged to William and Peter. (In any case, she had lost on both grounds.)[34] Between 1881 and 1884, Dorothea McCord, Huldah's daughter, twice sued William and Peter Young for false imprisonment and assault, and twice she won large jury verdicts. However, each time the decision was overturned on appeal, and in 1884 she, William, and Peter came to some kind of out-of-court settlement.[35]

Then, in 1889, thirteen years after Jacob's murder, Huldah and Dorothea were back in court before the chancellor of the New Jersey Court of Equity. The bill they filed claimed that they were entitled to a decree against William and Peter, that William and Peter held the land that Huldah and Jacob had once farmed "in trust" for the two women, that William and Peter be ordered to specifically perform the contract Jacob had made with his father, and that the two surviving brothers account for the "rent, issues, and profits" of the farm during the time that they had wrongfully held it in their possession.

William and Peter demurred. That is, they responded that the law was completely on their side and that, even if Huldah and Dorothea proved all of the facts they alleged, they still could not win. However, William and Peter also told a contrasting story and presented a different set of "facts."

In 1848, as William and Peter Young remembered it, all of Henry's children had lived with him in his "mansion house," and his sons "all assisted their father in the cultivation of the lands." (In order to diminish the significance of Huldah's stake in the property, they described her as still living with her father, William Miller, in New York City even after the marriage.) At that time, Jacob desired to farm for himself, and Henry agreed to rent him a neighboring farm he had bought. Jacob and Henry agreed that Jacob would pay one half of the annual product of the farm as rent. Henry had generously provided Jacob with horses, cows, and hogs, and he had killed Jacob's meat for the first year. He had given Jacob tools, flour, and provisions, as well as bedding and other furniture. Jacob, Huldah, and Dorothea lived on the land on those terms until April 1, 1866, when the terms of tenancy were changed. From then on Jacob paid $250 rent annually, plus one half of the taxes, and this revised tenancy continued up to his death. Throughout all those years, Jacob paid rent as a mere tenant. (According to William and Peter, however, he was often much behind in his payments. "Their father often complained to them as well as to others that Jacob was a very poor paymaster as a tenant.") Father Henry always exercised "acts of ownership," and throughout those years Jacob made few improvements, and as a result the farm deteriorated in value. None of the money Huldah had inherited was used by her husband to improve the property.[36]

Chancellor McGill was thus confronted by two very different stories of the relationship between Jacob Young and his father. In his 1889 opinion on the demurrer, the chancellor moved in two contradictory directions.

On the one hand, substantively he agreed completely with Huldah and Dorothea and entirely rejected most of what had appeared in William and Peter Young's demurrer to the bill. It appeared, he wrote,

> that Jacob Young, confiding in his father's promise, entered upon the farm in 1849, and remained in possession of it for twenty-seven years, until he was murdered upon it, and that thereafter, till his father died, his widow and heir maintained the same possession. During that time he cared for, repaired, cultivated and improved it, expending thereon not only his own earnings, but also moneys that he had obtained from his wife. The contract was wholly performed to the time of his death, upon his part, and apparently, in the utmost good faith. It is manifest that after such performance, non-compliance with the agreement, upon the part of the father, would work a most grievous fraud.

Furthermore, the chancellor held that these facts imposed what lawyers call a *constructive trust* on William and Peter, a continuing obligation to do that which would prevent fraud, in particular, to make a conveyance of the land to Huldah and Dorothea. They ought to make good on Henry's obligation to convey the land to Jacob. Along the way, the chancellor cited *France v. France* and *Davison v. Davison,* among other precedents that supported his conclusions.

On the other hand, he agreed with William and Peter that Huldah and Dorothea had waited too long. They were guilty of what lawyers call *laches,* unexcused delay, in bringing their case. "For nine years" William and Peter had "openly asserted a claim to the farm adverse" to Huldah and Dorothea, and "during all that time, for aught that appears to the contrary in the bill," Huldah and Dorothea had "acquiesced in that adverse claim." The demurrer had to be granted. Huldah and Dorothea had lost the land again.[37]

But there was a third act. In 1893, four years later and seventeen years after Jacob Young had been murdered, as well as forty-five years after Jacob and Huldah had begun farming on the banks of the Delaware, Dorothea McCord and Huldah Young were back in court. This time they came with a long brief that detailed all of the bad legal advice they had received from various lawyers around New Jersey, none of whom (until they found their present counsel, Louis M. Schenck) had helped them frame the case in a way that could help them. This time Vice Chancellor Pitney decided to excuse their laches: They, not their attorneys, had always "been prompt to seek counsel, and equally prompt to act upon counsel's advice." "The advice they received was not always the same, but whatever it was they acted promptly upon it; they visited their counsel frequently and furnished them with written statements of the evidence, and seem to have been urging on the suits as fast as they could."

Consequently, Huldah Young and Dorothea McCord won, but only in the sense that William and Peter lost. (That might have been enough, certainly for Huldah and Dorothea, who, in the vice chancellor's eyes, had been "treated with great great harshness," so much so as to engender "not only bitter feelings but a desire for litigation.") Just as their rights had survived all those years, so did Jacob's debts. As the vice chancellor wrote, the result, in the end, "may be a substantial defeat" for Huldah and Dorothea "for the reason that it is not probable that the farm is worth taking upon these terms; but I cannot allow the circumstance to influence me." When last seen in 1895 (in scattered material in the New Jersey Archives), Huldah and William were still negotiating with each other, and Huldah was still not in actual possession of the land.[38]

After *Young v. Young* and on into the 1940s, there were other cases, like *Gedicks v. Roberts-Horsfield,* in which equity courts enforced an older person's promise to convey land to a child or other younger relation. Here is one.

In 1919 Howard Lee Danenhauer, known as Lee, lived with his family in Philadelphia. A 1908 graduate of the University of Pennsylvania and a civil engineer, he had a sole ambition: to become a horticulturalist and to hybridize irises. His parents had a summer place in Mays Landing, close to the Jersey shore, where they let him plant a few rows of irises on the property. According to Lee, however, the land was not really good enough for what he wanted to do.[39]

By 1921 Lee had found a place in Paoli, in Chester County, Pennsylvania, where he could potentially do what he wanted. He would sell his house in Philadelphia, and he, his wife, and their infant daughter would move to Paoli. He took his father with him to inspect the property. On the way back, his father asked him whether he would not rather move onto their summer place in Mays Landing and turn it into a nursery. If he went to Mays Landing, he need not worry about taxes. His father hoped he would take his brother George into the business with him, but Lee remembered his father as having said that he alone would eventually own the place. His mother, who held the actual title to the summer place, agreed with his father's plan.[40]

After thinking about the proposal, Lee decided not to move to Paoli. He sold the house in Philadelphia, and he and his family moved full time to New Jersey. In summer they would share the place with his parents, and his brother and his brother's family would visit. However, he, his wife, and their child would live year round on the property, which he worked to make his own.

At the time that he moved, the house was unpainted and dilapidated. The land was uncultivated and covered with brush. The Great Egg Harbor River had flooded large parts of the land, and the road from the highway was often impassible.

What did Lee Danenhauer do? In his words, he "cared for the land, cultivated it, cared for the property, improved it, that is, the buildings, improved it, added additional buildings, hired and bought machinery to care for the land." He rebuilt a sluice, cleared fifteen acres, perhaps more, and also brought three acres into "finished cultivation." He paid to have four to five other acres plowed. He brushed out the road, trimmed the brush, and fertilized the land. Two old buildings were demolished and removed, and old trees were cut down. A new house and a shop were built or rebuilt. By his account he spent approximately $20,000 on the property. His father helped in small ways, but Lee insisted that he had paid most of the costs. He imported iris stock from France and England. In the mid-1920s a famous professor of horticulture and irisarian from Cornell University, Austin W. W. Sand, had come to inspect and to admire his hybridizing work. By then, Lee Danenhauer had a business selling irises, peonies, narcissi, and dahlias. His reputation for the quality of his horticultural endeavor was growing, and he had also written magazine articles.[41]

His witnesses described happy scenes and regular acknowledgments by his parents that the property was or was to be Lee's. A local minister had conversations with the father: "Pop [Lee's father] would take a great pleasure in taking me about the place and showing me the improvements which his son Lee had wrought on the place, and he delighted at the success that he was meeting in carrying out his plans." The minister's wife heard Lee's mother describe the place as "Son's place" ("Son" was clearly Lee, not George). A neighbor described what the place had looked like in 1921. It had "looked like any other Jersey land, lot of brush land." How about the house? "Just like an ordinary country house to me, see millions of them, Mays Landing had thousands before they paved the street." However, after all of Lee's work, "it looks like a home now, to be frank with you. . . . [A]nybody would move into it and have all the comforts in there." The neighbor, who had observed all of Lee's labors, said that Lee had done "more than I would do."

Lee's boyhood friend Elliott remembered bumping into "Mother Danenhauer on the back porch" at the time that Lee had put in a water pump. "She was in the act of scaling fish, that was the first time she had met my wife, and she was all perturbed because she had on a gingham dress, and hair disarranged, and I started to josh her as I usually did, and then we started to razz her . . . and she seemed to think I was in earnest." She then told the friend about all that Lee had been doing, "how fine he had made the place, how happy Father was, and how happy she was that he had come down to live there, and then I started to rag her about electricity, why in the deuce don't you get electricity down here, we even have it up to our place in the country, and she said, 'I don't think Lee can afford electricity now, but maybe some day when we are gone he will fix that all up.'"

In addition, an older man who had helped Lee set up the iris farm heard the mother say to Lee, "When we are gone, this will be your place." Another friend heard the father speak to the son about "your place." A neighbor also had a conversation with the mother in 1925 or 1926 about how the son was pollenizing his plants. "She said that would be eventually for his own benefit, doing that way down there, he would get the benefit of it later on, it will be his place." An architect who had grown up with Lee and used to go camping with him and who was just back from having lived in Honolulu, heard Lee's mother say that it was "wonderful to think that my own son is going to live on this property and carry this property on, due to the fact that we both have so much love for this place. . . . [I]t certainly is wonderful that . . . he is going to live on this property and develop his flowers, and it is wonderful that he is interested in it."[42]

Lee's mother died in late December 1927; his father died less than three weeks later. His mother's will left the property first in a life estate for his father, then he and his brother George were to share a life estate in the property, and then, after their deaths, the estate would go to George's children after a $5,000 gift to Howard Lee Danenhauer Junior, Lee's son from a first marriage. George was made the executor of the will. The land would never be Lee Danenhauer's if the terms of the will were carried out.[43]

Why had Lee's mother written that will, effectively reneging on the promises that she and her husband had made loudly and insistently? The transcript offers at least three not fully articulated answers. In the first place, the place in Mays Landing had been shared family space. One senses that for the mother certainly and perhaps for the father there was a sense that it should not become Lee's property alone, and this connected to a desire to treat the siblings equally. Lee might—and did—argue that he had spent and invested, while his brother had not. However, Lee had not, for reasons that were not articulated in the transcript, brought his brother into the business as he had been asked to do. Second, as the will made clear, Lee had an adolescent son from a first marriage. In cross-examination, Lee revealed that he was entirely estranged from his son, and one passage of his wife's testimony suggests that the older Danenhauers were estranged from their grandson as well and may indeed have instigated the estrangement. Yet one can imagine that the grandparents' guilt played some part in the story.[44]

Third, Katherine, Lee's second wife, had apparently provoked some family conflict. At least one defense witness had implied that Katherine was not providing for or caring well for the older couple. Katherine herself acknowledged that she had been brought up in a more genteel household and had difficulty adjusting to the Danenhauer ways. She told a story in her testimony about what had happened when her own brother had once carelessly left a boat unattended. Her father-in-law had talked sharply to her. She had replied, "Understand this, Father. . . . I will never take anything like this from anybody. . . . My own father and mother don't talk to me like this, and I will not take it from anybody else." She then, as she remembered it, went upstairs and told Lee she was going home to their house in Philadelphia (this was evidently before they had moved to Mays Landing). But the moment passed. Everyone continued to get along. Katherine emphasized that she and Lee's mother never "had a word" even though they had lived together in the same house.[45]

Even more important may have been an impolitic or a presumptuous act of politeness on Katherine Danenhauer's part. One evening, as George Danenhauer, Lee's brother, and his wife were leaving what they all still regarded as the family summer place, Katherine extended "a very cordial invitation to come back and visit them again." That invitation caused shock within the family. What shocked them was her assumption that the house that she and her husband lived in was (already) theirs. His mother took George aside and said that that was a "rather peculiar remark" to make. Yes, he agreed, it was "rather odd for my sister-in-law to be inviting me to my own home." Then his mother said, "Well, it will never be her home. It will belong to both of you jointly." Why was it odd to be invited to the home, he was asked on cross-examination. "You were not living there, were you?" And, of course, Lee and Katherine were, full time. He replied: "It always had been my home, I was welcome there." He had always considered it his mother's home. He "went there every time I felt like . . . anyhow."[46]

After the reading of the will, Howard Lee Danenhauer went to a lawyer, who soon brought a complaint before the New Jersey Court of Equity. Eventually he would get a decree from a vice chancellor, affirmed by the New Jersey Court for the Correction of Errors, that his parents' promise to him should be specifically performed. He had a right to the property. He had earned it through his labor and his reliance. His mother's will was, in the court's rendition, an attempt to defraud him of what was rightfully his. The opinion explaining the decree relied on *Vreeland v. Vreeland,* J. Pierson Vreeland's case, but also cited *Davison, Van Dyne, France v. France,* and *Young v. Young,* among other precedents.[47]

These particular cases came into being because older people had put children on land without conveying title. Not conveying title perhaps gave the parents the illusion of control and stability, the sense that the younger people could not leave; certainly they could not simply sell the land and move on, at least until the old people died. However, over time the younger people, acting in conformity with the older people's apparent wishes, had shaped their own identities with the lands that the parents had not quite given them and made the properties their own, emotionally, experientially, and in terms that an outside world would recognize. It is not hard to imagine the younger people's shock and disappointment when they discovered that they would not be given what had been promised them. They had acted as if they had become owners; they had made the property their own because they had been promised that it would be theirs.

Each case revealed a more complicated story about change over time that lay behind the apparently simple story of a younger person or younger couple merging their labor with land, making it their own. By the time the younger people discovered that they were not getting what they believed they had already been given, much had changed in their familial circumstances. Alignments within families had shifted, and new families had formed. People had died, remarried, and quarreled. Debts had been incurred, and inopportune comments expressed. Perhaps those younger people were less shocked than they appeared in litigation that the older people had not followed through on their earlier commitments.

Still, at least in cases such as those discussed in this chapter, in the end the courts would agree that the younger people had in fact become owners. From the perspective of the New Jersey courts, Frances Roberts-Horsfield, Jacob France Junior, Huldah Young, and Lee Danenhauer had each in their own way "performed" legal and cultural scripts that entitled them to property. They had worked or used lands in the economically and culturally appropriate ways that marked the lands as theirs. They had passed arduous tests that demonstrated that they had made property theirs. To deny them title would be to legitimate acts of fraud by others.

Why focus on such cases about a summer home, neighboring properties, and unused land? These were not cases about getting younger
people to move into the family home or about bringing them in as
caretakers or caregivers in exchange for a promise of a future inheritance. Indeed, when the younger people came to court, they came as
members of separated nuclear households, as individual property owners, and sometimes as businesspeople. They did not come as household
workers, as children on whom older people had grown dependent in
retirement, or as participants in shared households.

Each of these cases, like many others, began with the likely prospect of a move away by the younger person. Parents or uncles and
aunts responded by using the resources that ownership of property
offered them. They worked to preempt a move by making the child a
better offer—the use and ultimately the ownership of family or neighboring property, although one should also emphasize the extent to
which they couched that offer in fuzzy and liminal terms that left
them in control of the situation. Albert and Antonia Gedicks, Jacob
France Senior, Henry Young, and Mr. and Mrs. Danenhauer were all
doing what older people did in a mobile and market-driven world where
children conventionally moved away. One can, if one wishes, understand their acts as instances of family altruism that are perhaps explicable through a metahistorical evolutionary biology. However, they
were also acting in historically specific ways to counter one great fear
of old age in the nineteenth and early twentieth centuries: loneliness.

These cases are the revealing detritus of older people's efforts to
plan against what was understood as an almost inevitable and baleful
accompaniment to old age. Unlike Lydia Sigourney, they did not praise
God for their isolation and abandonment. Instead, they worked with
what they had to prevent those circumstances from occurring. When
they found themselves likely to grow old alone in a God-forsaken portion of New Jersey, when they faced the prospects of their children
moving away because of marriage or opportunity or just the "natural"

tendency of the young to move, property—keeping it while not quite giving it—offered the hope of a solution. Like James W. Davison and Ruth Buzby, they used their resources as best they could, including promises of inheritance. If one wanted to keep younger people near in what was, as Antonia Gedicks put it, a "lonely country," it was important to offer "inducements."

Chapter Four

Things Fall Apart

From a younger person's perspective, staying with or near and work-ing for aging parents or other older people might have seemed a secure investment in the future. To repeat James Davison's lawyer's words, he had stayed because "he was making some provision for his own settlement in life . . . as well as discharging the duty of a son to-wards his parents." At least by the time of litigation, many of the younger people looked back to missed opportunities: jobs and careers given up, land sales not undertaken, or marriages put off. They had chosen to forgo one or more of those more conventional alternatives not just because of their parents' needs or wishes but also because doing so—or rather not doing the things they would otherwise have done—offered the prospect of a profitable and secure future. They had chosen among various alternatives and made rational economic decisions to work at home. Moreover, their parents' words, as remembered, were unquali-fied. They had offered (Stay with me, or live near me on lands I now own, and in the end I will give you what you deserve, what you have earned by staying). The children had accepted. And then the children had worked, while trusting in specific and clear commitments.

For old people, the goals were equally obvious and easily stated if we imagine them, too, as rational calculators when plans for old age were put into place. Accumulate enough property so that the promise of a legacy might give one some capacity to control one's children's life choices. Then keep a son home to take over the farm or the business. If that son had a wife or acquired one later on, put her to work as well. A wife was important because a son without a wife probably meant the absence of someone capable of housework and of intimate care.

Alternatively, get a daughter, perhaps one with a husband in tow, to come live at home. Or perhaps get that daughter to postpone marriage. Keep the other children nearby to the extent one could by making some distributions early. (Obviously, doing this last depended on resources and wealth.) Satisfy those other children so that they would stay nearby in case of need, but do not put them into direct competition with the son or daughter who stayed to do the work.

Those without children or without available children had other options. By the early twentieth century more and more older people were looking elsewhere—beyond their biological children—to find caretakers, caregivers, and those who would serve as working family members. The obvious choice throughout the era was to acquire a child by other means. Many of the cases involved promises made to children who had been more or less informally adopted. Sometimes, as in *Gedicks v. Roberts-Horsfield,* a child came into a new family because of the death of the child's mother. More often, as in Ruth Buzby's case, the reasons these children became a part of a new household were never fully explained. Some children, like Frank Ehling in *Ehling v. Diebert,* came as employees and over time became something more, close to being an adopted child, as the older people became dependent on them. In John Van Duyne's case his childless uncle and aunt arrived shortly after his birth and told his mother and father that they wanted him. Likewise, James Taylor, a pioneering Trenton ceramics manufacturer, took his granddaughter Ella away from his daughter when Ella was a baby. When Ella's birth father was asked, more than thirty years later (both Ella and her grandfather were dead by then), about what had happened, he answered, "They wanted the child. . . . It [*sic*] was a pretty, affectionate child; they wanted the child but took it as their own." Later Ella's mother was asked, "What was the understanding between your father and mother and yourself at the time Ella went there?" She answered, "We had no understanding; he just took Ella for his own."[1] In another case, an uncle and aunt were asked to take a niece into their family in Ireland after the niece's mother had died. While in Ireland, they decided to keep the little girl and make her their own. Six or seven years later they returned to New Jersey and "bargained" with the girl's father that "if he would . . . surrender her they would adopt her as their child, and maintain and educate her and make her the beneficiary of their joint and separate estates."[2]

Another possibility was to turn to a housekeeper. Older widowers often made this choice, and one suspects that they may have done so as a way to avoid antagonizing their children, who would resent the old man's taking a new wife. Over time, however, housekeepers became family members. They would be offered a farm, a business, or a bank account in lieu of wages if they would stay and provide care. When they accepted, however, they might discover that all they would get, after many years of largely unrequited labor, was an inadequate equivalent of unpaid wages rather than the property they had been promised. Courts were loath to turn an employee into an heiress.[3]

Sometimes the older person would have turned, perhaps in desperation or confusion, to true strangers. There are cases of tenants whose elderly landlord suddenly appeared and said, Take care of me for the rest of my life, and I will give you the house.[4] Sometimes it was a neighbor or the daughter of a neighbor who would be approached.[5]

Moving in with others—into the household of a son, daughter, or other relatives—was usually understood as a bad choice for older men and women to have to make. They struggled to avoid that alternative, although widows without complete control of family property often had little choice. One wanted authority over dependents; one did not want to be placed at their mercy. The retention of as much power as possible in a situation of "inevitable dependency" was a core goal.[6]

Obviously, the economic power of an offer of property provides an incomplete explanation for the arrangements usually made and carried out. What was at stake in the negotiations between young and old was never just an economic bargain between rational actors.[7] Older people negotiated with the young to receive love and to be cared for in a loving way, not just as a job. Love—incorporating feelings of duty, kindness, sympathy, concern, and affection—also played a crucial role in old people's strategies.[8] Love was context, and love was a tool. Love may sometimes have been the goal of the negotiations. The older persons sought to reassure themselves that a child or someone else cared about them. They wanted to know that care was being given for reasons other than an anticipated exchange of property. Uncertainties about love underlay many of the endless negotiations and renegotiations recounted in the trial transcripts. (We might speculate, for example, that James W. Davison's accusations against his daughter-in-law Jane constituted his awkward attempt to make his son, James, choose him over her. James W., like all of us, wanted to be loved. Perhaps, as the head of the household, he wanted to be loved most—or at least more than his daughter-in-law.)[9]

However, for the young who worked for the old, love was a great legal danger. If a court was going to give them what they had earned, they had to appear as independent, individual, and canny bargainers. On the witness stand and in depositions they had to hold their love for the old, even for their parents, at bay and even deny it since otherwise lawyers would use it against them. They had to resist being revealed to be what they often really were—family members who had done what they had for deeply emotional, as well as material, reasons. They and their lawyers worked to mask the fact that they were children who were returning care and love to their parents, who had once cared for and loved them.[10]

The soon-to-be or expectant old planned for old age, and a plan in-
volves an imagined future. It is not hard to give content to what that
imagined future would have been for older New Jerseyans of the late
nineteenth or early twentieth centuries: They would live on comfortably in retirement without undertaking excessive labor, with loving
children and grandchildren around them, without pain or discom-
fort, and with their wits about them. The chosen one—the son, daughter, or other younger person who had been promised the farm, business, or bank account—would lovingly and competently take care of
them, as would that person's family. Things would happily drift on
into an indeterminate future.

We can be confident that the plans that older people made for their
care sometimes worked out to the relative satisfaction of all concerned.
Younger people stayed; older people received the care they needed; property was eventually conveyed.

Nevertheless, cases arose because planning is one thing, reality is
another. In fact, plans, bodies, and minds often fell apart. What actually happened depended on changeable resources, timing, continued
competence, the availability and the life plans and the commitment of
younger people, and the physical and mental health of all of the parties. Those contingencies produced scenarios; those contingencies
produced court cases. Plans would be undone because an older person's needs became too great for a particular child or relative to handle, or a painful last illness made it impossible for the older persons
to do what they had promised to do, or the child—the designated
caregiver—found it impossible to do what (from the older person's
perspective) needed doing. Wills would be left unwritten and deeds
unconveyed, because of the sudden onset of mortal illness or dementia. Sometimes deeds were conveyed too early, and then the older
persons found themselves at the mercy of a child who no longer cared
or could not deal with the work of caring. Even caring children could
do little to slow or forestall the destructive forces of disease, decline,

or the onset of what medical anthropologist Lawrence Cohen calls the inherent "insanity" of old age. To have achieved old age and retirement, even with children or others close at hand and committed to help and to care, did not necessarily mean one had achieved happiness or even a modicum of control over a chaotic future.[11]

Many voices in the law and in the popular culture struggled to resist or to deny that chaos. Nineteenth-century images of the stages of life always made old age into a predictable mirror of childhood. Judges and other participants in the culture liked to talk about "second childhoods" and the ways the dependency of old age recapitulated the parent-child relationship in reverse. "The parent becomes the child, 'with the same dependence, over-weening confidence and implicit acquiescence' which had made the other, in infancy, the willing instrument of the parent's desires."[12]

Still, everyone must have known that old age was actually a distinctive phenomenon that is very different from childhood, which had (then as now) a more predictable course. How long old age would last, looking forward from the vantage point, say, of one's forties or fifties, was anyone's guess. Old age could easily stretch forward several decades with relatively little organic or intellectual loss. Everyone would have known a few vigorous and engaged older people who flourished well into their eighties or nineties. The fantasy and the hope were that one could create a basis for that long and happy period through planning and accumulation and that one could earn the right to a happy and placid old age. On the other hand, mortal disease, injury, disability, dementia, insanity, and incontinence—let alone more or less sudden death—could arrive at any moment. People did not die when they should, and they did not die in predictable ways. Moreover, being old could mean many different things. The "stages" vision of the life course offered a mental picture of control and expectations of smooth and gradual transitions. What really happened, however, as everyone knew, was often sudden, dramatic, and unexpected: Years, days, or

perhaps just a moment of happy "retirement" might be rapidly over-
taken by painful diseases and losses, for which there was no remedy
or cure.[13]

For good and sufficient reasons, an older person had made repeated
promises to secure the presence, care, and attention of a younger person. The older person had delayed making a will or conveying property so as not to lose control. However, sometimes (actually often if
the case records suggest an underlying reality) and suddenly it was
too late. Things fell apart. The older person became too sick or foolish
to make a will or to transfer property. That person would then die
without a will or with the wrong will or without sufficient resources to
command the continued and needed attention. Alternatively, even
if the person remained sufficiently competent to produce a will or a
deed, the power and control that had moved from the weakened older
person to a younger caretaker meant that the older person might have
been understood as subject to the caretaker's "undue influence." In
that case the will or deed might be declared invalid.

Many cases were about one version or another of that "too late"
situation. In addition, the chaos of having to manage the needs of the
old, once enmeshed in a situation where rational planning was at an
end, was everywhere in the case records, although often hidden in
judicial opinions.

In *Slack v. Rees* (1904), two brothers sued to invalidate the deeds to
two pieces of property given by their dying father to their sister, Ella
Rees. In the laconic and orderly version of the "facts" of the case re-
counted in Chief Justice Gummere's opinion, written for New Jersey's
Court for the Correction of Errors and Appeals, the father, George H.
Slack, had long suffered from syphilis of the spinal cord. His mental

and physical powers were weak, but he was still competent to "dispose" of his property.

The question was, had he been subject to his daughter's "undue influence" when he made the conveyance to her? Chief Justice Gummere thought that he had. He noted that during the three months before his death, the father had been an "inmate of his daughter's home" (this was, as we will see, something of a misinterpretation or misstatement) and dependent on her "for the care and service which a man in his weakened physical and mental condition constantly requires." As a consequence, the "normal relation of parent and child . . . had been reversed, and the daughter had become the guardian of the father." When that reversal occurred, the presumption of law—the default rule—was that any gift made by an aged parent to a child was the product of the child's undue influence over the parent (just as, during childhood, any gift from an infant to a parent was presumptively due to the parent's undue influence). It would also be the daughter's responsibility to prove the contrary. Had she done so? Had she met her burden of proof, which negated the presumption of undue influence? When the case had been tried before Vice-Chancellor Reed, the court had ruled that she had indeed met that burden. According to Reed, there was no evidence that the daughter had "exercised any dominative influence" over her father. Whatever influence she had "acquired" over him was through her "filial devotion," and it was, as such, "entirely legitimate" that the consequence of her devotion was that she had been rewarded. Gummere made clear that he disagreed with the vice chancellor's conclusion and that he would have reversed the vice chancellor's decision in Ella Rees's favor. However, the other judges on his court were divided on the question.

Therefore, Gummere worked—successfully—to find an alternative rationale to justify reversing the vice chancellor's decision, one that the whole court could join in. That reversal rested on the fact that the father had conveyed the property to his daughter by deed without retaining any control. No "power of revocation" had been "reserved." He had given his daughter everything he owned and left himself without any resources except for a small Civil War pension. The fact that he died the day after giving the property to his daughter did not change the imprudence of what he had done because, when he made the conveyance, he did not know when he was going to die. True, he had just had a "prostrating attack," but, according to Chief Justice Gummere, his physicians had not expected the attack to kill him.

After the attack, as soon as he was well enough, as Gummere reconstructed the facts of the case, George Slack had called for his attorney, Henry D. Phillips, who had previously helped him acquire his pension. When Phillips came, George Slack told him that he wanted to convey his property to his daughter, Ella Rees. He had asked the attorney whether it would be better to do it by deed immediately or in his will. Phillips answered that Slack should convey the property by deed. And so he did. However, according to Gummere, the attorney's advice was clearly incompetent and in fact bordered on malpractice. "If the opinion of his [Slack's] physicians . . . had turned out to be accurate, he would[,] for the rest of his life, have been dependent upon the charity of others." Thus, because of the attorney's incompetence, the deed had been drafted in favor of the daughter without any useful "independent advice" at all. There had to be a reversal of the vice chancellor's decision in favor of the daughter, and George H. Slack's estate would be divided equally among his three children.[14]

Behind that legal conclusion—that reversal by an appellate court—lay a characteristic family mess. George H. Slack had been a carpenter and a contractor in Trenton. In 1902, when he died, he was in his late sixties. One of his sons, Robert, had moved to Ohio. His other son, also called George, had worked with and for him. According to that son, testifying after his father's death, his father had intended to divide his property equally among all of his children. However, father and son, George and George, had also quarreled over money matters and were not on good terms. According to son George, his father was illiterate and could write only his name. The son had always had to do all of the writing and reading, which gave him "the power in the business." Yet his father questioned everything he did, including his son's honesty, which had made the son furious.[15]

Meanwhile, for close to two decades George's older sister Ella had lived with their father and mother in their Bayard Street house in Chambersburg (a residential neighborhood of Trenton). She had married and raised a daughter, while living with her parents. There was much disagreement about the terms on which Ella remained in her parents' home. Some witnesses described Ella's relationship with her parents as "always of the very sweetest," whereas others insisted that daughter and father were "always quarreling and fighting." Much testimony was devoted to a demonstration that Ella had not been a perfect caretaker, that she did not get along well with her parents, and that she was selfish. Most of all, she had abandoned her parents when they had most needed her care, and her father was afraid of her.

There is no direct evidence in the trial transcript of any early promises by Ella's parents to compensate her for her years of care and her labors. On the other hand, at some point, her father had conveyed his property to his wife. Ella's mother had then made a will in favor of Ella. We might speculate that those legal acts were intended as ways to give effect to a promise to reward Ella for having stayed to care for them. (George H. Slack was around eight years older than his wife, and he had long suffered from tertiary syphilis. He may have assumed that his wife would survive him.) However, for reasons that will become clear, his deeds conveying his property to his wife were never filed, and his wife's will was destroyed.[16]

According to many witnesses, father George's disease had led to a general decline in his capacity to conduct business. He was not insane, but he was growing deaf, and he had lost interest in the world.

According to son George, by the mid-1890s, when he was in his early sixties, his father had grown "cranky and hard to get along with, and he would go into the stable and flog the horses until the neighbors would interfere, and my sister would have to go and stop him." Once, when she went down to the stable to stop him, he told her "to get to hell out of there." He was, according to George, "drowsy and sleepy all the time, he would get up in the morning and eat his breakfast, and then would lie down on the sofa and sleep until dinner time, and then get up and take his dinner, and then lie down again until supper time, and then he would get up and eat his supper, and then would go down town . . . and when I would take him out, as I would in the wagon, he would be drowsy and sleepy, and he would act in this way all the time, and he used to tell me when I spoke to him about it that he could not help it, and then sometimes he would get downhearted." He did not clean himself, he was a glutton, and "they fairly had to force him to wash himself, he was so dirty, they could not get him to take a bath, and he would sit at the table and they would have to carry the things right away from him." Others reported that his mind was "almost totally gone." He did not know when he had had enough to eat and "that he would eat as long as anything was left near him after a meal." Ella had difficulty "in getting him to change his underwear."[17]

Meanwhile, George H. Slack's wife, Ella's mother, was becoming "insane." What that meant in modern diagnostic terms is impossible to reconstruct from the trial transcript, but certainly her mother's behavior made Ella's life in the household difficult and eventually impossible. The mother was obviously still active, whatever her mental state. According to the brother who lived in Ohio, his mother continued to do all the work in the house, in contrast to his sister and her daughter. At one point, he reported, his mother had told him that "she was working like a nigger for the whole family." Others disagreed and described Ella as doing all of the work. She had, according to Ella's

husband, Albert Rees, "sacrificed her life by staying there and not going to a home of her own." She found her mother impossible to deal
with.

In any case, some time in 1899 or 1900, Ella, along with her husband,
Albert, and her daughter, Caroline, moved to a house on Tyler Street in
Trenton. Why did she do so? Her brother Robert claimed that she had
been ordered out of the house by her father, but Ella denied this and
claimed that she had left of her own accord because she could no longer take the living situation. Her father told her "as long as Ma's mind
was in the state it was, . . . it was best for us to part." As Ella concluded,
"My mother was insane, and I could not get along with her."[18]

Then, in early November 1901 Ella's mother wandered away from the
house. She began to walk toward Lambertville, up the Delaware River
from Trenton, and eventually was found in the cold water of the river,
near Titusville, by a gentleman "who sets traps for muskrats." She was
taken to a farmhouse, where her clothes were dried. She was given
something warm to drink, and then she was taken back to Trenton.

Ella came back ("I came home") for six weeks to care for her mother.
On Christmas Eve 1901 Ella's daughter, Caroline, became ill, and, as
Ella put it, "I was called home" to her own house on Tyler Street. When
she left, her father said, "When you come back . . . you will move back
home with me again." However, Ella replied, so she remembered, "No
father, the way Ma's mind is no one can get along with her here, she
knows she's boss, and no one can get along with her, and I cannot
come back here."

At that point George H. Slack made his daughter a promise: "If you
will come home, I will deed my property to you." But Ella was un-
swayed, at least as she remembered it in testimony, and she answered,
"No, father, I won't accept that" while he and his wife survived. "I said
I wanted them to live and enjoy all they had." He said that his Civil
War pension would be enough, but she said she would not do it.[19]

Even though she had refused to live in her parents' home even with a promise of property, she did come back two or three times a week throughout the winter and spring of 1902. She cleaned house and cared for her increasingly unsettled mother. Then, in spite of her resolve to live apart, her mother "got so bad" that she had to move back into her parents' household. Finally, in early summer 1902 her mother was put into the Trenton Asylum for the insane, where she died on August 10, 1902. (At least by the time of the trial, her brothers blamed Ella for putting their mother into the asylum and for allowing her to be a public charge there. According to Ella, those had all been their father's decisions.)[20]

Ella was questioned closely about her conduct on the day her mother died. Her behavior at that moment became, for her brothers and their lawyers, an indication of her lack of loving care. She had received a call at ten in the morning that her mother was dying at the asylum. However, the train to the asylum left before she was ready to go, and there was not another one until two in the afternoon. By then, her mother was dead. Also, her daughter had had a dentist appointment.[21]

On the day of his wife's death, George H. Slack left his own home and moved into the house on Tyler Street, where Ella and her husband lived. Two days later, he collapsed in the bathroom of their house. Once he had recovered a bit, he called for doctors and for an attorney to make the transfer of property to Ella. That done, two days later he was dead as well.

At her father's funeral, her brothers had asked her whether she knew anything about the property their father had left. She said yes, but that "Pa" had told her not to say anything until after the funeral. Her brothers insisted, and she told them that the property had been left to her. Robert, her brother from Ohio, asked her whether she "thought that was right." She answered that she thought it was "because I had staid home and sacrificed all my life for them." Robert told her "then and there" that he would "fight" her.[22]

Thus, a case came into being, one that ended with Ella's losing the property her father had deeded to her.

The bet that many younger family members must have made when they stayed home to care for their parents was that the older people would not live too long. Sometimes the result of that wager would have been the discovery that a father or mother was just too healthy or strong or that the "someday" in "someday, all this will be yours" drifted off into a too-distant horizon. Productive years were being spent in the position of a domestic servant, perhaps without marriage, certainly without a career or the happiness of a home of one's own. Sometimes the continuing health of the old must have led to a decision to leave and to give up on the uncertain and distant prospect of an inheritance. However, younger persons could as easily find themselves in a much worse situation when the older person broke down but did not die. Then they might be stuck taking care of a demented or painfully sick patient day after day, occasionally for many years. They would be unable to escape the unending work of cleaning suppurating wounds or incontinent bodies, of endless washing and cleaning, drug dispensing, and comforting (all the work that today we mostly assign to others who are paid and who, we hope, can go home at night and leave the miserable conditions behind).

Adult children may have been independent and theoretically mobile. They had no legal duty to remain. However, for reasons that have little to do with any contract or with rational planning or calculation, once an older person had broken down, a younger caretaker would have found it difficult to get away. Old and young alike all lived in a moral and a material world where family care was the only care available for older people who had become dependent. Few would ever have contemplated allowing a parent or other close relative to go to the poorhouse.

Later, sometimes many years later, when these young (or no longer young) persons sued for a compensation or a legacy that had not come or defended against the charge that the legacy received was the result of "undue influence," they would have detailed the work that had been required as the older person fell apart. Such descriptions reveal a regimen of work and attention almost unimaginable today, one that was carried out in chaotic but distinctively private households.

In 1897 the New Jersey Prerogative Court had to decide whether James Ledwith had been subject to "undue influence" when he left a will that gave most of his property (the proceeds of a liquor business and a few tenements in the Lower East Side of New York City) to his surviving daughter, Annie Claffey, and provided only a small gift to the children of a son who had died several years previously. Two daughters, one of whom had died in 1892, had stayed with him and cared for him for many years. At the time of James's death in 1894, he was clearly suffering from "senile dementia" and considered incompetent. However, the court had to determine when his competence had ended. Was it before 1890, when he had signed the "will" that left his property to Annie and her sister?[23]

Some thought James Ledwith was completely incompetent as early as 1886. Testimony related that he had wandered around at that time, was found eight miles from his house, and was taken off to the poorhouse, where family members eventually found him and brought him home. In the fall of the same year, he got off a train but did not know where he was. Again, he was taken to the poorhouse. Was he drunk or just deranged? Again, he was brought back home. Others thought his mind began to "give way" in 1887. One witness told about Ledwith's difficulty in making his mark when he had to sign documents. He was no help at harvest time; instead, he "occupied himself in the aimless transfer of things from place to place." Daughters and others had to watch him constantly, "as though a child." He wore inappropriate clothes; he put eggs in his pocket. He would throw things on the floor.

A witness saw him "go to the fireplace, and take a clock from the mantel, and put it on the stove, and then dip his hands in some pots of cream behind the stove." While the witness was churning [butter] at his house, he put rotten apples in the churn. "Apparently unconscious of the propriety of his conduct, he used the floor of his house in answer to the calls of nature." Another witness stated that in 1889 "the old man was so far demented that he failed to remove his clothing when he relieved his bowels." (Others disagreed and believed him still sharp and competent at that time.) By 1890, his daughters did not trust him to go to the village alone. When he went to be shaved, someone had to go along. Ephraim C. Bass, "a western cowboy" who had married a local girl and was at the time of the trial a motorman on the Brooklyn electric railway, reported that Ledwith would get up at nine or ten; his daughters would wash and dress him, and then he would wander away and get lost. He was unable to do anything properly. "At times he had to be taken to attend to the calls of nature, or would act as an infant, in disregard of his clothing." Another witness was hired to build a fence to keep him out of his daughter's flower garden. He remembered that "the old man soiled his clothing . . . without apparently understanding what he had done." A priest who saw him about ten or twelve times in 1889 and 1890 thought he "was then in his second childhood; that he was not irrational, but, as a child, did childish acts, without fully understanding." Another witness described how he had "to be constantly watched, because of his mental irresponsibility, to keep him from being harmed and doing harm." (Meanwhile, others reported he was still quite competent at the time of the execution of the will in 1890 and that he could talk with great intelligence and coherence.)

As the court concluded, "It will suffice to say . . . that the witnesses decidedly vary in their impressions" of James Ledwith's condition as of 1890, when the will was written. Everyone, on the other hand, agreed that by 1892 he was incompetent. However, as of 1890, the court ruled, he was sometimes competent, sometimes not. Many of those who insisted on his incompetence had some interest in promoting litigation in the case. Still, the court did not see sufficient bias in their testimony to destroy their credibility.

Unfortunately for Annie Claffey's claim, however, she had often told others that she was convinced that her father was crazy and incompetent. All agreed that she and her sister were hostile to her brother's family, his widow, and his children, those who had been excluded from any legacy by the 1890 will, and she had often expressed her hostility to her father. She had told many that she wanted her father to write exactly the sort of will that eventually appeared. He was entirely in her power and that of her now dead sister. "For years his daughters had been his constant companions . . . they had managed his business affairs for him, and had performed the most menial and disgusting offices in ministering to his comfort . . . in every sense he had become dependent upon them." All of that became evidence for the conclusion that James Ledwith's apparent will must have been produced through the undue influence that Annie and her sister had exercised over him. Thus, the court rejected probate of a will that had finally compensated Annie for all her work in caring for him. She would have to share her father's estate with her dead brother's children.

In this case, as in others, the court came close to asserting that Annie had "undue influence" precisely because she was a faithful caregiver of someone who was becoming, if he was not already, dependent and incompetent. Such decisions could put such caregiving women (and occasionally men) in an impossible situation, when wills or other dispositions were challenged. A competent person should not have had to be cared for, and, if James needed care, then he was dependent on, and likely to be influenced by, the one who cared for him. That was easily construed as an "undue" influence, one that had led to an unnatural disposition of the estate. (This was even more so when the dependent was a man and the caregiver a woman.) Why else would the will have been written in the caregiver's favor?[24]

In *Waldron v. Davis* (1904), to take a second example, a family successfully sued the estate of an older aunt by marriage for the extra care involved in keeping her for the last ten years of her life. The aunt had long lived in the house with them, paying room and board. For years all was well, but then, things fell apart after the aunt returned from a summer vacation.

Suddenly, the aunt "couldn't seem to care for things . . . she wasn't tidy and neat about her room, and she couldn't help in the work as she usually had done." She seemed terribly worried all the time. According to the daughter in the family, "My mother would have to work with her for an hour or an hour and a half to get her quiet." Soon she was unable to care for herself and her room. Then she could not be left alone. That remained the case for the next five years—until she died. She "soiled" the carpets in four rooms and the hall, which ruined them, and destroyed some of the furniture. About 1898 she became more violent, noisy, and troublesome at the dinner table, so the family could not have other boarders, and "she made the whole family nervous . . . sick . . . from care and worry." She would sing, though not in words, the "Star-Spangled Banner" and "Hail, Columbia" night and day until the neighbors complained, and she would scream and cry. No doctor was able to help. She would mumble, hum, and croon. She could not feed herself. She would walk around the house and then sit down and fall on the floor. "In caring for her if she was soiled and we wished to remove her clothing it would often take two to handle her, because she would kick so. She would fist and scratch and pull hair, and all sorts of things like that, and she would walk from one end of the room to the other while we were trying to remove her clothes; one had to hold her feet while the other would get her clothes off." According to a son, who was also a doctor, by the end, after years of full-time care, when they gave her a spoon to eat with, she would hit them. She would wander about; she needed to be restrained. They had to watch her constantly for fear that she might burn the house down. In the son's professional judgment, it was never safe for them ever to leave her alone.

According to the doctor son, she should have been removed to a hospital or an asylum, but the family did not like the idea of a relative being in such an institution. The daughter testified that her parents regarded it as their duty to keep "Aunt Eliza" in their home "in sympathy and kindness and Christianity." They felt "they could not put her out."

What had begun as a boarding relationship between family members became instead a kind of psychiatric hospital. The household had become entirely defined by the obligation to care for this demented old woman. For that "extra care," the New Jersey courts eventually ruled that extra compensation beyond the payments made for ordinary room and board was allowable. The amount for ten years of "extra care" was set at $574.68.[25]

If one looks at such situations from the perspective of older people rather than from that of the caregivers, the anxieties attached to the prospects of such sudden but apparently uncontrollable and irreversible changes must have been overwhelming. What would one do? What would happen? Who would care? Would anyone stay when one needed care? Where else would one go if one were abandoned by those who had promised to stay?

Without property, the poorhouse or its equivalent loomed. However, even with property, one was at the mercy of those whom one most needed.

Captain Peter Van Pelt went to stay with his tenants, Christina Appleton and her husband, after he had been "chucked out of the house" by his "son and daughter-in-law." Van Pelt suffered from "valvular disease," which caused "dropsy and cardiac asthma" and resulted in a hugely and painfully enlarged scrotum and testicles, which required constant washing and bandaging.[26] Noah Collins, who was eighty years old and feeble from malaria, had been living with Andrew, a son, but he felt that he was treated cruelly by both Andrew and Andrew's children. Consequently, he turned to another son, John, to take him in. John, with what the Court for the Correction of Errors and Appeals called "almost impious candor," refused to have him until Noah had transferred four lots of land to him. "You can either fish or cut bait," John reportedly told Noah. "Sign them papers, or go out of doors; for I won't keep you while you've got property."[27]

If one did not convey property, people might leave. If one did, one lost control over the situation. And once children had their hands on the property, what happened next?

One of the leading "undue influence" cases, cited often in later decisions, was *Mott v. Mott* (1891). Ann Eliza Mott was in her early seventies in 1880. Until then she was an independent woman of average "mental force," and she had, according to Vice Chancellor Green, two prominent character traits—affection for her children and tenacity in keeping control of her property. Like others we have seen, her favorite expression seems to have been "that she would keep the loaf under her own arm." However, then, over the next few years, things changed for her. She sustained a fall, which broke two ribs and injured her spine. Thereafter, she suffered from "neuralgia or headache, dullness, inattention and forgetfulness." She had the "usual forgetfulness" of people's names characteristic of those her age. Beyond that, she also had trouble making herself understood; she had lost the ability to convey her ideas on "ordinary matters." She would lose her way in the streets of Hackensack, where she had long lived. She was subject to unreasonable fancies: She imagined that a sermon was directed at her; she worried that someone was robbing her of her vegetables, wood, and coal even though they were kept under lock and key; she believed people were conspiring to turn her out of her lodgings and put her belongings in the street; she begged for money from church deacons; "and on one occasion [she] cried because she had not been asked to go to a children's Sunday school picnic." She had become, in Vice Chancellor

Green's words, susceptible "to influence if sought to be exerted by one who had her confidence or affection."

At least in the vice chancellor's highly wrought and sentimental reconstruction of what next happened, Ann Eliza Mott's son, Damon, played on her weaknesses. He alienated her from her daughter, kept her from going to stay with the daughter, and convinced her that her daughter and her family were going to rob her. He told her that if she left him she would never see him alive again. She responded to the pressure by conveying all of her property to him in exchange for his promise to care for her and to furnish her a home without charge.

According to Damon Mott, he gave his mother exactly what she had bargained for. According to the court, on the other hand, Ann Eliza Mott had fallen into a trap. What was the "care, support, and maintenance" that she was to receive? What did she get for her bargain? "Without female help or female associations, she was placed in charge of his house, cooked his food, mended his clothes, became the merest drudge, doing everything but the washing, and really earned all she received as the consideration of the transfer of her property." Only when "the weather grew so cold that fires had to be started" would he bring in any household help for her. She became sick in February. She rallied, but her mind was gone. Now she really needed "care, comfort, companionship." According to Green, "The period had arrived when his bargain would not be profitable." However, except for a housekeeper Damon did nothing. When Ann Eliza's daughter came to visit, she found her mother at ten in the morning in the "sitting-room not yet put to rights," wearing nothing but a "morning wrap on, nothing but her night dress." She was alert enough to recognize her daughter, and her first impulse was to go away with her. Ann Eliza cried when she realized that she had no money.

The test of whether there had been "undue influence," according to Green, was whether the contract Damon Mott had made with his mother was not only free "but fair, and made with the utmost good faith" as well. Damon obviously failed that test. He had misused the natural reversal that occurs with old age, a reversal we have seen mobilized in cases throughout this chapter. The aged parent "naturally looks with confidence to a son or daughter for advice and protection." The parent becomes like a child. In addition, just as the transactions of children with parents would always be closely scrutinized by a suspicious and interventionist court of equity, so would it be for Ann Eliza Mott as an aged parent.[28] Damon Mott had violated his duties as a child who had become, in effect, a parent. He would lose the property his mother had transferred to him. Moreover, her guardians (for by then she had been declared no longer competent to hold her own property) would gain control of her estate.[29]

For older people worried about the onset of disabilities, victory in a case like *Mott v. Mott* would have been faint comfort. It might have been easy to offer the prospect of land or a farm in exchange for care when one was healthy and vigorous or, better yet, when one did not look too healthy and vigorous. But why would children stay when one had become really sick or needy? In addition, how could one know that they would do what one hoped caretakers would do? When one most needed help, one would be least able to command it. Also, whether one did or did not give the property, one would, in the end, be at the mercy of others. It was, as *King Lear* taught, a recipe for insanity.

Disquiet and anxiety were not just what happened to a few "legal failures" that ended up in court. Disquiet and anxiety colored nearly every transaction between older people and adult children and lay beneath nearly every story about planning for old age. No older persons could ever be sure that those they needed would be there when they needed them. In a situation where everything rested on the control of property, the lurking, inchoate knowledge must have been that the time when such control had to be mobilized would also be when one was likely to have lost the power to exercise that control. Whether or not one had children and loved ones around one, even if one had sufficient resources, even if one was momentarily hale and strong, growing old was a terrifying prospect. This was particularly so in a legally constituted world in which care was private and familial and in which, at the same time, a mobile and economically explosive free society meant that no one had to stay home and provide care.

Part Two

Death and Lawyers

How do you think all that sickness and dying was paid for?

Tennessee Williams, *A Streetcar Named Desire,*

1947

Chapter Five

A Life Transformed

Old age, planned or unplanned, had ended. One or more adult children had stayed at home and lived and worked there (or on other nearby family property). They had paid attention to the elderly parents and perhaps given direct bodily care. Certainly they had heard promises.

But now the old one, the property owner, was dead. What happened next?

Sometimes, as in the *Davison* case, conflict had already occurred before death, conflict that led to an attempt to remove an adult child and family from the home and from any disposition of property.

Sometimes, on the other hand, death revealed a will that acknowledged the care and love received and then went on to compensate an adult child for the years spent attending to the elderly parent. Sometimes, prior to death property had been set aside or granted by deed to the adult child who had stayed and cared. In other cases, even though the older person had done nothing before death to compensate the adult children for their labors, others, the managers of the estate—the executors or administrators—would have acknowledged the work done and the dead person's responsibility. The adult child would have been paid out of the estate.

The caregivers who had received what was due them—who had been paid or been deeded property or named as heirs—still ran legal risks, and they might well have needed legal advice. Creditors of the deceased often sued, claiming that what looked like compensation for work, for what were called "services rendered," was really a family conspiracy to avoid paying a lawful debt. The transfers or the payments to the adult child were, these creditors claimed, nothing but attempts to shelter resources owed them. Siblings, too, or others with frustrated expectations of inheritance might insist that what looked like an executed contract was actually an "advance" on an equal property division after death. They had been defrauded by their brother, sister, adopted sibling, or whoever had stayed with the older property owner. The one who had stayed had received support and care—room and board—at home. Whatever work that person had done was at most compensation for the privilege of living at home rent free. What the now dead property owner had really intended was to divide the property equally among all of the children. When the deceased had transferred property at death or prior to death to a caregiver, that weakened, vulnerable, and dependent old person had been unduly influenced or threatened. The court had to intervene, so both creditors and siblings often argued; otherwise, they would be defrauded by one who had merely stayed at home and manipulated the old person.[1]

However, younger people who had stayed at home and provided care for older persons had routinely received nothing. They had been forgotten or excluded from the will—or there was no will at all. The promises they and others had heard had been forgotten or not been acted on or been countered by a quarrel large or small. If there had been a will giving them what they thought they had been promised, it had been destroyed; if there had been a deed describing the property promised them, it had not been delivered. Or, what was still a common occurrence throughout the nineteenth century, one illustrated by *Young v. Young*, a younger person who had been the expected beneficiary of an older person's promise and was supposed to get the property on the older person's death had died before the older person. The older person, often under the influence of other younger people, often siblings of the dead younger person, would then have changed the will to avoid letting the property fall into the hands of the now dead younger person's spouse or other heirs.

Some unknowable percentage of those who had been promised property and then received nothing (or much less than they believed they had been promised) accepted the situation. They might have interpreted their "loss" as God's will or the price of family harmony. Daughters more than sons undoubtedly fell into that category and found themselves intimidated by brothers or their own lack of knowledge of the law or access to legal counsel.

For many others, though, daughters no less than sons, the next step involved a consultation with a lawyer about their legal rights. They believed they deserved what they had been promised—the farm, the land, the shop, the savings account—or at minimum they deserved a monetary equivalent of the work they had done. They were, after all, adults, and adults were paid for work. That was a legal principle that everyone in the society understood.

Going to talk to a lawyer about a potential legal challenge must have been a difficult decision to make. There had to have been a high threshold of upset, outrage, and loss before they took that first step. Going to a lawyer meant bringing to public attention what should have remained out of public view. Going to court likely meant having to talk—and to be cross-examined—about intimate "dirty" aspects of care and life, about incontinence, dementia, and bedsores, for example, not to mention the ordinary and extraordinary irritations and quarrels that result from people living together in close circumstances. Few if any adult children would have found the prospect of such talk— making private matters public—anything but horrifying. One might suspect, as well, that it was no easy thing to challenge dead parents'

disposition of their assets. Grumbling about the unfairness of a disposition was one thing. Litigating, trying to undo that decision by mobi-
lizing state power, was quite another. It would ordinarily have seemed
disrespectful to a father's or mother's memory to strategize about how
to undo decisions that parent had made. In addition, everything we
know about the legal culture suggests that belief in testator's freedom
was widely shared. If the old persons had chosen not to give what they
had talked about giving, that was their right even if it was a stupid or
an unfair decision.

On the other side, going to a lawyer—contemplating litigation—
after the death of a parent or other household head could be justified
within the normative order in which many Americans lived. Challenges
to the probate of a will were common and would have been a part of
most adults' knowledge and experience. Within the Anglo-American
legal culture, the death of a property owner was already a time of change
for any family. At minimum, property had to be retitled, whether by
will or by intestacy. The probate moment had a "use it or lose it" quality. Once that process had taken its course, property would have been
conveyed from the dead hands of the estate into new, presumably
more possessive and active, hands. However emotionally difficult it
might have been at that moment to go to court to lay legal claim to
property or payment, later moments would be still more so. In any
case, often, what had held a family together, that is, the presence of
parents or their hold on family property, had disappeared with death.
Some of the cultural constraints on intrafamily litigation—particularly
sibling against sibling—would have lessened. The death of a parent
was a good time to talk with a lawyer.

Our stories, the ones we know because they produced trial records,
all began when one or more adult children entered the legal field by
talking with a lawyer. What was the law—in its institutional, normative, and cultural dimensions—that the adult child would have learned
about in a lawyer's office? What confronted such a client around 1930

or 1940, when the dimensions of legal practice in this area had matured and a rich body of precedents and illustrative and contradictory cases existed?

This chapter and the next two constitute something of a thought experiment: a rendering of what a knowing, learned, and ridiculously talkative lawyer would have presented to a client as "the law" when the client asked for advice. Or perhaps, slightly more plausibly, these chapters lay out the normative and doctrinal understandings that a lawyer would have discovered or demarcated from research that he or his law clerk had conducted, after having had a first consultation with a client.[2]

The first question a lawyer might have asked, after the client-to-be had told a shortened version of her or his story, would have been "What do you want?"

The client's answer would usually have been something like "the land (or the home or the estate) I was promised." The lawyer might then have asked a second question: "Would you be satisfied with payment for the work you actually did?" Let us begin by imagining that the client answered that question, as many presumably did, "No, I want the land I was promised," or, "No, she promised that I would be her heir."

What could be done to undo the old (and usually by now dead) person's decision or indecision? To get the land or the estate itself, rather than monetary damages, typically required an action for "specific performance" in a court of equity before a judge called the chancellor (or later in the nineteenth century, before one of several vice chancellors appointed by the chancellor).[3] An order for specific performance commanded whoever now held formal legal title to the property to convey it to the adult child. The child would get what had been promised, the property that the child had worked for and earned. An equity court's order of specific performance required that it be particular to the situation. So, in *Davison v. Davison,* the order was to the two brothers of James Davison who had been given the farm by their father, James W. Davison, although the particularities of that order also incorporated the fact that James Davison, the son, would receive the property, given the terms of the promise made to him, only on his father's death. Alternatively, in *Roberts-Horsfield v. Gedicks,* the specific performance order was directed to Cecilia Gedicks, Albert Gedicks's widow, and required her to mark off and to convey the lot on which the Roberts-Horsfield's house was located. Or, in *Danenhauer v. Danenhauer,* it was property belonging to Lee Danenhauer's mother's estate (of which brother George was the executor) that was ordered to be conveyed to Lee Danenhauer.

An order for specific performance was understood to be an "extraordinary" act of judicial power, since the ordinary course of legal action, which would occur on the common-law side of the New Jersey courts (i.e., before county courts of common pleas and the New Jersey Supreme Court), was to order nothing more than money damages for harms caused. One justification for such extraordinary orders was one version or another of a notion of fraud: that a legal title holder held the property either fraudulently or because of the fraudulent behavior of the parent or other older person who had conveyed the property to the present legal title holder. The special powers of a court of equity were needed to undo the fraud. The command of specific performance was directed to a wrongful but legal title holder. It ordered that person to undo the wrong—to do substantive corrective justice—and to convey possession to the petitioner, who ought "in equity" to own the land. A court of equity had a mandate to look past the formal legalities, including who had legal title, to uncover what were called "the equities" in the situation. However, such an order also depended crucially on convincing a chancellor or vice chancellor that a monetary remedy—damages—would be an inadequate form of compensation for the losses the adult child had suffered.

To make the case for an order of specific performance, a client's lawyer needed to prove detailed and particular facts about work done, the specificity of promises, and the lives that had been shaped by promises. Most of the time, a lawyer would put the client and other witnesses on the stand to talk about what had happened in order to show the underlying unfairness of the situation. The lawyer had to construct a convincing story—through testimony—that the client had worked and expended resources on the land or other property with a clear understanding that the client was investing in that land. Alternatively, the lawyer had to demonstrate that the client provided care for the older person with the unmistakable understanding that the work was being done in response to an unambiguous and publicly known promise made by the older person. The story had to produce the damning implication that those who had ended up as legal title holders had profited unjustly from that labor; they had defrauded the client.

The "case" for an order of specific performance became particularly fraught and uncertain in family histories of claimed care and promises. Necessarily, such claims rested on testimony of oral promises, of commitments unwritten and unformalized that could be known only through memories recounted in testimony given many years after those promises had been made—if they had ever been made. Judges were properly suspicious of the truth of the stories of care and work that supposedly justified such an order. Witnesses swore to tell the truth before testifying, but there was no stopping them when they perjured themselves. Put aside the likelihood—even the certainty—that some on the witness stand lied consciously. In many cases, it was not dishonesty but uncertainty, forgetfulness, and wishful thinking that testimony revealed. Who could really know what had been intended, what had been said, and what had been promised twenty, thirty, or forty years earlier? Memories faded or were shaded to produce the right outcome. As a vice chancellor wrote in a 1932 case, "Conscience offers feeble resistance to self-interest." At about the same time another vice chancellor opined as follows:

> Oral agreements of the character here relied upon are by reason of their own peculiar nature dangerous and all too often made the instrumentalities for the perpetration of frauds. As such, they threaten the very stability and security of estates, and incidentally cast grave doubt upon the power of man to dispose, as he sees fit, of that which is his own. By means of them and the testimony of witnesses who speak under bias and great temptation, yet conscious of their practical immunity from detection, the savings of one's entire lifetime may be pilfered and even snatched away from his heirs and next of kin.[4]

Such statements of judicial dismay—and there were many similar ones—rested on more than just a generalized professional distrust of a kind of testimony that everyone knew was often either dishonest or based in fantasy and desire. Like every American jurisdiction, New Jersey had enacted a version of a seventeenth-century English statute known generically as the Statute of Frauds. Central to it were two provisions that required all contracts to convey land and all conveyances (devises) of land to be in writing, not oral. The language of the statute was peremptory. The Statute of Frauds was intended to be a law of universal application, one that held without exceptions. Sellers and purchasers would learn from it that they needed to write everything down and make their transactions legible and public; otherwise, their business deals and undertakings would fail. Their behavior would be shaped by the inflexible nature of the statute.

One goal of the original seventeenth-century Statute of Frauds had been to eliminate interminable tests of indeterminate testimony, tests of the sort that continued to characterize the evidence in the nineteenth- and early twentieth-century cases about old-age planning and care. According to the statute, conveyances not in writing had been declared to be void, not merely voidable or challengeable. Void meant nonexistent, without legal effect, wiped out. Rigorous enforcement of the Statute of Frauds, many expected, would stamp out older informal and oral practices of transferring property. When no one would be foolish enough to rely on an oral agreement to convey land, the statute would have achieved the ends its drafters had intended.[5]

However, in seventeenth-century England, as well as nineteenth- and twentieth-century New Jersey, that is not what happened. Landowners and their children continued to use oral promises to make family agreements. A few of those were ones that courts of equity felt ought to be enforced in spite of the statute because not to enforce them would turn the Statute of Frauds into a statute "for" frauds. Within families (as well as in several other contexts), it was understood to be wrong, uncivil, and inappropriate to insist that a promise be written down. When parents, siblings, or others then used rigid or formalistic understandings of the statute to deprive adult children of property they had spent lives working to earn, courts of equity intervened at least occasionally.

The Statute of Frauds was intended to be a law of universal application. Courts of equity were as bound by the terms of the Statute of Frauds as were courts of law. Nevertheless, almost from the moment of the drafting of the first Statute of Frauds in England, courts of equity, first in England and later in other jurisdictions, including New Jersey, developed a counternorm to the primary norm of rigorous and universal enforcement of the statute. That counternorm was captured by the term *part (or partial) performance*. Oral promises would be enforced when the promisee had performed in such a way as to reveal a preexisting agreement to the court. "Part performance" succeeded— that is, it countered the rigid norm of the Statute of Frauds and gained an adult child ownership of land or an estate—where the distinctive nature of the performance (that is, the caregiver's arduous work, for example, or the career the caregiver had abandoned because of oral promises made) pointed directly to the provable reality of the under-lying promise.

The norm or doctrine of "part performance" was always controver-sial. Many courts "deplored" it. It was "repudiated" in several American states, mostly in the South.[6] Joseph Story, whose treatise on "equity jurisprudence" helped shape the subject throughout nineteenth-century America, wondered whether it would not have been wiser to leave "the statute to its full operation without any attempt to create exceptions." He realized that an unqualified statute would have "enabled" some to commit fraud. However, such instances, in which the Statute of (or against) Frauds became a statute *for* frauds, would have become, Story suggested, "more and more rare as the statute became better under-stood," as children and others realized that they could not rely on the oral promises of others. In any case, "a partial evil ought not to be permitted to control a general convenience."

Story also worried whether such "exceptions" produced by the doc-trine of part performance harmed the actual victims of fraud. These exceptions certainly increased "the temptations to perjury."[7] Other treatise writers inveighed against the circular quality of invocations of "part performance." By its nature, the claim of part performance rested on the prior existence of an oral contract. The actions performed that constituted part performance—for example, the care provided to an elderly person—had to have been performed in response to a preexisting understanding or agreement. Yet, at the same time, the work explained in testimony would be used in argument to prove the existence of such a preexisting understanding or agreement. "Thus the acts relied on prove and are proved from the agreement at the same time."[8]

The relationship between "part performance" and the Statute of Frauds was a matter of continuous debate by English and American legal commentators. On the one side, the doctrine of part performance offered a way to undo injustices sometimes produced through enforce-ment of the Statute of Frauds. Any judge or chancellor living in nineteenth-century America knew that older property owners induced life-changing behavior by means of oral commitments that they and their heirs later ignored. That is exactly what had happened in cases like *Davison* and *Young*. Adult children had been made oral promises that land or other property would eventually be conveyed to them. Those adult children had performed as fully as they could. If they did not in the end receive what they had been promised, then courts of equity should act—by making orders of specific performance—to prevent the defrauding by parents, siblings, and other heirs who mobilized the instrumentality of the Statute of Frauds. It was too easy to turn the terms of the statute into "a guard and protection to fraud instead of a security against it."[9]

On the other side, the doctrine of part performance challenged the utilitarian goal of the Statute of Frauds, which was to force everyone toward written documents. The exceptions the doctrine of part performance created—the gaping holes in enforcement—shifted the inducements that should have driven everyone toward written contracts, written conveyances, and a recorded public record of commitments. As lawyers representing adult children manipulated "part performance" claims in equity cases, they worked to allow exactly what the statute was supposed to prevent. As a result, trials became occasions for dueling memories of faded and fantastic promises.[10]

The case law in New Jersey began with a series of cases in the 1850s and early 1860s in which chancellors used the doctrine of part performance to explain why the Statute of Frauds should not be applied, even though all of the promises were oral.[11] However, in the generation after *Davison v. Davison*, the decisions of the New Jersey Court of Equity generally moved in the opposite direction. In *Eyre v. Eyre* (1868), Chancellor Zabriskie rejected the claim of two brothers for lands promised them by their father. "This salutary statute [meaning the Statute of Frauds] should not be lightly dispensed with." The statute's "wisdom" threw "doubt over the doctrine of equity, that part performance will take a case out of it." A similar case around the same time involving a promise apparently made to a son-in-law also failed because of the chancellor's regard for the "wholesome provisions" of the statute.[12]

It is hard to know whether the difference in tone between the chancery opinions of the 1850s and early 1860s, as opposed to those over the next twenty years, was the result of changing fact patterns—that is, changes in the stories and situations that clients brought to the courts—or of changes in judicial personnel. Perhaps it also had something to do with the increasing professionalization of the judiciary and the development of a treatise tradition and a national legal culture, all of which tended to favor the apparent clarity of rigid enforcement of the statute and to disfavor the fuzziness of the doctrine of part performance.[13] One should not overstate the changes. There were still instances in the 1880s and 1890s in which equity courts ordered specific performance, although this occurred more often in situations in which land was given—incompletely—to a son (as in *Young v. Young* and *Vreeland v. Vreeland*), less often in response to care work or other work within the home. However, by the end of the nineteenth century, two matched but opposing sets of precedents were available in the New Jersey equity courts. Claims that part performance justified and proved the existence and the enforceability of a contract to convey land succeeded under one set of precedents but failed under the other. In the best of circumstances, even with a very strong record of work and care, as well as many unqualified statements of promises made, a petition for specific performance by adult children was still more likely to fail than to succeed.

So, how could one acquire the land or the estate one had been promised? The answer, according to our knowledgeable lawyer, would have been to provide a court of equity with unimpeachable or unimpeached proof of a life transformed. What was this transformed life that one needed to reveal? Ideally, the adult children, the claimants, had to show that who they were by the time of the trial could be understood only through the lens of a contract. To put it more precisely, it was the lawyer's job to elicit testimony that revealed a life whose dimensions were shaped by a contract with a promisor, that is, with a propertied older person who had made an offer of land or an estate.[14]

An enforceable contract to convey land or to make a will required both an offer (for example, Stay with me, do what I want, care for me, and I will give you the land) and an acceptance (for example, Yes, sir, or OK), followed by performance or "execution" of the contract. A promise alone, no matter how well proven, was not sufficient if there had not been "acceptance" by the promisee, the adult child who stayed.

However, in the absence of a written document, how could one demonstrate acceptance, that necessary "Yes"? What proved acceptance? Courts were wary of testimony that simply reported on a spoken "Yes." Chancellors and vice chancellors wanted rich descriptions of lives spent doing things that could be explained only as resulting from such agreements. However, at least within the realms of nineteenth- and early twentieth-century family life, everything that one might point to as work done within the households of the old and of their caretakers was of ambiguous legal significance. Children who did what their parents wanted, who were dutiful and obedient, and who worked at home revealed nothing about the necessary existence of a prior agreement. Obedience was what children did at home without the need for or the presence of a contract.

Besides, work was what happened at home in nineteenth- and early twentieth-century households. Nothing determinative could be read from the fact that a child had stayed home or from the fact of work done there. As a vice chancellor wrote in one 1905 case involving a son who claimed that his parents promised that if he would give up his business, live with and care for them, and manage their "cheap" boarding house in New Brunswick, they would on their death give him their houses and lots: "That the services of caretaking of his father and mother, and looking after their business, were performed by the complainant, proves no contractual relation. Those services are in the law presumed to have been rendered in recognition of family duty and affection. No implication of an undertaking on the part of the father or mother, to whom such services were rendered, to pay for them, will arise."[15]

Nor did courts consider the fact that a young woman had given up or postponed marriage to stay and care for her parents or other older relatives as probative or revealing that her life had been transformed. There were, after all, many possible reasons why a young woman had not married. Perhaps she had found it less strenuous to stay at home rather than struggle economically in the world outside. Perhaps the young woman was in effect speculating on a legacy, sticking around and working at home in the hope that she would be remembered.

Still, lawyer and client had somehow to show that the client's life had been shaped irretrievably and distinctively by the undertaking that followed on an accepted promise. They had to demonstrate that but for the promise and its acceptance, life would have been different, and they had to show the costs—psychic and economic—that resulted from having stayed and provided care. The proof of a life shaped and restricted by an agreement to stay and work on the family farm or in the household or business served to reveal both that there had been acceptance of the offer and that the undertaking had been costly and determinative for the promisee.

The 1857–1858 case of *Van Duyne v. Vreeland* became the obligatory first citation for complainants' lawyers who attempted to make such a proof. That was the case of a "son" informally adopted shortly after birth by an uncle and aunt, who had promised the child's birth parents that they would make the child their heir. For a quarter century after he was taken into John Vreeland's household, John Henry Van Duyne had behaved like a dutiful son to his uncle and aunt, and the uncle had written several wills in John Henry's favor. However, after John Henry's aunt died and as his uncle became old and querulous, they began to quarrel. John Vreeland, the uncle, then remarried and wrote new wills that excluded John Henry Van Duyne, his nephew and adopted child. Finally, he conveyed all of his lands to John and Elizabeth Brickell, the son-in-law and daughter of his new wife. In the deed that marked that conveyance, the lands were valued at $6,000 (which both John Henry and Vreeland's neighbors thought seriously undervalued the property), but no money changed hands. Instead, Vreeland gave the son-in-law a mortgage in exchange for a written promise by the Brickells that he and his second wife would be taken care of for the rest of their lives. "Things" were "fixed" so that John Henry Van Duyne "could not get anything."[16]

At that point, John Henry Van Duyne brought a petition based on his "part performance," asking the chancellor for specific performance of an agreement to make him his uncle's heir. There had been, he claimed, an enforceable contract between his birth parents and his uncle. Moreover, he was both the rightful beneficiary of that agreement, which included a promise by his uncle that he would be his uncle's heir, and he had fully performed what the contract had asked of him, which was to be a dutiful and obedient "son."

John Henry Van Duyne won the ensuing case because his lawyer constructed a compelling trial record that demonstrated that John Henry's life had been fundamentally changed by John Vreeland because of the promised legacy. He would not have been adopted but for Vreeland's promise to his parents that he would be Vreeland's heir. John Henry's birth mother testified that she would never have given him up without that promise. Her claim was never challenged. Witness after witness reported on Vreeland's refusal to let John Henry learn a trade because he was needed at home and would never need a trade since he was going to inherit the property. Witness after witness testified that John Henry's birth father had excluded him from his own will because of Vreeland's promise. Witness after witness also insisted that John Henry himself had "devoted the prime of his life to the service of . . . Vreeland. He served him twenty-five years, upon the faith of an agreement, made at the solicitation" of John Vreeland with his own birth father.[17]

John Vreeland, the uncle, had tried to justify his change of mind, his decision to cut off his adoptive son and to turn for care to his new wife's daughter and son-in-law, by raising various acts of disobedience and disloyalty on John Henry's part. John Henry had not loved him enough or cared for him enough, he claimed. Those acts justified John Vreeland in his decision to transfer his property to his new stepdaughter and stepson-in-law.

But the chancellor was not persuaded. John Vreeland had wanted a son, and he had turned John Henry Van Duyne into that son:

> The defendant and his wife took the complainant, when but a few weeks old, and had him baptized, calling him by the defendant's own name, and standing for him. When he was a year old, they took him from the care and protection of his parents, to their own home. They adopted him, and brought him up in ignorance of his true parents. They claimed from him, and received the submission of a son. He never renounced his obligations to them as standing in the place of his parents. He resided under their roof until he was nearly twenty-one, obedient and exemplary in all respects. His own parents abandoned all control over him. His father, at his death, left a will, and relying upon the agreement that had been made with the defendant to provide for the complainant, he left all his property to his other children.

John Vreeland and his lawyer had "carefully sifted" John Henry's whole life, looking for any "delinquencies" that justified not fulfilling Vreeland's agreement with John Henry's birth parents. In the chancellor's judgment, however, they had found little to discredit John Henry, and what they had found was trivial. Few sons could have shown a better record of "filial obedience." John Vreeland had made John Henry Van Duyne into exactly what he had wanted, and it was the rankest fraud to deprive John Henry of the benefits of the agreement. Furthermore, although the agreement had been an oral one, it was not within the Statute of Frauds; that is to say, it did not become a "void" agreement, because of John Henry's "part performance."[18]

Later courts restricted Chancellor Williamson's relatively expansive understanding of what was evidence for a life sufficiently transformed, even as his opinion remained an obligatory citation. In particular, New Jersey's courts of equity would rarely find in the life of an obedient, caring, informally adopted daughter or son a life sufficiently transformed. By the early twentieth century, one can draw from the cases a general implication that those taken into new homes as foster or informally adopted children had already benefited from the change and had gained care and education from new and usually wealthier foster or adoptive parents. Such changes did not entitle a child to the benefit of oral promises to be an heir. Too, given the new availability of legal adoption, the fact that the adoptive parents had chosen not to formally adopt a child—following statutory forms—weighed heavily against a holding that the parents must have intended to make the child their heir. The dutiful behavior of such children did not reveal the promises they claimed had been made to them (whether the promises were made to them directly, to birth parents, or to the managers of orphanages).[19]

Nonetheless, *Van Duyne*, along with a few other cases, did establish a way of determining what constituted sufficient "part performance" to elicit an order of "specific performance" from a court of equity, one that privileged the notion of a life transformed. That approach continued for much of the next century.

Cooper v. Colson (1903) was a case that many early twentieth-century lawyers and courts used with *Van Duyne* to mark the boundary between a life so transformed as to justify specific performance and one insufficiently transformed. This was the case of a housekeeper, Margaret Sayre, who had been promised one of her employer's three farms if only she would stay and care for him. She stayed with him for more than two decades until his death from the consequences of what we today would probably call Alzheimer's disease or dementia. In an earlier chapter, testimony from the trial phase of *Cooper v. Colson* was used to illustrate the promises made by the old to solicit care. Here we look at the law that the case produced.

After all of the testimony had been taken, Vice Chancellor Reed summarized the ways in which Margaret Sayre's life had been shaped by her relationship with Joseph Colson: She first went to work for him in 1872, when he lived on a rented farm in Salem County. At the time she was paid three dollars a week in wages. In early 1875 he quit farming, and she left and got a job in "service" elsewhere. In 1876 Colson went into the "marl" business. (Marl is a crumbly rock or soil that consists mainly of calcite or dolomite, and is used as a fertilizer for soils deficient in lime. Demand for marl boomed as demand for fertilizer rose in the farming areas of New Jersey.) Sayre returned to work as his housekeeper at two dollars a week with the understanding that, after two years, in lieu of wages she would receive whatever she could make from the poultry she kept. Then Colson went back to farming. He bought one farm in 1881 and asked her to raise chickens there for one half the profits. She refused the offer. Then he said that if she would do as he wanted and stay with him, he would leave her a farm. She accepted that offer. However, a year and a half later Sayre changed her mind and decided to move to Montana. Again Colson convinced her to stay. Once again he did so by promising that "if she stayed with him and took care of him as long as he lived," he would give her a farm. Over the next years, they continued to discuss which farm she would take of the three he eventually owned. They lived on one or another of those farms until the mid-1890s. Throughout all of those years, she did all kinds of work that went well beyond what a housekeeper ordinarily did. When Joseph Colson became demented and unable to care for himself at all, she moved into a house in Woodstown, where she nursed and cared for him until just before the end of his life, when he had to be moved into an insane asylum. There he died without a will.[20]

What did that history mean? To Vice Chancellor Reed, it meant that all of the elements of a contract had been proved. He ordered that the administrators of Colson's estate convey to her a deed to the "Peterson" farm, one of the farms he owned at his death.

However, the lawyers for the Colson estate appealed to the New Jersey Court of Errors, which reversed, by a vote of eight to two. Margaret Sayre would not get her farm. Justice Fort's opinion began with the understanding, drawn from his reading of the treatises, that there were two "acts" of part performance that would take a "parol agreement" (that is, an oral agreement) "out" of the Statute of Frauds and allow a court of equity to decree specific performance. One such act was "actual open possession" of the land or other property; the other was "permanent and valuable improvements" made to the land. Each of these he regarded as easy cases. He then drew from the early New Jersey cases the conclusion that there might in addition be "special acts of personal service and the like," which, "when performed upon condition that land would be conveyed," might entitle "the party so performing" to a decree for specific performance. He believed both that *Van Duyne* was the best exemplar of that claim and that *Van Duyne* revealed that when the result of "performance of the labor and service under the agreement" had been "to change the whole course of the life or life work," then the case was one "within" the rule as to part performance even without possession of or improvements to the land.

However, here there was no such transformation of a life. Margaret Sayre was a housekeeper when she started; she was a housekeeper at the time of Joseph Colson's death. All the work she did, including the intimate bodily care of her longtime employer, was coherent with gendered expectations of what women did as routine aspects of their lives, whether as paid employees or as kin. There was no doubt, Fort conceded, that her services were performed "in part, though not wholly, in reliance upon compensation by way of the conveyance of a farm." Still, what she had done was neither "exceptional nor extraordinary. . . . She in no way changed her mode of living, or course of life, or life work," and so she would not get the farm she had been promised.[21]

Fort's much-cited opinion was interpreted by lawyers and judges to restate a test that required "exceptional" tasks as the proof of a life transformed. Performing tasks that were coherent or predictable within roles or jobs assumed within a family failed that test. Proof of the work done was never enough. One had to demonstrate that the work done could be explained only by the prior presence of the promise to convey property.

By the middle of the nineteenth century, men who gave up jobs or careers to care for older property owners at home were often understood as having passed that test. Returning home had become, in the culture and in the law, an exceptional undertaking at least for young men who ordinarily left home and entered labor markets. By contrast, women who gave up or postponed marriage to stay and care for older relatives were not often recognized as having made such an undertaking. There were too many possible routine and unexceptional reasons that a marriage had not occurred. Specific performance required an unusual story and an unusual relationship, an undertaking that could be understood only through the lens of an unquestioned promise to convey valuable property.

At least in the hands of the chancellors and vice chancellors of the New Jersey courts of equity, that did not always become an impossible test for all women, and even a few women who had done carework would win their cases. In *Winfield v. Bowen* (1903), decided at about the same time as *Cooper,* Vice Chancellor Stevenson held in favor of a young woman (a school teacher and "a woman of intelligence and fair education") who in 1872 began doing the books and correspondence for an older and illiterate tugboat captain, Simon Cosgrove, who was a friend of her parents. Minnie Winfield had continued to do that work for the next fifteen or sixteen years, always without pay, even though the tugboat captain was very well paid for his own work. In 1887–1888, Cosgrove retired from the tugboat business and moved in with Minnie, her husband, and her children in a small house that she and her husband, a fruit broker, kept in Jersey City. For the next six years she "supplied" him with "board, lodging, washing, and mending." She also nursed him in illness. Yet, she was never paid for anything she did. Meanwhile, he regularly and publicly promised her a house without ever telling her that he already owned one. Then he died without giving her anything.

The problem the vice chancellor faced in *Winfield* was to decide whether Minnie Winfield's labors were performed "as a mere gratuity" to Cosgrove, "this old family friend, this bachelor," without expectation of compensation. Alternatively, if with an expectation of compensation, had she worked "merely with the expectation that such compensation would be voluntarily made . . . in the form of a gift by will or otherwise"? Then again, had she done the work because he had made a promise to her? The vice chancellor admitted that he found the case a difficult and a close one. In the end, though, he decided that the only way to prevent fraud would be to decree specific performance and order Cosgrove's estate to convey to her the house he had owned while he lived with her in her small house.[22]

Laune v. Chandless (1926), to take a second instance of a successful suit, told the story of Elizabeth Laune, a woman with a small child, who in 1906 moved into the home of her sister Catherine and her brother-in-law, Charles W. Chandless. She was in her early forties at the time; they were about twenty years older. Her sister soon died, and Elizabeth stayed on and "looked after" her brother-in-law until his death in 1922, offering the ordinary care that women in such situations gave. Her claim that he had contracted with her to leave her all of his property if she stayed and cared for him was corroborated by witnesses, and he had actually written a will that gave effect to that understanding. However, the will lacked some formalities, and so it was ruled invalid. She had received nothing. However, Vice Chancellor Bentley decided that there should be specific performance in this case because Chandless probably "executed what he meant to be a will because he was under moral and legal obligation so to do." Bentley's opinion included an apology for having expressed doubt during the hearing of the case whether Elizabeth Laune had carried the "unusual burden" that cases of this sort required. His opinion suggested that he was still a bit anxious and uncertain. On balance, though, he decided that she met the test enunciated by Justice Fort in *Cooper*. She was not a housekeeper who had remained a housekeeper, and so she received her due.[23]

However, in other cases about caretaking, the caretaker's claims failed. In *Boulanger v. Churchill* (1916), to take one example among many, Romeo Churchill had a conversation with his niece's husband shortly after Romeo's wife had died. Romeo needed someone to look after him. Would his niece, Mary Elizabeth Boulanger, do that? If she would, if she would "come down and take care of me," he promised, "she shall have this property when I go." Her husband and her uncle negotiated, and the husband then went back to discuss the matter with Mary Elizabeth. They agreed to move in with Romeo Churchill.

For the next four years, she took charge of the household and also nursed him. According to the husband, "Romeo was like a baby around the house, requiring a lot of attention." An attorney was called a week before Romeo's death to write a will that conformed to the promise he had made, but no will was completed because he was still trying to decide about how to dispose of a few incidentals. Then he died without a will, and Mary Elizabeth sued for specific performance (she had died before the trial, so the case was concluded in her husband's name).

The court ruled that nothing in the "voluminous" testimony indicated that the labor or services she had performed were "exceptional or extraordinary" or that her whole course of life or lifework was changed by performance of the agreement. Unlike *Van Duyne*, where there were "services of affection rendered by a child to its parent," here everything done could be measured by its "money value." An award of damages for unpaid wages was the appropriate way to compensate for Mary Elizabeth Boulanger's work.[24]

A housekeeper who worked hard as a housekeeper and who cared for her employer, even for many years, did not reveal a life appropriately transformed. She retained a remedy for her uncompensated labor by suing for unpaid wages. As both Justice Fort and the lawyers for the estate had insisted in *Cooper v. Colson*, Margaret Sayre ought to bring an action *quantum meruit* for all she had done, particularly in the last years, when she was caring for and nursing a demented man. A common-law court could determine her right to damages, which would be figured by the relevant market standard (for example, what nurses and housekeepers in Salem County were paid at that time). On the other hand, hard work alone did not earn one the right to a farm.

Chancellors and vice chancellors always scrutinized the testimony, with a particular eye to uncovering the strategic uses of notions of a life transformed. When they found such uses, they pounced. So, in *Johnson v. Wehrle* (1931), Vice Chancellor Backes had to rule on "companion bills," one by Joseph C. Johnson, the nephew of Catherine Beaver, who, until he was sixteen, had lived with Catherine and her husband. The other bill was by Mary Brice, Catherine Beaver's sister. The claim that Joseph Johnson and Mary Brice made was that there were two oral contracts, one giving the homestead plus the income from an estate of $15,000 to Mary Brice for the rest of her life, the other giving the residue of the estate to Joseph Johnson. Each testified for the other, since neither Johnson nor Brice was a competent witness for himself or herself.

To the vice chancellor, what each said seemed too perfectly structured to fit within the doctrinal strictures, particularly those articulated in *Cooper v. Colson.* In the nephew's case, the court found a "feeble effort" to take the case out of the Statute of Frauds. The nephew claimed that his "attention to his aunt's affairs" supposedly "altered his course in life and resulted in neglecting an oil burner business, to his loss." The vice chancellor noted, however, that he was still in business and, "as a side line," worked as a detective. The testimony had disclosed neither the nature and extent of his business nor any "degradation in occupation" that had been caused by his "devotion to his aunt and her affairs." In Mary Brice's case, the claimed change in her life was that her sister, Catherine Beaver, expected her never to leave her alone. As a result, she had lost her freedom. Yet, it was not apparent to the vice chancellor "that she was not at liberty to go at will, as she chose, and that she had not all the freedom and perhaps more than she enjoyed when working for strangers." He concluded that Mary Brice, "this hard-working worn-out old woman," had "found surcease, comfort and contentment in the home of her sister, where she was willing to be of service in the expectation of being rewarded by her rich sister, who, mayhap, held out the prospect. At all events, she did not step out of her ordinary vocation." If, in the end, her work had become "more arduous than in her other jobs," it was "estimable by a jury" in a case of *quantum meruit,* that is, through a suit for damages. Her situation, according to the vice chancellor, was "ruled" by *Cooper v. Colson.*[25]

We can watch the demand for the demonstration of a life transformed played out contrapuntally in the hands of opposing counsel in the 1940 case of *Ehling v. Diebert.*[26] Frank Ehling had gone to work for Ignatz Kulat, a butcher in Jersey City, in 1913, when he was fourteen.

According to the "bill of complaint" Ehling drafted with his counsel, the politically connected Charles Hershenstein (Hershenstein was "personal advisor" to the infamous Boss Hague of Jersey City), he had "often" lived with the Kulats as a youth and "was in their constant companionship and mutual estimation." At that time the Kulats were a childless couple in their fifties. After Ignatz died in 1917, Frank continued to work for Bertha Kulat, Ignatz's widow, who had inherited everything from her husband, including the butcher shop, two family houses adjoining the store, and three other "family houses," all in Jersey City. (At her death in 1939, her estate was worth approximately $130,000, not including real estate.) Frank may have been fired or let go by the manager of the store at some point but was subsequently rehired. He claimed that he ran the butcher shop for Bertha, although most of the testimony suggests that he probably did not.[27]

What he did do for the next twenty-six years was to become Bertha's constant companion, which was certainly not an easy task. She was estranged from all of her living relatives. Many of them resented the attention she paid to Frank. They particularly resented her known and repeated promise to leave him all of her property. According to his petition, he had relied on that promise, and the result was that he managed the butcher shop, and "he gave of his personal time, attention[,] and devotion . . . as if he were her son." He took her "walking, riding, picnicking and to places of amusement." For many years he continued to be paid the same salary ($12 a week) that he had been paid at Ignatz's death. Eventually his salary varied from $25 to $35 a week, but he never demanded a higher salary, "nor was there any inclination on the part of Bertha Kulat" to pay him more, according to his petition, "because of the mutual understanding of their relationship and of his eventual and conditional accession to all of her properties and possessions."

In 1925 he married Grace Maxwell, with Bertha's consent. During his courtship, he would take Bertha along, and her constant presence in the marriage continued thereafter. His "attention, time, and devotion to Bertha" did not "diminish." For the next fourteen years, she accompanied the couple whenever they went to the movies. She went "motoring" with them every Sunday and in the evenings when the weather was warm. "Hardly a night in years . . . passed when Bertha Kulat failed to speak with complainant on the phone . . . merely to have a conversation with him before they retired, even though they were together in business all day long." When she was ill, he was the only one she tolerated to care for her. In addition, she treated the child of Grace and Frank's marriage as her own grandchild.

Then came the key passage in Ehling's petition:

> All of these acts, services and sacrifices made by complainant over a period of 26 years for the benefit of and on behalf of Bertha Kulat materially changed and altered the course of his life. He had nurtured no friendships, forsook the opportunity of establishing his own business, worked without fair and reasonable compensation, so that he is today without any independent funds or income; neglected the normal intercourse of his own family, and even created differences and misunderstanding in his own home and between himself and his wife, and lost the respect of her parents and friends, and impaired his health.

In 1938 Bertha Kulat had a will drafted, but it did not conform exactly to the promises she had supposedly made to Frank Ehling. However, it did express her desire to leave Frank Ehling the bulk of her estate. It made a variety of gifts to charities, to some relatives, and to Frank's daughter and his wife and left the residue to Frank. That draft will was modified several times by several different lawyers, always leaving Frank as the residuary legatee. However, then she suffered a fall and died without having signed a will. The result was effectively to defraud him, to cheat him of what he had worked for and of what had changed his life. He was, therefore, according to the "petition," entitled to an order of specific performance that would make effective the intentions she had expressed but not carried out in her unsigned will.[28]

Everything about Frank Ehling's story was reframed in the answer of Harry Diebert, one of Bertha's relatives and the administrator of her intestate estate. This answer was drafted with the aid of Diebert's equally politically connected but Republican lawyers, John Drewen and William Rurode.[29] In Diebert's rendition of the enmeshed histories of Bertha Kulat and Frank Ehling, Ignatz Kulat had hired the boy Frank solely "to run errands and render such unskilled and menial tasks as are generally required in such a business." Frank had been discharged by Ignatz some time prior to the latter's death. Eventually Frank learned the "butcher's trade" and was rehired, but he was always kept "in a subordinate position"; he was never a manager. Meanwhile, Bertha found it increasingly difficult to leave her home. She bought a car but never learned to drive it. Frank Ehling became her chauffeur, which was why they were often seen together. She was not specially attached to him; she did not feel particular affection for him. To the contrary, she became "increasingly apprehensive and fearful of him." She kept him employed "only because of sympathy for his wife and child, and because of the belief that in the event of his discharge [the] complainant would succumb still further to the vice of drink and descend to utter ruin." He was a drunkard who had been committed three times to the psychopathic ward of the Jersey City Medical Center. His drinking had caused a separation from his wife. While drinking, he had become "obsessed" with the fanciful notion that he could make Bertha convey all of her property to him. She had resisted and died without a will, however.[30]

In making the case for Frank Ehling before Vice Chancellor Thomas Kays, Frank's lawyer, Hershenstein, relied on the testimony of Grace Ehling, Frank's wife. Before her marriage to Frank, he asked, had she observed "the conduct" between Frank and Bertha Kulat? Drewen, the opposing counsel, immediately objected to the question: If the testimony was intended to show "a disposition of favorable intent of the deceased toward the complainant," it was irrelevant since intent to

make a contract did nothing to prove the actual existence of an agreement. Hershenstein explained that he only wanted to show the affection that existed between them, but the vice chancellor sustained the
objection.

Hershenstein tried again: Had Grace had conversations with Bertha
with respect to an agreement with her husband? Grace answered: Yes,
she had. The first time had been right after she received an engagement
ring from Frank. She had already noticed "the over-affectionate" ways
between Frank and Bertha. She asked Bertha why "he and her were so
together," why Bertha was the inevitable accompaniment to their courtship. Grace and Frank could not go out by themselves. "We always was
a three-some." Bertha told her: "I have promised him that I will take
care of him and that everything I have will be his, providing he takes
care of me and gives me the due respect and love any son would give his
own mother." Grace detailed several later conversations, all to the same
effect. The last one took place as Bertha was leaving the hospital just
before her death: "She was coming home to live with us; give up the
business, and take care of us for the rest of our days. That was her last
promise."

Grace Ehling then began to explain how the time her husband spent
with Bertha Kulat had harmed their marriage. Immediately there was
a lawyers' colloquy about relevance. Hershenstein argued that this
was important information because the cases had held that instances
"where a person, the promisee, gives up some things in life, changes
his course of conduct, disrupts his own life, begins a new sort of life"
demonstrated the "part performance" that revealed a contract enforceable in equity. He meant to show that the agreement between Bertha and
Frank had disrupted his life and his marriage to Grace. The court rejected the explanation and sustained the objection. Hershenstein tried
again: Did you, Grace, and Frank give up your time for Bertha? Again,
an objection; again, sustained. "I think, your Honor, it relates exactly to

what your Honor said this man gave up." The vice chancellor replied: "No. I just think your argument is ridiculous."

So, Hershenstein asked, what had Frank done? Grace answered: He devoted two-thirds of his evenings to Bertha Kulat. How so? "Taking her out, taking care of her when she was ill, when she was blue and melancholy, he would go and spend evenings with her, call her on the telephone every evening, and completely disrupted my home." "Court: strike out the last." At ten o'clock every evening, if they were not already out with her, Bertha would call. The conversations would last one to two hours. The court questioned that statement. Could it have been so long, so much? Hershenstein responded: "That is exactly what I asked this witness. It was a remarkable thing." "It certainly is remarkable," the vice chancellor agreed. "Very remarkable," Hershenstein added. After further testimony about the ways Bertha regarded Frank as a son and about her conflicts over writing a will, Grace returned to Bertha's constant presence. They saw her practically every Sunday for eighteen years. They took many photographs together, though the court would not let Hershenstein introduce them into evidence.

Under cross-examination, Grace continued to insist on the nightly telephone calls. Drewen, one of the lawyers for the estate, asked her about a trip to Florida shortly before Bertha's death. Had she gone to Florida because of her husband's heavy drinking? "No, not exactly." However, it was the case that Frank had been drinking heavily for three to four days just before she left. The lawyer tried to get Grace to admit that Frank had been drinking for weeks. She denied that she had had him committed to the psychopathic ward. He went there voluntarily—twice. Bertha had asked him to go in for alcohol treatment. He had not gone to Bertha's funeral. Why not? Was it because he was intoxicated? No. He had stayed away because "he was not welcome." According to Grace, Bertha's relatives were the cause of his absence. Was it not true that their marital difficulties were the result of his conduct, his drinking? "Not all. . . . The majority was due to the over-affection of Mrs. Kulat, which made my life very miserable."[31]

Other witnesses confirmed conversations with Bertha Kulat in which she described her intentions—her promises—to leave everything to Frank Ehling, although the testimony over how much responsibility he had over the business revealed discrepancies. Descriptions of Bertha's desire to adopt him as if he were her son also varied. With regard to his behavior, everyone conceded that he sometimes went off on "sprees" that usually lasted a couple of days, although a few were longer. Lawyers for the estate tried to get George Maxwell, Grace's father, to concede that for years Frank was mostly unable to work. One witness for the defense, an employee at Kulat's Market, the butcher shop, stated that part of his job was to go to saloons to find Frank Ehling and take him home. In fact, once he was off on a bender for around five weeks. During that time he would occasionally show up at the shop. "He would go in the kitchen, then he would maybe get something to eat, and walk out again."

The manager of the store testified that he had once told Bertha that she ought to get rid of Frank. She had answered, "Oh, if I put him out, his wife and child will suffer for him" and that "she did not want to see them in the gutter." When Frank Ehling testified about his work habits, he claimed that he had missed work for only a couple of days at a time. He had a nervous condition that led to his drinking, a condition that worsened a little in Bertha's last years. On cross-examination he conceded that he had been away from work "sometimes a month." He went to the psychopathic ward because of nerves, not alcoholism. "My dear man," the lawyer interjected, "isn't it a fact that, while this case was pending, and during the adjournment of the case, you were on a spree of excessive drinking?" No, Frank answered. Nonetheless, the manager of the butcher shop had seen him in a tavern at that time. What was Frank doing there? Answer: "the same as he was doing."[32]

The opinion of Vice Chancellor Kays entirely rejected the argument of lawyer Hershenstein for specific performance and dismissed Frank Ehling's "bill." The "headnote," or abstract to the opinion, nicely captures its holding: "Equity will specifically enforce a parole agreement to make a will in order to prevent fraud upon one who . . . has in good faith performed . . . and changed his position to his disadvantage. . . . Oral agreements . . . are always regarded with suspicion and subjected to closest scrutiny. . . . The acts of [the] complainant do not constitute such a performance as would take an oral agreement on the part of the deceased out of the statute of frauds."[33]

The case then moved to the New Jersey Court for the Correction of Errors and Appeals. Hershenstein's brief for a reversal made three points.[34] First, he claimed that the proof was "conclusive" that Bertha Kulat had made an agreement to leave her estate—or the bulk of it—to Frank Ehling. The fact that the draft wills did not precisely reflect what she had apparently promised did not matter. (Here he cited *Van Duyne v. Vreeland.*)

Second, and more important, the proof of change in Frank Ehling's life was so strong that a denial of specific performance constituted a "gross fraud." Thus, there had to be a decree in spite of the Statute of Frauds. Hershenstein's brief acknowledged that there were "some differences" in how various courts in diverse cases had interpreted the burden that had to be met in order to take an oral agreement "out of" the relentless operation of the statute. However, whatever standard one chose, Frank Ehling met it.

In addition to all of the work he had done for Bertha Kulat, he "became devoted to her as a son." He took care of her and "gave her all the attention, companionship and sacrifice which a mother and son relationship entails. For 22 years he spent his days, evenings, Sundays, and holidays with her." When he married, he "compelled" his bride "to pattern her life after his." One consequence of Bertha's "constant monopoly of his time" was the disruption of his marriage. His was a life transformed. The testimony revealed "how heinous a fraud would be perpetrated" if the Statute of Frauds barred "his present enjoyment of the *quid pro quo* promised him by the decedent at the commencement of the history of his devotion to her." In addition, the authority for this conclusion was found in *Davison v. Davison,* along with other cases. Indeed, the situation of James Davison, who had been "turned out of his home without a dollar's compensation and without means of subsistence, after rendering services to a needy father," provided a "perfectly applicable" analogy to Frank Ehling's situation.

And point three? The defense, Hershenstein conceded, had shown that Frank Ehling was often intoxicated. But what of it? Even if one assumed that Frank had often been so drunk that he had been unable to work, that was not a breach of the relevant agreement, which was not, in its essential features, about work in the store or about abstinence. "The essence of the agreement" was that Frank Ehling should be "devoted" to Bertha Kulat "as a son." His "intoxications" did not "destroy that devotion." Bertha's "manifested concern" for Frank's "welfare, well-being and health" in fact offered the "strongest evidence that she at no time regarded any conduct of his as a breach of the agreement." Behind this last point lay an unspoken claim that his drunkenness— his alcoholism—was caused by and a manifestation of the demands that Bertha had made of him and that it was, in the end, revelatory of how his life had been transformed by these commitments.[35]

The brief on the other side, by Drewen and Rurode, began with a quick characterization of the relationship: Bertha Kulat had always been "generous and hospitable" toward Frank Ehling and his family. There was no proof that he had not been "fully compensated" for what he had done or that his wages were not entirely appropriate for his employment. It might be the case, though, that he had been spoiled by his "long association with an over-indulgent employer." In the end, however, he was just a drunkard who had imposed himself on Bertha.

Then Diebert's attorneys moved on to characterize the past cases (the precedents) in which an oral agreement to make a "testamentary disposition" (a will) had been enforced. Those cases, they insisted, were ones in which an "intimate blood-relationship" existed between the parties. In some, an effective "conveyance" of land would have taken place on the strength of the promise (as in a case like *Young v. Young*), or "long years" would have been spent "in domestic association and help; or unrequited service and labor, for example—on a father's farm" (as in *Davison v. Davison*). These cases demonstrated how far short Frank Ehling's case fell. (One might note that they entirely skipped informal adoption cases like *Van Duyne,* which might have been better applicable to Frank Ehling's situation, and instead relied entirely on cases involving direct parental [blood] kinship.) The law, they were sure, was unmistakable and justified rejecting Ehling's case. Expressions of "testamentary" intent (oral promises) offered no evidence of a binding agreement. The proof of the existence of an agreement had to be clear and convincing. Someone like Frank Ehling, who rendered services out of the hope of a legacy, had not changed his life sufficiently to justify specific performance.

In any case, there was "abundant reason" for the vice chancellor's decision, they continued. Hershenstein's brief they characterized as totally confused. It was "quite impossible" to tell whether its theory was the existence of an actual agreement (which, they claimed, was what the previous decisions required) "or the so-called 'relationship of mother-and-son,' or just 'friendship,' all independent of agreement. Certain it is that the brief in no particular is addressed to the basic tests imposed by the decisions." As a result, what Hershenstein had written had reached "absurd extremities."

Why had Bertha Kulat not made a will in Frank Ehling's favor? Here is how Diebert's lawyers reinterpreted the testimony about what had happened using a mix of the popular psychological categories of the 1930s: It was "not at all unlikely" that Bertha Kulat had taken "a fancy" to Ehling. "Such things cannot be readily explained," and it was "of no consequence whether the phenomenon . . . arose from senility, frustrated maternal instinct, neurosis, or plain foolishness. Let us say—however unjust it was to others—that she felt most favorably inclined" toward Frank Ehling. Concede all that, the lawyers continued, and that inclination still did not produce "an obligation" or an agreement. It was only "an impulse toward morbid generosity." Even so, she had not entirely lost her sanity. "One dominant misgiving restrained her" from succumbing to her impulse. She knew that Ehling was a drunk who was moving "from bad to worse." She probably hoped that the prospect of a will would "encourage the cure of his weakness." Eventually, however, she saw that her hopes had failed, and what she saw kept her from signing the wills that she had had drafted. The "real reason" she did not "execute" the will that would have given Ehling what he had hoped for "must be as plain" to Frank Ehling as it was to them. "Whatever hope Bertha Kulat had of restoring Ehling to a sober life" had given way to "despair." "At the time of the injury that resulted in her death *Ehling had been on a continuous rum debauch for five weeks, the longest ever.*"

There was, these lawyers concluded, nothing to show an irretrievable alteration in Frank Ehling's "status or the course of his life":

> Beyond the exigencies that rule every life that must provide its own living, appellant is not shown *once to have done aught he did not wish to do or aught he would otherwise not have done.* There is nothing to show that he could at any time have bettered his situation, or that his place in the employ and friendship of Bertha Kulat was less than a great good fortune and advantage to him. [Italics in original]

The Court of Errors agreed unanimously. Those who represented Bertha Kulat's estate had won; Frank Ehling had lost. Moreover, the court said nothing to make it likely that Frank Ehling would ever be able to get even a damage remedy from a common-law court.[36]

Two years later Frank Ehling was dead.[37]

In a lawyer's office, a client would have learned that it was difficult to establish a transformation in one's life significant enough that a chancellor or vice chancellor would have recognized it as revealing an "executed" contract. It would not have been sufficient that one had felt trapped by obligations, by a relationship, or by the promise of an inheritance. A transformed life had to be more. The New Jersey courts emphasized identities that would not have been assumed and lived but for specific promises made. Proving the "but for" was hard.

Behind the lawyerly arguments about lives transformed and untransformed lay murky and muddied motivations and lives. We can imagine that the adult children in these cases had stayed for multiple and contradictory reasons: often out of love or the desire for a stable place to live or perhaps because of others living nearby, because they had no parents, or because other prospects were still more speculative than the promise of property after death.

The property owners (the purported promisors, the parents, the employers) may have been in love with them or thought of them as mere employees—or both or neither. Who knows whose love was unrequited or inadequately requited? Female caregivers may have found it particularly difficult to unpack their sense of a culturally powerful, general moral duty to care for others from the idea of a "freely" assumed contractual obligation.

The life transformed was also and at the same time often the life they had been raised to lead. What it meant that a young woman had given up marriage to stay at home with elderly relatives was inscrutable to the courts. In addition, the case law—the legal doctrine—refused to consider not marrying as evidence of a part performance. (And yet one wonders whether, behind the justifications articulated in their opinions, such choices did not weigh on judges.)

Men may have had it easier in the sense that courts did, at least sometimes, recognize the foregone opportunity of a job or a career away from home as evidence of a part performance. Furthermore, by the mid-nineteenth century, staying at home to care for the old (or, more often than not, bringing one's wife along to care for them) was no longer articulated as a moral or legal duty for young men. Still, for them as well, it must have been an odd and contradictory experience to claim that the devotion and attention they had paid to the older people who loved and needed them was motivated merely by a promise.

It would be the lawyer's work in representing such clients, male and female, to repress much of that emotional complexity. It would be the lawyer's job to identify contractual motivations and to make them appear as the dominant and real ones, those that had transformed lives.

That may not have been so difficult much of the time. These were, after all, also stories about young or younger people who believed that, but for the promise of an inheritance, they would have done something else, probably something better, with their time and their lives. They were in the lawyer's office and willing to go to court because they believed they had been cheated. Because they had stayed but not gotten what they had been promised, they had been robbed, perhaps of their lives. But for promises made, they would have gotten better jobs, learned trades, moved to Montana, not become a drunk, and had happier marriages. They knew, at least by the time they were in the lawyer's office preparing testimony, that taking care of elderly people had been a distraction at best from the lives they were supposed to lead. Staying home ought not to have been destiny even for the younger women. Staying home with old and needy kinfolk (or elderly employers) had not helped careers, marriages, or much of anything else that was important or valuable.

The "part performances" that entitled them to rely on oral promises were, in their nature, performances against ordinary self-interest. That is why it seemed and still seems plausible to apply the language of fraud to those situations in which promises that solicited care were not carried out.

Yet, the love they had felt for those they had taken care of and the satisfactions they had experienced at home, as well as their sense of continuing connection and obligation, would keep leaking out in the testimony.

Chapter Six

Compensations for Care

T he lawyer asked again: What do you want?

This time the client-to-be answered: I want to be paid for the work I did in caring for the demented or dirty or difficult or sick or demanding old person. That should be easy. Or at least, easier than asking for the land. Right? I worked. I cared. I should be paid for my time, for my trouble, for the years I have lost.

What would that answer have meant for lawyers and clients living and working in early twentieth-century New Jersey?

Everywhere in nineteenth- and early twentieth-century America adult children sued estates for unpaid wages. Those adult children—daughters and sons, as well as grandchildren, adopted children, relatives distant and close, and unrelated individuals—brought actions *quantum meruit,* actions for "as much as he has deserved."[1] A suit for unpaid wages would often have been understood as a second-best alternative. What many of the complainants had really wanted, the better alternative, was land or other property. That was what they had been working for. However, it was not easy to turn labor in the home into a successful claim to property. What they would have to settle for was a cash equivalent of back wages, and even that form of compensation was most uncertain.

In the trials that resulted, courts heard testimony about promises made, negotiations and wills drafted and changed, and foregone opportunities elsewhere, and they heard much about quantities of work and care. However, there was almost never a written contract put into the record. All that judges and juries had to go on were narratives about work performed and the reasons that people had done so.

What were such narratives supposed to prove? What was the evidentiary significance of work in the absence of a written contract of employment? By the mid-nineteenth century, such questions usually had a direct legal answer. At least for free American adults who worked outside the home, work presumed a right to compensation. To be a free adult meant that one should be paid when one worked for someone. To put it somewhat more legalistically: "When one" was "employed in the service of another for any period of time, the law" implied "a contract of hiring and a promise to pay." A worker had a right to be paid for work actually done, for the "services rendered." When services were rendered, the recipient or beneficiary of those services, the employer, became obligated to pay the employee. Not to pay would be a form of unjust enrichment—of fraud and of servitude.

The law presumed that no one volunteered to work for free. Furthermore, if the employer had not paid for the labor actually completed, the employer was liable for an action *quantum meruit*. That is, the employer could be made to compensate the worker on the basis of the work done by the hour, day, or month. Or, if the employer had died with such accrued wages unpaid, then the executors or administrators of the estate were similarly subject to such an action. Either way, the compensation that resulted from a successful mobilization of the cause of action was understood as righting the wrong that had been done to an employee. The employer had benefited from the labor and therefore ought to pay.[2]

Was that true within a family as well? Did it hold for the kinds of work that adult children did within the households of their parents and other older relatives? Here a second baseline understanding or default rule qualified or limited the initial answer: "An agreement to pay for services rendered and accepted is presumed . . . unless the parties are members of the same family or near relatives." As Chancellor Williamson put it in *Updike v. Titus,* a much-cited 1860 case:

> The law implies no promise to pay for services rendered by members of a family to each other, whether by children, parents, grand-parents, brother, step-children, or other relations. No action can be maintained for such services, in the absence of an express contract or engagement to pay for them. The rule rests upon the simple reason that such services are not performed in the expectation, or upon the faith of receiving pecuniary compensation. Ordinarily, for a service rendered, the law implies a promise to pay, corresponding with the value of the service, but for services rendered by members of a family to each other, no promise is implied for remuneration, because they were not performed in the expectation, by either party, that pecuniary compensation would be made or demanded.

He concluded that authorities for this proposition were "so numerous" that there was no need for any particular citations.[3]

This qualification was presented as if it were an expression of simple common sense. Family work meant noncompensable work that was done for reasons other than expectations of pay. One family member could, of course, pay another family member. No law forbade doing so. In addition, there was nothing to keep one family member—an elderly person in need of care, for example—from making an explicit contract to pay—in the present or in the future, with wages or land as the "consideration"—for care or for other services. However, to fail or refuse to pay for work completed or services rendered did not necessarily imply the existence of an unpaid obligation or a debt unsatisfied. Work done in the home by family members did not suggest the presence of an underlying contract for wages and did not subject the beneficiary or recipient of the services rendered (or the executors or administrators of the beneficiary's or recipient's estate) to an action *quantum meruit*.[4]

When someone worked anywhere but at home, the cultural and legal implication was that the work would not have occurred but for the expectation of pay so long as the someone was a competent and free adult.[5] Why would one labor for a stranger except for a promise of compensation? By contrast, when someone worked at home—although what was "at home" could include "on the farm" or "in the shop," as well as "in the bedroom and kitchen of the house"—the presumption, again, both culturally and legally, was that the work came about because of desires and obligations distinctive to family life. That meant that compensation was not presumptively the reason for the work. After all, there were many culturally significant reasons—among others, love, duty, sharing, and investment in the future—that explained why one might have worked "at home" without the expectation of pay.

Judges, lawyers, and litigants alike regularly sang familiar sentimental songs about the distinctiveness and the significance of the loving home in a variety of keys and registers. They knew, as all competent participants in the legal culture knew, that the work that made a home differed ontologically from commodified labor performed for strangers. Outside of the home, a judicially enforced contract law held sway; in the home, reciprocity, care, love, and duty shaped the commitments that came with intimate relationships. To look to contract law and to expect a court to adjudicate what one family member owed another for the work done in maintaining that family must have seemed, by its very nature, an odd and perilous task, one that risked destroying the very bonds that united a family.[6]

How, then, could one adjudicate the claim to compensation of adult children (or other near relations) who had remained at home even though they could have left to pursue opportunities elsewhere? Were these adults still at home? They were not in a relationship of dependency and might well have their own family—children and a spouse. In a society founded on mobility, where sons and daughters routinely moved away from their parents' homes when they became adults, what did it mean when they had not done so? Or what did it mean when they returned to the parental household after a period of time away? Had home become presumptively a place of employment, with parents as employers, or did home remain "home," in which labor occurred for reasons other than the expectation of wages?

The starting point for any legal analysis of these questions was that to be an adult child meant that one carried no legally enforceable duties toward one's parents. Children surely felt obliged to care for those who had once cared for them. In theory but almost never in practice, a town or other local government could require compensation from children if a parent were put on poor relief—had to go "to the poor house." However, parents had no inherent rights to the labor or care or the cash of their nonminor children. The point was stated with marvelous clarity in an early New Jersey case, *Youngs v. Shough* (1835). Jacob Shough had constructed a coffin to bury Margaret, the mother of Philip Youngs. The coffin cost ten dollars and fifty cents. After Philip's father's death, Margaret had married a man named Sigers, with whom she had lived until her death. Sigers had contracted with Shough to pay for the coffin. However, about a year after his wife's death, Sigers auctioned off his belongings and left the county, leaving his debt to Shough "unpaid, and probably forgotten." Shough then went to Philip Youngs, and Philip apparently promised that when he had been paid for his own work, he would settle with Shough for his mother's coffin. Yet when he did not, Shough sued him on this promise.

Shough won a judgment before a justice of the peace, but Philip Youngs appealed that judgment to the New Jersey Supreme Court, which reversed the JP's decision. Philip Youngs's promise to Shough was "a promise without consideration to support it; nothing was given by Shough, nothing received by Youngs." The promise was "what the law denominates a naked promise," one that Philip could not be compelled to perform. Philip had no "moral obligation" or responsibility "for a coffin for another man's wife [that is, for his own mother's coffin], while there was a husband living, who had taken this mother from her children, and appropriated her society, her labor and services exclusively to himself and his affairs." All of the legal and moral obligation lay on Sigers. Therefore, Philip Youngs was entitled to a reversal of the judgment against him. The appellate court then went further: The only justification for the demand made on Philip Youngs derived from the fact that Margaret was his mother. "But a son is no more liable in law for his mother, than father, brother or uncle. One relation cannot run another in debt without his consent or request; otherwise any man might be undone by his father or mother, brother or sister."[7]

If an adult child could not be compelled to pay for his mother's casket, what then of the adult child who sued a parent or a parental estate for unpaid wages? In *Williams v. Barnes,* an early (1832) North Carolina case involving a son who had stayed home to help his mother (by being the overseer of her slaves), the trial judge had instructed the jury that he was a competent adult who was free to negotiate with his mother, another competent adult. The jury, according to the trial judge, should not infer any meaning from the parental relationship; the jury should consider the relationship between mother and son as in effect one between employer and employee. Yet to Thomas Ruffin, the famous chief justice of the North Carolina Supreme Court, such instructions were clearly wrong and required reversal. "Compensation" was "expected from strangers." They had "no right, legal or moral, to another's time." Still, a jury should be free to consider the terms of the relationship between parent and child, including "their whole conduct before and after the arrival of the child at full age," in order "to rebut the presumption of a promise, which would arise in the case of a stranger." The jury should be free to give that relationship "the

weight" it was "entitled to" and to use "their own feelings as sons and
fathers, and . . . their knowledge of our state of society."

Ruffin himself could not contain his "involuntary emotion of de-
testation of the odious irreverence and ingratitude of a son, who says
to a widowed mother the day he is twenty-one, 'pay me now for all I
do.'" He continued: "Is there no bond but that of the law? No gratitude
for bounties already bestowed, no filial piety, no affectionate regard—
nothing to keep the son under the maternal roof, but the prospect of
gain? And if gain be the object, does it follow that it was to be in the
shape of annual wages and none other?" Who was this son anyway,
who insisted that the court deduce a contract from his presence at
home? Ruffin paraded a variety of possible answers before his readers.
Perhaps the son had been too lazy to go out and find work in the world.
Perhaps he was incompetent, not "fit for other business." Perhaps it was
only because of "a continuation of parental favor" that he had been allowed to remain in the "comfortable" parental home. Perhaps in letting
him stay, his mother gave him more real compensation than he would
have been able to earn as wages in the labor market. On the other hand,
perhaps he had stayed as an investment or a speculation on an inheritance. He might well have expected a "liberal legacy" because "his tenderness and assiduities made him a favorite."

Then Ruffin switched to an instrumental or utilitarian tone. Adulthood had not "as yet" severed the tie that connected a child with parents.
Legal control ended, "but the relation and all the feelings incident to it
remain, to give a character to, and raise presumptions concerning
their acts towards each other." "It cannot be possible," he wrote, "that
the head of an harmonious household must drive each member off, as
he shall arrive at age, or be bound to pay him wages, . . . unless he
shews that it was agreed that he should not pay." Such a position would
"dissolve that connexion, the duties and the enjoyment of which are
the cement which unites families." It is, he intoned, "the interest of society at large to preserve that union, and make it as close and cordial

as our selfish natures will allow." Ruffin admitted that he did not "trust" himself to say "yet" that the absence of a formal and written document was itself evidence that there was no contract. However, when, as in this case, a son "merely" continued to reside with his mother and to buy supplies for himself on her account (that is, when he likely received room and board from her) and when he did not put into evidence that he had assumed "*all* the severe duties usually exacted from overseers, and may therefore have acted rather as master than served as man," in such a case a court should rule that there was no evidence of a contract. Moreover, Ruffin believed that claims like those made by the son in this case should be strongly discouraged. "To sustain them tends to change the character of our people, cool domestic regard, and in the place of confidence, sow jealousies in families." If he had been the trial judge, Ruffin would have encouraged the jury to reflect on the family relationship.

Thus, there had to be a new trial. The lesson to adult children would be clear: Do not assume that work "at home" raised a legal expectation of pay. Stay at home, if one wished. In the end one might receive an inheritance to justify that decision. However, if one wanted compensated employment, one should go elsewhere. Otherwise, one should contract explicitly, in writing, with one's parents. To put it differently, parents did not need to worry that their children had to be paid for the work they did as members of a household.

However, even in this early North Carolina case, discordant notes were heard. Ruffin's opinion did not actually say that an adult child did not gain an implicit entitlement to wages by staying home and working. The most the case stood for, read narrowly and putting its sentimental rhetoric aside, was that a trial judge should not prevent a jury from considering the parent-child relationship. Furthermore, Ruffin's associate, Justice Joseph Daniel, had written an unqualified dissent to the opinion. In the dual roles that characterized judges in early North Carolina, Justice Daniel had in fact sat as the lower-court judge who had delivered the jury instruction that so incensed Ruffin.[8] According to an unrepentant Daniel, when a child became an adult, the child became bound to maintain himself or herself, "and the law likewise" released "the child from the obligation of giving . . . labor and services to the parent." When a child, according to Daniel, worked for the child's parent as an adult, "the law" inferred "a promise by the parent, to pay as much as the labor of the child" was "reasonably worth." The parent-child relationship was not "an exception" to the general legal presumption that work implied an obligation to pay.[9]

Far from settling the question in North Carolina, in later cases Ruffin's opinion was often cited to be qualified and distinguished in holdings that allowed compensation to adult children. In *Hauser v. Sain* (1876), a case about a granddaughter who had stayed home to take care of her dependent and eventually insane grandfather, the court went out of its way to rule that "the weight" of the law had been on Daniel's side in spite of the "sentiment and feeling excited in the heart of the Chief Justice [Ruffin]" by the circumstances of the case.[10]

Meanwhile, at about the same time that *Williams* was decided, a similar case challenged the Massachusetts Supreme Judicial Court. *Guild v. Guild* (1833) came up as a motion to set aside a jury verdict awarding damages to a daughter. The case, according to Chief Justice Lemuel Shaw (like Ruffin, a very famous and influential nineteenth-century judge), had taken too much of the court's time. It had long been held "under advisement," while the members of the court continued to discuss what so divided them. Now, at last, Shaw thought he had found a way to bring about a united decision.

The problem that confronted the Massachusetts court was what inferences to draw when an unmarried adult daughter continued to live "in her father's family, performing such useful services" as it was "customary for a daughter to perform, and receiving such protection, subsistence, and supplies of necessaries and comforts" as it was "usual for a daughter to receive in a father's family." Did the law raise a presumption that she was entitled to compensation from her father's estate for such services? Alternatively, did the administrators of his estate have the burden of proof to show that such services occurred without any expectation of pecuniary compensation?

On those questions the court had apparently split evenly. One side believed that, once a daughter had reached the "legal period of emancipation," she and her father presumptively dealt with each other just as "strangers" would. The other side insisted—"(confining the opinion to the case of daughters, and expressing no opinion as to the case of sons, laboring on the farm or otherwise in the service of a father)"—that a daughter's continued residence and labors in her father's family could be accounted for "upon considerations of mutual kindness and good will, and mutual comfort and convenience, without presuming that there was any understanding, or any expectation, that pecuniary compensation was to be made."

Shaw worked to find a middle ground between the two sides. All of the judges agreed, he began, that a jury was certainly entitled to infer a promise to pay from relevant circumstances that revealed that her services had been of such a nature that compensation for them was expected. Such circumstances would vary but would, he expected, fall into one of three predictable categories. She might have been a servant in the home, presumptively expecting wages. She might have been a boarder, expected to pay her parents for her "accommodations and subsistence," or she might have been a "visiter [sic], expecting neither to make nor pay any compensation." (Shaw believed that "the latter predicament," shaped by the culturally predictable mobility of young people, embraced the greater number of situations that courts would see.) Testimony would reveal what the relevant circumstances were. In the end, it was relatively "unimportant" whether the jury would be instructed that such facts suggested an "implied promise" or merely a rebuttable "presumption of such a promise." (Since the court remained equally divided, the verdict in favor of the daughter was not reversed.)[11]

Similar cases were a continuing presence in New Jersey. In *Ridgway v. English* (1850), as we have seen, a daughter sued her father's estate *quantum meruit* for the wages not paid her during the years she had stayed in her father's household and worked. The daughter and her new husband had put into evidence her father's promises to compensate her for her willingness to remain after her mother's death to help her father in the household. However, to the court, those promises did not reveal a relationship that required the payment of wages. Nor did the work she had done reveal such a relationship. According to the majority, in language that echoed Shaw's in *Guild,* an adult child—over the age of twenty-one—remained in a parent's home in one of three roles: as a hired servant, entitled to wages; as a boarder, who would be expected to pay for room and board; or "as a child unemancipated in fact, in which case she is neither entitled to wages nor liable for her board." Absent proof to the contrary, the third was presumptively the role an adult child assumed. "The law will not presume any change in the existing relation of the parties from the mere fact that the child is [over] twenty-one." A daughter at home would have to prove that she was "emancipated," and there were really only two ways for her to do that. She would have to find waged labor outside of the home and retain her wages for herself, not sharing them with a parent, in which case she ought to have been considered a boarder, bound to pay her father for her maintenance. Alternatively, she would have had to contract directly and explicitly with her father for work done in the household, in which case she would have become a "hired servant." However, the testimony at trial revealed that not "one word, even, passed between the father and daughter" with regard to compensation.

The decision in *Ridgway* came with a second opinion, in this case a concurrence, that described the evidence that could have been mobilized to justify a jury verdict that awarded damages to the daughter. Justice Carpenter agreed with the rest of the court that this daughter had no right to be compensated based on the record before them. Yet, what circumstances, what evidence, he asked, would authorize a jury to infer an enforceable promise? It depended on the state and condition of the family, the character of the services, the conduct of other daughters and whether they had shared in the labors done for the family and received any compensation for their work, and the specificity of the parent's or parents' statements. In particular, Carpenter emphasized, it would help if a father's statements had been made prior to the commencement of the services rendered. If there had been an "inducement by which he had retained her in his family," then there might well have been a "record" that would have justified compensation. Such evidence, he concluded, would have refuted the idea that services were given "gratuitously." In this case there was insufficient evidence to justify such a decision. In future cases it was up to the lawyers to build better records.[12]

Over the next century, young women and men continued to sue for unpaid wages even in the face of precedents that appeared to indicate that they would not win, and they continued to find lawyers who would represent them in those suits. Many lost their cases. However, the apparently clear cultural script that determined that work in the home was not real work—that is, not compensable—unlike work away from the home, sprouted exceptions and qualifications.

Adult children's suits for compensation after the death of a parent or other older household member produced a continuing conversation among judges, lawyers, and litigants about the nature of the adult child: as an adult, that is, as a competent individual who might be either a worker or someone who had chosen to give the gift of care, and also as a child, that is, as someone who continued to "belong" to a family or to a family member. Hard, almost metaphysically hard questions about freedom, care, and duty emerged from these trivial and common situations. What was adulthood? What did it mean to be "in" the family? What were "exceptional" tasks that would not have been undertaken but for the expectation of compensation? What were "voluntary" undertakings? Did a voluntary undertaking imply an underlying contract and an expectation of compensation? Or was it by nature a gift?

When an adult child took care of an older person, was it work? That is, was it "free labor"? Or was the older person (and that person's estate) "freed" of the obligation to pay? That is, was it "free labor" of a different sort?

Here is how L. Dewitt Taylor, a lawyer representing an intestate estate in an 1886 lawsuit, challenged the claim of a daughter in her mid-forties that she was entitled to be paid $3,000 on a note her now dead mother had given her. The note was meant as payment for the daughter's care and work. However, according to Taylor:

> If obtained under the pretext that it was for services rendered by the daughter to the mother, it was void because the daughter never rendered any services to the mother, but such as it was her duty to render in the position she occupied in her mother's house; that she was unmarried and unemancipated; that she and her mother stood to each other in the relation of parent and child; that there was no express contract ever made between them that the daughter should receive compensation, and that she could therefore receive none; that she was fed and nourished at her mother's table; that she was clothed and cared for at her mother's expense; that she was in feeble health a good deal of the time, and required the attendance of a physician, for whose services the mother paid; in short that the benefit she received from her mother greatly overbalanced any services she rendered.[13]

The keyword in Taylor's argument was "unemancipated." This was a term with a long and tortuous history, a history only loosely connected to the post–Civil War understandings that built from abolitionism, the Emancipation Proclamation, and the Thirteenth and Fourteenth amendments, and a history almost entirely distinct from the emancipations identified with the 1960s.

For Taylor and his audience of judges, emancipation defined the boundary between a child's dependence and an adult's responsibility and independence. The middle-aged daughter, who, he argued, did not deserve the money she had apparently been promised, remained a daughter, a child who lived in her parent's house as a dependent. Thus, he insisted, she should not be paid.

For us, the boundary between childhood and adulthood may be marked by a variety of events and transformations: the right to vote, military service, sexual maturity, wages, living on one's own, freedom from a parent's authority, perhaps marriage. For both parents and children, the crossing of that boundary can be experienced as emancipatory: Children are freed from their parents' supervisory authority, while parents may understand themselves as emancipated from their duties of support. However, for us that boundary is fundamentally about chronological age, about a birthday celebrated, about an "age of majority," although we also still talk as if there were a vaguer but knowable moment of psychological and cultural maturation that might mark the switch.[14]

In the nineteenth century, chronological age—a birthdate that marked the end of minority—was important as well. A father or mother could not demand that a child who had turned twenty-one remain to serve and care for them. At fourteen, sixteen, or eighteen, depending on changing laws and mores, parents could no longer stop their child from marrying. In the 1886 case in which L. DeWitt Taylor made his argument, the daughter could have emancipated herself by marrying or by leaving home even before reaching the age of twenty-one. In fact, the Court for the Correction of Errors and Appeals ultimately rejected Taylor's claim that this middle-aged daughter was still unemancipated. Justice Dixon's opinion for the court insisted that the note the mother had given her daughter constituted a "just debt" against the estate. The services that the daughter had "rendered" over the many years since she had "become of age" justified it. Dixon noted that such services "might have been rendered out of filial affection solely"; still, she was, in his eyes, presumptively an adult, someone who had worked for pay.[15]

Nonetheless, Taylor's language, as well as Justice Dixon's, also carried traces of a notion of emancipation that was functional—that is, about how and with whom one lived—rather than formal or objective—that is, about having passed a particular age. Their rhetoric was rooted in a much longer and older legal history in which chronological age offered an imperfect marker of adulthood and adult power.[16] The foundation of "emancipation" as a legal category lay in archaic understandings of patriarchal power. Although a father always had the right to emancipate his son at any age, in much the same way as he had the right to open a cage and allow a pet bird to fly away, he had no duty to do so. "Emancipate" was a transitive verb. It was something done or not done to a subordinate (sons and daughters, as well as foster and adopted children and apprentices) as an act of power and an expression of a possessory right. Early on it overlapped with notions of manumission, the right of masters to free their slaves.[17]

Over many centuries, that older notion of emancipation grew muted even as it remained a concept in the law. Emancipation became "the naturally attainable state of having come of age and maturity, at the latest after twenty-five years." It constituted an ending of paternal power. In addition, fathers and guardians could not retain permanent power over their adult children. By the nineteenth century it had become clear that parents could not keep their children under their control after they had reached maturity. Self-emancipation by the child, daughters as well as sons, had become something close to a legal right. Indeed, it became a contested judicial question whether parents had any continuing rights to demand their children's pay or to control children who had left home to find work or marriage before they turned twenty-one, the age of maturity.[18] In addition, when the adult children returned home, they presumptively did so as free individuals who were no longer in their parents' control and who would have come "home" only to be in a work relationship. That would be the case even if they went home at the "demand" of a parent who needed them. One could not become unemancipated.

Yet, did that mean that an adult child who remained within a parent's house and had never left was necessarily emancipated? What of those who did not exercise the mobility that was becoming the hallmark of being an American? Chief Justice Joseph Hornblower of the New Jersey Supreme Court reflected on such questions in an 1837 poorrelief case about a woman of fifty-two, described by her eighty-fouryear old father as "of weak mind, . . . an idiot" who had never left his household. Before one reached age twenty-one, only marriage or the acquisition of a settlement in another town produced emancipation. After age twenty-one, one was emancipated "by separating . . . from and ceasing to be a member of . . . father's family." However, if the child remained single and made "no contract inconsistent with the idea of . . . being a member of, and in a subordinate situation in . . . father's family," and if the child remained in the father's home for "so long, whatever may be his age, would the child remain a member of the household of the parent"? "The age of twenty-one," he concluded, was "fixed upon, and spoken of in the books, not as the period *when* emancipation takes place; but as the age, at or subsequent to which, the child may emancipate himself by withdrawing from his father's family, and setting up for himself in the world."[19]

Children who had not acted on their right to be emancipated, usually by leaving, marrying, or getting a job and keeping their own wages, presumptively remained unemancipated. That was one core reason that the daughter in *Ridgway v. English* could not recover. She had remained a child "unemancipated in fact" when she remained in her father's household after her mother's death, notwithstanding her chronological age and the work she had done. This was "well settled law, at least in this state, and was not questioned at the trial, or upon the argument."[20]

It was all a matter of "presumptions." Absent evidence to the contrary and absent evidence that the relationship between parent and child had become a businesslike one (e.g., demonstration of an explicit contract), a child who remained in the household remained an unemancipated child regardless of the child's chronological age. In theory, it was easy to overcome the presumption that a child in the home was unemancipated.[21] There were a number of "facts" that, if presented in testimony, would be dispositive. An unsupported child was perforce an emancipated child. A father (or mother if she were the household head) had the right to turn a child out from the family "and from the shelter of his roof" once the child turned twenty-one. A parent had no duty to provide continued care, and a parent's liability ceased with the child's age of majority. From then on it required "either the express or tacit assent of the father to the continuance of his child in the relation of his unemancipated servant."[22] Conversely, an adult child had no legal obligation to stay at home to care for an aging or aged parent. All that had to be shown to prove emancipation, in theory, was that the child had left, had married, had pursued a career, or had made contracts with others, let alone with a parent.

However, if nothing had changed in children's work or marital lives, they remained presumptively children in the household. In that case, they would not be likely to succeed if they later sued to be compensated for "services rendered" in parental households.

In determining the force of such presumptions (what legal scholars today call "default rules"), gender conventions and assumptions played a powerful role. Young men who gave up opportunities away from home in a free labor market to return or to stay at home were often recognized as presumptively entering into a contractual work relationship with their parents. In *Updike v. Ten Broeck* (1866) (sketched in Chapter 2 for the promises made by a seventy-year-old father), a son sued his father's estate for seven years of work done between 1831 and

1838, a period that began with the son's twenty-first birthday. At trial, the judge had instructed the jury that if they determined, as they would, that there had been a contract between father and son, then "the relation of parent and child ceased, and that of master and servant commenced to exist." The presence of the master-servant relationship meant that Ralph Van Dyke Ten Broeck, the son, had become an employee and was entitled to be paid. The jury had awarded him $1,100 for his seven years of labor.[23]

What had happened in 1838? According to the father, as related in testimony, the son, known as Van Dyke, had "defamed" his father by spreading a story that he was guilty of "adultery, at his own home with his housekeeper," who apparently had later become the father's new wife. Had the father committed adultery (technically, fornication)? Had the son defamed him? Looking back nearly thirty years, the court could not say. In the end, the New Jersey Supreme Court did not care to arrive at a conclusion. The judges in the majority on the court concluded only that, on the one hand, the evidence of adultery had probably not been strong enough to justify the son's leaving before being ordered away. On the other hand, there was "no legal proof . . . that the son had spread the story." Since the father had wrongfully "repudiated" the son (given that he had no proof that the son had wronged him), Van Dyke had been wrongfully terminated as an employee. That meant that Van Dyke Ten Broeck could now, in 1866, years after his father's death, recover for his services *quantum meruit.*

Did it matter that as of 1831 Van Dyke Ten Broeck had never left his father's home? Was he therefore unemancipated? In his opinion for the majority, Justice Bedle resisted any suggestion that Van Dyke was a child bound by law or nature to stay with his father. In addition, witnesses' testimony was mobilized to demonstrate that Van Dyke presumptively remained because of an explicit promise to pay for his work. The court gave weight to the testimony of Jack Ten Broeck ("colored"), who described a typical exchange between Van Dyke and his father:

> "I want to go away."
>
> "[W]hat do you want to go away for?"
>
> "I want to go away to do for myself . . . all the rest of them are doing for themselves, and I want to do for myself, too."
>
> "I can't spare you; you're the only boy who'll work; I can't spare you; I have a large farm; I am getting old; as long as I live, I'll keep the loaf under my own arm; when I die you shall be well paid."

According to the court, Van Dyke had not remained because that is what a son naturally did; he had not remained merely because it was a convenient or an easy thing to do; and he had not remained because he was speculating on a hoped-for inheritance from his father. He remained because he and his father had made a deal (although the court left the terms of that deal unspecified). Van Dyke was understood as an economically capable employee wrongfully discharged and therefore entitled to payment under a contract.[24]

The presumption that an adult child remained a child within a parental household was easily overcome for such young men. Young women found it less easy. As one judge wrote, "The female children of many parents often remain . . . unemancipated long after attaining majority, rendering services to the father and supported by him." For such services, they would have no right to compensation.[25] The courts did not consider a young woman's postponement of marriage as equivalent to a young man's decision not to go away "to do" for himself in the world of work. Even when a young woman went away to work or pursue a career and then returned, her departure might not be enough to secure her emancipation and justify a later claim for compensation.

In *Gardner's Administrator v. Schooley* (1874), a young woman, Sarah A. Schooley, had gone off to learn a trade. She stayed away from home for three months. Then her mother's illness and eventual death made it necessary for her to return. Thereafter she stayed and served

in her father's house, where she lived along with her brothers. Their
father, who was a "day laborer" for the railroad, possessed a small
house on a one-quarter-acre lot. His sons paid no board to him (although they did help furnish the house), nor did they compensate
Sarah for the washing and mending that she did for them. There is
also nothing in the case to suggest that they "rendered" any "services"
to their father. Instead, the sons, whom one can read as effectively
emancipated, "retained all their earnings for their own use." Sarah
served them, as well as their father, in the small house where they all
lived. Her father, who had promised "that if his life was spared he
would give her something to show for her services," eventually gave
her a mortgage on the property. However, after his death, creditors
challenged the mortgage, and the court ruled that she was entitled to
nothing. No contract had existed between father and daughter. Instead, the gift of the mortgage would, if judged valid, have defrauded
her father's creditors of their claims. The law would not "imply" any
"promise to pay for services rendered by a daughter to her father under such circumstances." Sarah had "returned to her father's house
while she was yet a minor, to live in and be part of his family, and she
so continued, unemancipated."[26]

This is not to say that women who remained at home to care for
aged or aging parents never won suits for compensation *quantum
meruit*. To take just one example, in 1879, the chancellor, sitting as the
ordinary (which is what the chancellor was called when he decided
cases in the Prerogative Court), affirmed the payment of $518 to a late
middle-aged Catherine McCohn for the care of her very old mother
(she was ninety-three when she died) for the last five years of her life,
ever since she had fallen and become permanently lame. Mother and
daughter had always lived together, and Catherine had long taken
care of her. She could have been understood as never emancipated.

However, the court concluded there was clear evidence both that
the mother intended to pay Catherine and that Catherine expected to

be compensated. Several witnesses testified that the mother had told them that she meant to do something for Catherine. The court placed particular weight on the fact that the mother's lawyer had repeatedly dissuaded her from rewriting her will in Catherine's favor, "telling her that Catharine could bring in her bill against her estate for her services, and that the neighbors knew and could testify to their value." The case was, according to the ordinary, within the "rule" set in *Ridgway* and other cases about children presumptively unemancipated. Yet, that rule did not preclude recovery if circumstances were such that a contract ought to be presumed. Here the court cited a series of cases, including *Updike v. Ten Broeck*. It was all a matter of "intention." This was not the routine case of a "daughter, supported by her mother, and rendering service in the household." It was rather one in which a daughter provided "necessary services" to an "old and helpless mother," services that would otherwise necessarily have to be provided by "a stranger for compensation." Since the mother would have had to pay someone, it was reasonable to suppose that she had agreed to pay her daughter.[27]

By the time of this last case—in the late 1870s—the historically resonant language of "emancipated" and "unemancipated" began to disappear from New Jersey's judicial opinions in *quantum meruit* cases. It is not surprising, then, that L. Dewitt Taylor's 1886 argument failed. By then, lawyers who wanted to challenge claims for pay by children and other care workers were looking to a different discourse.

What was happening? Perhaps the courts could not resist the increasingly determinative power of age consciousness, the replacement of functional understandings of age and competence by more formal and seemingly objective notions of chronological age as fixing life transitions, including the age of majority. It may also be that by the 1870s inherited and long-standing legal understandings of "emancipation" and "unemancipation" were becoming increasingly difficult to articulate in the face of a constitutional polity now formally com-

mitted to universal emancipation. One discourse of emancipation over-
laid another. The older language of emancipation had carried with it
powerful but increasingly archaic patriarchal assumptions. The older
language had rested on a belief in what Blackstone once called "the
empire of the father," a belief that children ordinarily remained within
the private property–like domains of fathers (and sometimes mothers).[28] By the last third of the nineteenth century, however, a variety of
cultural and political forces—including a woman's rights movement,
the beginnings of a child protection movement, new and expanded
invocations of the police power that allowed at least some forms of
public and semipublic intervention into the privacy of at least some
households—challenged and effectively weakened parental power. As
this happened, the utility of the image of an unemancipated adult
child apparently weakened as well.[29]

The last New Jersey decision that depended on a judgment that an
adult child who had worked and provided care in the home was "unemancipated" occurred in 1894. The decision served as the penulti-
mate act in an endless and endlessly complex case about the estate of
James Taylor, one of the founders of the Trenton ceramics industry.
To simplify the story (which is not precisely about an adult child
claiming unpaid wages from an estate): The estate was sued by the
creditors of Taylor's business partner, Isaac Davis, because Taylor had
endorsed Davis's note. After having signed the note and not long before he died, Taylor had conveyed his large and recently purchased
family home on Clinton Street to his granddaughter, Ella F. Severs,
who would marry the much older Isaac Davis after her grandfather's
death. Isaac Davis's creditors argued that the conveyance of the home
was an attempt to defraud them. Ella F. (Severs) Davis had also died
by the time of the litigation, as had Isaac Davis, but her "heirs at law,"

her siblings, argued that the conveyance was not made as a gift, which would have fallen under the rubric of an attempt to defraud creditors. Rather, it was intended as compensation for the work she had done in caring for James Taylor and his wife, her grandparents.[30]

More than thirty years earlier, around 1861, when she was no more than one year old, Ella Severs had been taken from her own parents by her grandparents, and she grew up and spent her life separated (and apparently sometimes alienated) from her birth parents and siblings.[31] When, more than thirty years later, the lawyers for Isaac Davis's creditors asked her father whether her grandparents had treated her as a member of the family, he answered: "Took her to serve and take care of them." They clothed her and sent her to school, although witnesses disagreed about just how long she had attended school. According to her father, her grandparents pulled her out of school after two or three years because the "old folks" needed her to take care of them.

Witnesses disagreed about how hard she had to work. According to an aunt, Ella had not done anything "by way of making a living." She did little but "fancy work." Her grandparents "loved her so dearly that they didn't put no hard work upon her." Just painting and fine needlework, done for amusement, not for pay. She did not labor. "She wasn't very healthy, and wasn't able to labor very much." The aunt conceded that in the last years, when Ella was in her twenties, Ella had to do much household work and that she had always gotten the groceries and attended to other business. However, the aunt also insisted that her work was worth little. According to other witnesses, the old couple had no servants in the household until close to the end. In other words, Ella had "served" her grandparents in their household and had substituted for the servants they had not hired. Ella's mother answered the question "Who did the work in the house?" with a simple answer: "When Ella was large enough she done it." What was the nature of the work? General housework, including the work upstairs. Her grandmother generally did the cooking when she was able. However, when both of the grandparents got older, about the time that they moved into the house on Clinton Street, Ella had to wait on them. When her grandfather "came down in the morning he was a man that never could fasten his shirt, fastened in front, and Ella would always have to put on his pins and get his breakfast for him; to fasten his shirt together and do all everything pertaining to their needs." Her grandmother, a very large woman, suffered from rheumatism and was much disabled. "She went up stairs all right, but when she came down she would have to come down backward" and have to be assisted. Ella's mother tried to expand on the care Ella had given her grandparents, but the vice chancellor stopped her. He did not think the "quantum of care" made any difference. This case was about whether there was consideration for the deed. As long as there was some work, it would be enough.[32]

An attorney testified about having drafted the deed in 1886 that conveyed the Clinton Street property to Ella. It was done, he noted, at the direction of Isaac Davis, her grandfather's partner but not yet Ella's husband, in the rear office of James Taylor's pottery. The consideration for the deed was "the services rendered" by Ella to her grandparents, plus one dollar. When the deed was signed and acknowledged, the attorney remembered "Mr. Taylor saying, looking over to his granddaughter . . . she has been a good girl and she will do what is right. He had a smile on his face." Other witnesses reported that Taylor had told them that he had built the house on Clinton Street to be Ella's eventually. Why had he done so? "For her conduct to him and his wife. . . . He said he had not a child that could fill her place; he said for her kindness and attention to me and my wife. . . . [I]t was in compensation for her valuable services. . . . Because she had been a faithful girl—attentive— and her services had been valuable to him and to his wife."[33]

However, to Vice Chancellor Bird, the deed remained "voluntary," that is, not founded on a contract. Therefore, it could be attacked and nullified as a fraud on creditors' rights. He came to that conclusion for two reasons. First of all, Ella, although she lived into her late twenties, had never been emancipated from her grandparents, the two people who had been the only parents she had ever known. "The relation, which existed from the time the child was 1 year of age until she became 21, continued unbroken till her death." He quoted from *Ridgway* and other cases in support of that conclusion. Perhaps he made matters easy for himself by referring to Ella as James Taylor's daughter, not his granddaughter. In the second place, he reframed the case through the lens of *Disbrow v. Durand,* a recently decided "leading case" of the New Jersey Court for the Correction of Errors, with an opinion by Chancellor Alexander T. McGill. Bird believed that this new case "unequivocally" confirmed the older doctrine about unemancipated daughters. However, *Disbrow* looked at the question of compensation not in terms of patriarchal authority but of the expectations of "members of a family, living as one household." Within a household, where people shared and lived together, it was "the ordinary rule" that such relationships abounded "in reciprocal acts of kindness and goodwill, which tend to the mutual comfort and convenience." Work within a household was ordinarily "gratuitously performed." Where such a relationship appeared, "the ordinary implication of pay . . . for services" did not arise because "the presumption" that supported "such implication" was "nullified." The mutual dependence of those in such a family did not rest on their status as parents and children. Indeed, such mutuality arose even where the family was "composed of remote relations, and even persons between whom" there was "no tie of blood."[34]

All that Ella had done for her grandparents belonged to a world of care and love, far removed from the colder realm of calculation and individual compensation symbolized by a deed as payment for services rendered. It did not matter what her grandfather had said to his lawyer and to many others. It did not really matter whether or not she was emancipated. She had been part of a common family enterprise that depended on the work of all, and she had remained within that household. Her grandfather's decision to convey the family house to her had been merely a gift that could be challenged by the creditors of the man for whom her grandfather had stood as security (who would happen to become her husband).[35]

As Vice Chancellor Bird had predicted, *Disbrow v. Durand* quickly became a "leading case," invoked and quoted relentlessly over the next half century. Bird claimed that the opinion's significance lay in the ways it reproduced and continued an older understanding of the unentitled status of unemancipated "children." In fact, however, Chancellor McCall's opinion in *Disbrow* initiated a new style of analysis in *quantum meruit* and related cases. In place of the need to invoke an authoritarian family, a prerequisite for a claim that a child was unemancipated, lawyers and judges reimagined the family as a place of sharing. Those who worked to resist adult children's claims to compensation could now reframe those children as people who were confused about what was and was not compensable work. Adult children could be denied not because they were still children but because they ought to have understood themselves as part of a family, an institution whose premises and practices stood in opposition to a separated world of work and individual calculation. One presumption—one default rule—replaced another, the new one standing as a better reflection or invocation of what such judges and lawyers knew to be the real relations that shaped family lives, at least as of the end of the nineteenth century or the early years of the twentieth.

McGill's notion of "reciprocal acts of kindness and goodwill" offered a new way to characterize how and why work occurred in households. In addition, that new way reflected a growing recognition, certainly for middle-class lawyers and judges, of the separation of economically remunerative work from predictably smaller urban and suburban households.

Meanwhile, the opinion also expressed a perhaps surprising reframing of roles and identities within families. Older cases had tacitly differentiated between direct "vertical" blood relatives, in particular birth children, and other members of the household, including housekeepers, nurses, and servants, as well as more "distant" relations. In making such a differentiation, the cases had always presumed that both vertical blood relatives and all others shared an identity as "belonging" to the household of the property owner. However, the cases also presumed that a household by nature contained varieties of persons with varying relations to one another. (Remember all of the members of the Davison and Perrine households in *Davison v. Davison,* and note that no one had any difficulty distinguishing who they were or their roles or expectations within the household.) Vertical blood relations who lived at home had an implicit expectation (mediated, perhaps, by an awareness of testator's freedom) that they were going to inherit the property. Others in the household had, at most, a much more tenuous expectation of inheritance. They lived in the household for other reasons, including contractual reasons.

In that context, it made sense that courts would hold that no *quantum meruit* compensation was owed to an adult but unemancipated child or grandchild who had inappropriately claimed to "really" be a contractor. The unemancipated adult child or grandchild who wanted payment for services was pretending to be a different kind of member of the household than was actually the case, while probably still expecting to inherit as an "heir" (although in reality such cases usually occurred because the adult child had not inherited as expected).

On the other hand, in the world reframed by *Disbrow,* blood and lineage became almost irrelevant for the question of whether household work was compensable labor. Instead, courts asked: Did you belong to the family, or did you not belong? The home was reimagined as a site without remunerative work, except when a particular household became for some workers a site of work away from their own homes. That is, courts knew that there were nonhousehold members—nurses, housekeepers, servants—who came to a household because it was their place of work. For those "strangers," those employees who did not "belong" to the family, including those who came to do carework, the household was not their home. They had presumptively (in the judicial imagination) left their own homes elsewhere to go and do work in a household where they would be paid. By contrast, family members should not expect to be paid for the work they did both because the work was not of the sort that paid workers did ("reciprocal acts of kindness and goodwill") and because it was "gratuitously performed"; it was part of a gift relationship.[36]

The story that lay behind the actual case of *Disbrow v. Durand* encapsulated this emergent ordering. Sarah Disbrow, the plaintiff in the case, was the elderly younger sister of Smith Noe. (She was seventy-two in 1892, the time of the trial. He was considerably older when he had died a couple of years earlier.) She sued her dead brother's estate to be compensated for the twenty years she had spent keeping house for him in Rahway, "attending to all the work of the house" and caring for him.[37] The brief written by her lawyer, Benjamin Vail, reviewed earlier cases that had denied a caregiver's right to compensation. He insisted that all of those cases had depended on the existence of a parent-child relationship. Without the parent-child relationship, without a direct vertical blood relationship, the presumption of no pay was replaced by a presumption of expected pay. And that was the case for his client. Sarah Disbrow had lived with her brother only because of a work relationship founded on a contract. She had never made her brother's place her "home." Her "home was naturally with her son, and both he and his wife, as the evidence shows, urged her to come to them."

At trial, Mary Disbrow, Sarah's daughter-in-law, had testified about the work Sarah Disbrow had done for Smith Noe: "housekeeping, washing, ironing, baking, churning, etc., all the necessary work doing the house-work." There were no other household servants, but Smith had employed other men on his farm, and she had cared for their needs as well. She also nursed Smith Noe in his last illness, which lasted three or four weeks. (He was blind, but until shortly before his death he could get around "because he knew his place.")

Mary Disbrow, the daughter-in-law, had managed her own household ever since she had married Sarah's son twenty-five years before, so she qualified as an expert on what wages Sarah's services would have commanded in the local Rahway market. "Well, I had to hire such help and I had to give $12 a month, and I considered that not out of the way; it really ought to have been more." She added that the pay scale would be higher if nursing were added.[38]

Benjamin Vail's direct examination of Mary Disbrow began by asking whether Sarah, her mother-in-law, had ever resided in Mary's house. He wanted to get as close as he could to an evidentiary conclusion that Sarah Disbrow had another home (that is, with her son and daughter-in-law) and that Smith Noe's house was not her real home; it was, rather, just her workplace. Unfortunately, the testimony Mary gave did not help his case. "No sir," Mary answered. "I wanted her; she could not come. I needed her, but she could not come on account of keeping house for her brother."

Thomas Shafer, the lawyer who represented the estate, took off from that response in his cross-examination. What family did Noe have? "He had no family of his own; he was a single man." "Who lived with him?" "His sister; my mother-in-law." "Did anybody else live in the house?" "No, sir." (Actually, he had a brother who lived in another part of the house, and another sister sometimes lived there "when she had nowhere else to go; she went out nursing for a living." But neither counted as part of his family.)

A little while later Shafer returned to the same question. "Was not Mr. Smith Noe's house the home of Mrs. Disbrow; didn't she make her home there because she had no other home?" "No, sir." Where was her home? "With her son." How long had she lived with her son? Answer: Never. "She could not live with him." "She lived with Smith Noe all the time?" "Yes, sir." "Made that her home?" "Yes, sir." When Mary's husband, Sarah's son, testified that their house was always open to his mother, Shafer asked him, "Who constituted his [Smith Noe's] family at the time of his last sickness?" The son had to answer, "My mother and him." That probably made it inevitable that his mother would lose her suit.[39]

Part of what must have made *Disbrow* into a striking result was the fact that it involved a suit by one sibling against the estate of another. In legal theory, siblings owed nothing to each other. The sibling relationship did not appear in domestic relations treatises as one of the domestic relations. Siblings were as "strangers" to one another, without enforceable obligations, free to contract or not to contract as the spirit moved. As adults, they did not belong to the same family. Sarah Disbrow was, in law, no different from any employee—a paid housekeeper—who took care of an older man even if that older man was her brother. Yet, in the chancellor's opinion, she became a sister who had lived with and cared for her brother as a loving member of his household—not as a stranger. If adult siblings could be made into members of a shared household, anyone could.[40]

The core of what *Disbrow* meant for the judges and lawyers who considered it and used it over the next half century was that it provided a test. Those who lived together in a household presumptively dealt with one another as members of a common enterprise that precluded expectations of pay for services rendered. The legal question posed was whether a particular caretaker was part of a common enterprise—a family—or was she or he something else, that is, an employee.

In 1907, to take a representative example, Annie Mullen married. Her parents were "sorry" to lose her, and they decided to work out a deal so that Annie would stay and take care of her mother, who suffered from rheumatism. They made a promise to the young couple that if Annie and her husband stayed, the "place" would be left to her. Annie's husband, when asked what he thought of that, said that he would have preferred "to go to housekeeping," that is, for the new couple to live apart from her parents. But they negotiated and agreed that the new couple would not move to their own place. Instead, they would have the use of the kitchen and four rooms in the house, for which they would pay ten dollars a month rent.

For the next seven years, Annie Mullen's mother was able to move about the house on crutches and perform "most, if not all, of her work." Then she fell one day and became so incapacitated that she could not leave the second floor. Eventually she became entirely helpless and unable to leave her chair. For the rest of her life she would be entirely dependent on her daughter's care.

After her death, her daughter, who was the administrator of her mother's intestate estate, and who had not received the "place" she had expected, allowed herself $4,054, as payment at a rate of $30 a month for the continuous care she had provided between 1907 and 1918. She justified her "allowance" on the theory that she had been promised the house and that therefore she had moved in with a clear understanding that she would, in the end, be paid for having stayed.

However, when her allowance to herself was challenged, the Essex County Orphan's Court invoked *Disbrow*. According to the court, until the mother's last two years, when the services she needed became equivalent to those that would otherwise have been provided by a paid nurse (here the court cited *De Camp v. Wilson*), what the daughter had done was to live and participate in a common household, and for that there would be no payment. As a result, the daughter's allowance was reduced to $1,500.[41]

Those who had cared for the elderly but had not been paid as employees would have to explain why they had not been paid and why they had still continued to provide care. They could not rely on any presumption that work implied a promise to pay. Nor would a court presume that a nonrelation or a distant relation was there—caring—only because of an expectation of pay. Members of families, related by blood or not, ordinarily dealt with one another out of love or friendship and without expectations of payment.[42]

The language and the moral vision of *Disbrow* permeated the strategic choices made by lawyers who represented estates and heirs against litigants suing for compensation *quantum meruit.* In 1901, for example, Michael Gay of New Brunswick sued the estate of Hugh Mooney for $1,276.82, computed as the net balance on a bill for board for 283 weeks at $5 a week, plus 43 days of nursing at $4 per day, minus house rent of $311.60. Hugh Mooney had been Michael Gay's landlord, as well as his neighbor, and he was also the uncle of Bridget Gay, Michael's wife. One night Michael found Hugh lying "down in a heap of weeds." Hugh was drunk, and the people he boarded with (next door to Michael's house) had locked him out. According to Michael, "I thought it too bad to let him lay out, and I told him to come into my house, and it would be all right in the morning." So, Hugh Mooney went into Michael's house— and he never left. For the next five and one half years, he received board, washing, and care in Michael Gay's home. Michael stopped paying rent to Hugh. During those years, Michael continued to work on a steamboat. However, during the last 43 days of Hugh's life, when he was sick after a fall, Michael had to stay home to help care for him.[43]

Of course, it was actually Michael Gay's wife, Bridget, who had done nearly all of the work of caring for Hugh Mooney. At trial she was asked to describe what she had done. She answered: "Everything that should be done ... Three meals a day. ... Washing, mending, and cleaning and cooking." He slept in the bedroom. He had a room to himself. During his last illness, "He could not help himself more than a baby, and I would have to attend to him, and my husband would lift him up to give him a drink or feed him, the same as I feed my baby." In those last days, he had to be taken care of night and day.

Hugh Mooney never paid the Gays, but he kept promising that he would leave the house they were living in to their children. He regularly promised to make things "good" for them, although he had no money at the time. And then he died without a will, leaving them nothing.[44]

During the trial before the Middlesex County Court of Common Pleas, Schuyler Van Cleef, a lawyer for Hugh Mooney's estate, asked the judge to order a nonsuit on grounds drawn from *Disbrow:* "This was a mutual household . . . these people lived there, working and laboring among themselves, and the evidence goes to prove that." He also insisted that testimony with regard to promises to children had nothing to do with the case. His motion was denied.

The judge charged the jury while relying on *Disbrow.* The jury was asked to decide whether Hugh Mooney had entered Michael Gay's family "under circumstances that applied the rule of the ordinary mutual expectation of reciprocal acts of kindness and good will, tending to the mutual comfort and convenience of the members of the family." Or, in the alternative, had he gone and remained there "as a visibly impending burden for such board and nursing as were and would be applicable to his condition as one past the prime and vigor of life, and liable, by increasing age and infirmity, to become more and more of a dependence and burden upon others?" In formulating this charge, the judge had rejected the defense's formulation of a charge, one that again depended on *Disbrow.* The defense had wanted the judge to charge the jury that the presumption was that services were "gratuitously mutual" and therefore presumptively not compensable. It also wanted him to charge the jury that an unperformed promise to make a will to children did not give the children's parents any right of action for a suit *quantum meruit.* The jury then awarded Michael Gay $366, an amount small enough to suggest that the jury was uncertain about the terms of the relationship, except for the nursing.[45]

On appeal to the New Jersey Supreme Court, Justice Dixon affirmed the jury's verdict. The case came "within the rule laid down in *Disbrow,*" which he interpreted to mean that "in cases like the present a reasonable and proper expectation that there would be compensation must, and hence may be shown." In a brief to the New Jersey Court for the Correction of Errors and Appeals, the lawyers for the intestate estate naturally disagreed. They quoted the relevant passages from *Disbrow* and insisted once again that the point was that Hugh

Mooney was just a member of Michael Gay's household. On the other side, Gay's lawyers insisted that this was not a case of "family mutuality." It was, rather, one in which a "reasonable expectation of compensation" existed. There was "no family relation." Mooney was "a very troublesome boarder." One witness had described Mooney as a drunken burden: "He used to sometimes get a little full [of beer] and give a good deal of trouble." The evidence showed that he "recognized that he was a boarder, not living on the charity" of Michael Gay. Thus, the court should affirm the jury's verdict, which it did, unanimously.[46]

Watch, to take an extended second example, what happened when Julia Frean went to court in 1915 after she was disappointed to discover that Cornelia Hudson had left her only a pittance. Julia had been Cornelia's companion. She had lived in Cornelia's household in Bayonne for more than twenty years, ever since she had failed her teacher's examinations in Staten Island, where she had grown up. She was no relation of Cornelia Hudson; her parents had been Cornelia's friends.

After Cornelia Hudson's death in 1913 at the age of eighty four, a codicil to her will was found to include a gift of $100 to Julia, "as an act of friendship . . . which she is to forfeit if she sues my estate or my heirs, as she has no claim whatever against me or against my estate." Julia, who had expected much more from the will and who believed that Cornelia's son, Edward Hudson, had fraudulently inserted the codicil into the will, protested. Edward, who was executor of Cornelia's estate, offered Julia $500 "to pacify her." At first she accepted the offer, but later she repudiated it. Then she sued, asking for compensation based on six years of work as Cornelia's "housekeeper and companion" at $25 a month, plus three and one half years of work as a nurse at $15 a week. A Hudson County jury awarded her $4,159.18.[47]

On appeal to the New Jersey Court of Errors, Elmer Demarest, the lawyer for the estate and for Edward Hudson, asked the court to reverse on the theory that the trial judge should have ordered a nonsuit; he should never have let the case go to the jury. Demarest's brief began by insisting that Julia had been "practically a member" of Cornelia's family and had always been "treated as such" by all the members of the household. Indeed, in a later passage in the brief, she was described as treated better than other members of the family (which meant son Edward, who was the only other recognized member of the household). "No closer relationship can be imagined between persons without consanguinity, than that which the respondent [Julia Frean] admits existed between her and Mrs. Hudson."

Julia, the brief continued, was no nurse. She was "59 years of age, lame, and had no experience as a nurse." She knew perfectly well that "the services she was performing were given as though she were a member of the family." She was no servant; she ate at the table with the other family members. She and Cornelia acted as "mother and daughter." Julia understood herself as possessing "an equal right in the household with the other members of the family." What she did within the household she did "because of her affection and friendship for" Cornelia. She might have hoped for a legacy, but she knew, or ought to have known, that the "tenderness" with which Cornelia "cared for her" should have been enough. The main ground of appeal, then, was that Julia's "admission that the position of the parties [was that they] were in *loco parentis*" barred her right to anything more than the love and appreciation she had received from Cornelia Hudson. Thus there should have been a nonsuit.[48]

At trial one year earlier, the work that Julia Frean had done for Cornelia Hudson had been described by the one unmistakable employee in the household, a maid who had long done housework for the elderly Cornelia. What had Julia done? She had helped the maid do the cleaning, the housekeeping and running of the house, everything except washing and ironing. After that, Julia sat with Cornelia; she did sewing, crocheting, and all of the mending, "besides waiting on Mrs. Hudson." She also went out on errands for Cornelia, who never left the house. The maid had overheard many conversations between Cornelia and Julia with regard to payment for services. Cornelia apparently often said "she would give it to her [to Julia] if she had it[,] but she did not have it on account of her son, Ed Hudson, taking it from her." When he cross-examined her, Demarest had asked the maid to describe how Mrs. Hudson and Miss Frean and sometimes Edward Hudson all sat down together at mealtimes. Two next-door neighbors had added detailed portraits of the work Julia Frean had done, including serving at the table, clearing, dusting, cleaning the rooms and the silverware, and taking care of the son's clothes and his dogs. On cross-examination, Demarest had asked the first neighbor whether she had ever seen Julia do any work that a member of that family would not do. The second neighbor was challenged to justify Julia's claims that she had done the work of a professional nurse.[49]

Cornelia Hudson's longtime physician had testified that he considered Julia Frean to have been Cornelia Hudson's "nurse and attendant." What nursing work had been necessary? He answered: Cornelia Hudson could not go upstairs or outside without someone with her. She was troubled with dropsy. That is, her limbs were swollen below the knees, making it almost impossible for her to get from chair to bed. "I would not have considered her a safe woman in the last five or six years." Toward the end, she was not able to attend to her person. Most of the time she had control of her bowels, but not always. Then Julia attended and cleaned up. Julia, he had concluded, had been a good nurse. However, he thought there had been much conflict in the house about the question of payment to her.

In cross-examination, Demarest asked the doctor whether the services Julia had provided were not ones that any "woman member of the household could ordinarily perform?" No, he answered, not in the last two or three years. What made her good at what she did? Well, in part she had done it for a long time. She knew Cornelia's "habits, her nervous makeup and her physical condition better than any one else would." No one else could have done what she had. Demarest tried again: Was Julia like a daughter? He never thought of her that way, the doctor answered; he considered her a companion and a nurse in the household.[50]

Julia Frean then testified. She, too, detailed all the work she done, including directing the maid. She did all of the mending, and she would go out to do the shopping. She had expected to be paid for her time, but she was not, although she did receive two dollars a week for taking care of Edward Hudson's dogs. After 1910, in her rendition, she had taken full charge of Mrs. Hudson's bodily care: She had bathed her every morning, clothed her, and fed her, and sometimes she had had to change her bedding as Cornelia would soil the bed. She did all the work usually done "in an invalid's room."

Demarest had reserved the right to object to her testimony since it was an open question whether a plaintiff could testify in her own case. However, he then cross-examined her about her treatment within the family. He had her walk across the courtroom to demonstrate how lame she was. Too much so, he implied, to have been a real, that is, a paid nurse. She insisted she had been lame only for the past few years. They then went back through Julia's and Cornelia's life together. Julia had been remembered at holidays with gifts, she had given gifts to other members of the family, and she sat with them in the evenings. She was certainly no servant consigned to the back rooms. When Cornelia Hudson still traveled, Julia Frean accompanied her, and they stayed in hotel rooms together. For years she had not been paid, but she did "fancy work" that she sold, and she paid for her own clothing. Julia described in detail all of Cornelia's excuses not to pay her. Why then, Demarest asked, had she stayed? "Because she never wanted me to leave her, and at last she was so sick I could not leave her." Cornelia Hudson was very fond of her and treated her as a member of the family. She also considered herself a family member.

At that moment, one of Julia's two lawyers had had Demarest repeat the question, presumably to give her a chance to realize what she was saying since everyone knew that a family member had no expectation of pay. This time she answered that she was treated as a family member only by Cornelia Hudson, not by the others in the household. The services were "performed" for Cornelia alone. Demarest asked, "You considered that the services that you were performing for her . . . were as though you were a member of her family, as of her household, did you not?" She answered, "Yes." He repeated the question, then moved on. Had Cornelia Hudson become like a mother to her? "Yes, she was like a mother to me." "You had no mother, had you?" She answered: "No." The occasional spending money you received from her "you looked upon as spending money, the same as she would give . . . to any member of her family?" Julia answered, "Yes, between ourselves."

He pressed again: "You considered yourself, so far as she [Cornelia] was concerned, a member of her household, did you not? . . . Practically a member of the family, with the possible distinction that you were not a blood relative?" Julia answered, "No." She did not believe herself a blood relative. But had she felt on an equal level with the other members of the family because of what Cornelia Hudson was doing for her and what she was doing for Cornelia? "Yes." (One might imagine that Julia thought she was showing Edward that she was a better child to Cornelia than he had been.) At that moment, one of her lawyers tried to intervene on the theory that Julia evidently did not understand the questions posed (or the implications that could be drawn from her answers). The questioning went on: There was much conflict about money in Cornelia's last years. Julia tried to raise the possibility that Edward Hudson had forged the codicil to the will. She insisted that Cornelia Hudson had promised to take care of her in her will.

Demarest had then returned to the question of what had motivated her to remain and to take care of Cornelia: "And up to that time you were rendering to Mrs. Hudson these services because of your love and your affection and friendship for her, the same as you had done for a number of years previous, depending upon her to give you at the time she died some legacy?" Her answer: "Yes, she always said she would." She had known she could not depend on the other members of the family for support. It was only when she found out how little she had gotten that she had become dissatisfied. Until then she had never expressed dissatisfaction? "No, because she [Cornelia] always said she would take care of me." Demarest: "You felt while you were living with Mrs. Hudson that she was doing as much for you as you were for her?" Answer: "She died in my arms." Question: "But you felt that the tenderness with which Mrs. Hudson cared for you and the fact that she was giving you a home from the time you had been unfortunate was equal to anything that you could do for Mrs. Hudson in return, did you?" Her lawyer intervened again because the witness was "a little upset." (And one can presume he feared she was about to destroy her case for compensation.) She took a moment to compose herself. Then she answered: "Yes." (One can only imagine the slumped shoulders of her lawyers at that moment.)

On redirect, that is, when Julia's lawyers regained the opportunity to question her, they worked to reclaim ground. Under their questioning Julia described how, in Cornelia's last years, Julia's nursing services took up every hour of the day. She would be up several times at night, and there was no one brought in to relieve her. When had she become lame? "Oh, when I was taken sick, and then when I fell working for her and doing—I was worn out working for her and then I fell, and I have been lame ever since." It had happened in 1911. How much had her fancy work earned for her? Answer: Only forty dollars, earned one winter knitting sweaters.

On recross, under questioning again from Demarest for the other side, she admitted that if Cornelia Hudson were still living, she would not have sued. She had brought suit only because of the way she had been treated by Cornelia's heirs. This, once again, could be read as a concession that she had no contract with Cornelia. Then her lawyers asked one more set of questions (on reredirect): Why would she not be suing if Cornelia Hudson were still alive? "Because I expect I should be living with her yet, kept right on taking care of her." She did tell Cornelia once, though, that she would wait until she was gone, and "then I would sue her. I said I would not worry you now, she was worried enough."[51]

In spite of Demarest's efforts during the trial and her own concessions that love had shaped her conduct and her identity as a member of Cornelia Hudson's family, Julia Frean won. As is always the case, the written transcript cannot fully convey what the judges and the jury saw and what they knew to be "true." Moreover, effective lawyering can go only so far. We can surmise that Julia's expressions of love for Cornelia did not, in the end, counter perceptions of the fundamental unfairness of the will Cornelia Hudson had signed (whether or not it was an expression of her intentions). Justice Bergen, who wrote the opinion for a unanimous Court for the Correction of Errors and Appeals, rejected Demarest's argument that there should have been a nonsuit, that the judge in the Hudson County court should never have allowed a jury to consider the question of whether Julia Frean was entitled to compensation. Demarest's interpretation of the law "that no contract to pay can be inferred from services when the plaintiff was a member of the decedent's family" was answered by the fact that Julia "was not a relative in any degree" of Cornelia Hudson. The evidence was not conclusive that the services she had provided were intended as "gratuitous." A "fair inference" could be drawn from the testimony that there had been "an express promise to pay what the services were reasonably worth." In any case these were questions that could properly be submitted to the jury. Although *Disbrow* was not mentioned directly, one could read the opinion as holding that Julia Frean's lawyer had offered enough evidence to suggest that what she had done in the Hudson household could not be reduced to "reciprocal acts of kindness and goodwill, which tend to mutual comfort and convenience."[52]

Gradually, the *Disbrow* standard was confined to those who were living together as part of a nuclear family, exactly what the case had not stood for when it was first decided.[53] In 1917, for example, a Camden County judge heard the suit of Deborah Anderson, who wanted compensation for having cared for her great-aunt and, after the great-aunt's death, for her great-uncle, William Bishop. At the end of the testimony, Lewis Starr, the lawyer for the estate, asked for a nonsuit. He insisted that the case should not go to a jury.

The judge who heard the case was nervous about being reversed; he wanted to get things right. With the lawyers in tow, he worked through the relevant case law. Starr invoked *Disbrow* for the proposition that, as a "member of the household," Deborah Anderson could not recover except on an express contract to pay for services. Henry Stockwell, Deborah's lawyer, disagreed. Deborah was a great-niece of the wife of the dead property owner. That meant she was no relation at all to him. Thus, she was just an employee. The judge questioned that conclusion. Looking back at the holding in *Disbrow,* he said: "It does not so much turn on that as it does on the relationship which the parties bore to each other." Stockwell agreed but used that statement to distinguish Deborah Anderson's situation: "The testimony is that she acted as maid and did all the work."

Stockwell insisted that the dead man's statements revealed an intention to leave property to Deborah. However, the judge knew that was not enough. Stockwell tried again. Starr, his opponent, he argued, had tried to place Deborah Anderson "upon the same plane" as an unemancipated daughter, "who might be living in that home, who had all the privileges and performed the few duties that a daughter would perform." If that were the case, it might make sense not to pay her.

Yet that was not the situation here since Deborah was "related in no way" to Bishop. Starr answered: Stockwell had misstated the relevant law. *Disbrow* "expressly" held that the relationships included "were not limited to kinship." The focus, instead, was on "members of the family relation" regardless of their relation to the "head of the family" or whether they were "in the position of loco parentis." The judge agreed with Starr: "There is a presumption . . . that those standing in that relation are rendering free services as part of the family from promptings of the heart." Was there anything in the testimony to counter that presumption, anything that countered "the idea of gratuitous services"? Nothing, Starr answered. Certainly there was nothing sufficient. There was nothing to "rebut the presumption" that Deborah Anderson "was part of that family." What she had done was "perfectly in line with those services which a daughter would perform as a member of the family."

Further argument continued. The judge then granted the defense's motion for a nonsuit. The weight of *Disbrow* had overcome his own "inclination" to give the case to the jury. He did not like the law as it stood, but the law, he had concluded, had "thrown its protection around dead men's estates, that they shall not be charged unless clearly liable." He was bound by the "presumption of law that the services were rendered gratuitously and under no expectation of compensation."[54]

The New Jersey Supreme Court affirmed. However, the Court for the Correction of Errors and Appeals reversed and ordered a new trial. According to the high court, the trial judge had misinterpreted *Disbrow*. In spite of all his work, he had gotten the law wrong. Even though Deborah Anderson had grown up in her great-aunt's household and had lived there as something like an informally adopted child (the defense had emphasized the music lessons she had taken) and even though she had remained in that home well past adolescence, still, the work she had done, combined with the promises she had been made, had turned her into someone who might be compensated for her work in the home. Until her great-aunt's death in 1912 she had nursed her while also doing the housework. She had then stayed on in William Bishop's household for four more years, until a year before his own death. In that household, she had performed "all kinds of menial work." She had taken care of the heater and the range, taken out the ashes, done the kitchen work, and prepared the meals besides taking care of Bishop when he was ill. All that, combined with the promises that Bishop had made, meant, according to the Court of Errors, that it was open for a jury to find that she was to be compensated for her services.[55]

Like Bridget Gay and Julia Frean, Deborah Anderson became, within the confines of *quantum meruit* litigation, just an employee, someone who ought to be paid for work done. Over time, the *Disbrow* holding, which had seemed to suggest a broad and inclusive standard for defining family members, that is, those who did not need to be paid for family work, had narrowed. It had become easier for those who cared for older people within households to claim a right to payment, because the New Jersey courts were willing to define those who did the actual work of care as workers, not as family members.[56]

Over time, as a reflection of a moral and economic change, it became increasingly clear that old-age care was something that ordinarily ought to be paid for. Was old-age care still part of a family's work? Or was it becoming by nature an "exceptional" task outside of the normal work that family members routinely did for one another?

Chapter Seven

Paid Work

Consider Jane Alice Bissett on the witness stand in 1892, testifying about her life as her father's housekeeper and eventually his caretaker:

> Q. Who clothed you? A. My father. Q. Did you spend any money for yourself? A. If I felt like it I would spend it for myself, and ask for it as a daughter would ask her father for money. Q. You always would get it? A. Not always; he did not always have it. . . . Q. You were there not in the capacity of house-keeper? A. I was there as house-keeper and daughter. Q. And part of his family? A. Why, certainly.[1]

Who were these nineteenth- and early twentieth-century adult children—these younger people—who sued estates for land or for damages and insisted they were entitled to compensation or property because of care they had once provided older people in family homes? How do we characterize those who inhabited this peculiar middle space, these people who were neither family nor employees—or both family and employees? In a legal culture ideologically committed to keeping home and work apart, where work meant pay and home meant something else, sometimes love, courts—in New Jersey as elsewhere in the United States—struggled to fix identities that were multiple and contradictory. Often it must have been as confusing for the adult children as it was for those who had to judge them.

We can imagine that these adult children lived at the same time in at least two moral universes. In one universe, that of the family/household, they earned rewards—moral and spiritual, as well as material rewards—by sharing in a common family enterprise. The material rewards of having invested in the family might be frustrated. Older people—those in control of family property—usually did not have to act in accord with promises made or with apparent commitments. Testator's freedom remained something close to a trump card. The property owners—the parents, the older persons—retained the right to change their minds and to deny promised rewards. In the end there was no legal duty to share. Moreover, the fights after death might have ruined the moral and spiritual rewards of family life at least retrospectively. However, these adult children earned rewards, if rewards were earned, by joining in and being loving members of a family unit. They justified themselves within that normative universe by showing exclusive loyalty, by submerging their independence as competent adults, by emphasizing their continuing place in the family, and perhaps by continuing to be as children should be even when they had become chronological adults. (It is, therefore, not surprising that many women who served as caretakers also delayed marriage until the older property owners (parents or otherwise) had died.)[2]

In the other universe, in the moral universe that a suit for compensation *quantum meruit* to a common-law court or a petition for specific performance to a court of equity articulated, adulthood, that is, rights and identities as an independent and contractually competent actor, took priority. Subordination (just as too much love) within the household was inconsistent with an adulthood that produced a successful cause of action. As Alexis de Tocqueville famously put it in describing the effect of inheritance on the lives of young American men, "As the family is felt to be a vague, indeterminate, uncertain conception, each man concentrates on his immediate convenience."[3]

A good lawyer for the plaintiff or petitioner ordinarily worked to cabin a client within the second moral universe and to suppress the often multitudinous traces of the first. Yet, as we have also seen, the complexities of real lives kept leaking into the testimony, and that made the lawyer's work difficult.

Revelations of sharing and caring and love could become destructive to the case the lawyer wanted to make. Remember the anxious interventions of Julia Frean's attorneys as she described her love for Cornelia Hudson. However, in the hands of a clever lawyer, it was even possible to turn testimony about how subordinated and submerged an adult child had been into support for a successful right to individual compensation. Just as no competent individual or adult would have accepted the discipline of the factory floor without the expectation of pay, so it was with the adult child within the household. One ironic consequence of subordination and loyalty within the family was that it could occasionally become implicit proof of a labor agreement between an older person and a younger family member. Someone like Julia Frean, Deborah Anderson, or Jane Alice Bissett would not have stayed and done all of that work and accepted a role as a "dependent," if she had not expected to be paid.

For those on the other side, for the lawyers and their clients who opposed adult children's claims to property or compensation, there were many ways to mark adult children as greedy or ungrateful, morally obtuse or dishonest, or as forgetful of the primary moral universe in which they had actually spent their lives. For example: Because of bad legal advice or their own moral deficiencies, these adult children had insisted on rights to property or payment. Instead, they should have understood themselves as privileged to have grown up in or to have been part of loving homes. They ought to have recognized themselves as gift givers, not as crass contractors. In caring for older people, they had done good deeds as individuals. It sullied and darkened their moral status that they were now insisting on compensation for what they once had given voluntarily and freely, out of the goodness of their hearts, out of love. Furthermore, there always lurked the question of whether what the adult children now claimed had been solemnly sworn and promised commitments—contracts—had really been something else earlier, before death and litigation. Was it only after the fact—sometimes many years after the fact, after the relevant speakers were dead—that mere talk had been reconstructed as contracts?

So, in September 1942, the elderly, ill, and unhappy John H. Stertzer prepared a letter that began: "To Whom It May Concern." He wrote the letter three days before his only daughter, Margaret Robertson, would leave the house they shared in Hackensack to move with her new husband to Ohio, where he would be doing "war work." Stertzer's letter was written to explain why he had destroyed a will that would have given her his full estate and why his daughter should not be able after his death to reconstruct an imagined contract to be compensated for having lived with and cared for him. The letter sketched the life he had led from early 1929, when he and his wife had moved in with then thirty-one-year-old Margaret (then Margaret W. Wills) in Nyack, New York. She was then in the process of divorcing her first husband, and she worked for the Metropolitan Life Insurance Company. According to Stertzer, he paid all of the expenses of the shared household over the next two-year period. In 1931, after the death of his own father and stepmother, Stertzer took over a family house at 469 Main Street in Hackensack. The three of them moved there together, and his daughter gave up work outside of the home.

For the next years, according to his letter, Margaret "had no expenses whatever," and his wife and he "made it very pleasant for her." He bought her a car. He paid for two trips for her to visit a friend in California. He paid her dentist bill. He paid all of the maintenance costs on the car. He paid for regular vacations in Asbury Park. He paid for her clothes and her shoes.

He and Margaret continued to live together after John Stertzer's wife, Margaret's mother, died in early 1936. However, by 1940, "life" had become "unbearable." Why, he did not explain. Margaret called in a doctor from New York City "to examine me [Stertzer], . . . hoping that I would be put away." He had, he said, "a nervous breakdown," and while he was very sick, she had attorneys come to the house who forced him to sign a will that would have given her all of his property. Eventually, though, he "regained strength," and he found the "paper" he had signed. He had that will destroyed. Since then he had "lived a life of Hell." He added, in conclusion, that he had given her a power of attorney to collect rents for him at a building he owned on Main Street in Hackensack, but he had never been able to receive an accounting from her.[4]

Stertzer's letter leaves much unarticulated. Yet, it clearly contemplated the likelihood that Margaret would sue his estate after his death, and the point of the letter was to insist that she had been supported by him, that she had not been a good caregiver, that she had done nothing to earn a right to his estate, and that, at best, she had been just a member of the family who had been lucky and well taken care of. He had, as would be revealed in the trial that came after his death, as predicted, often told others of his intentions and his promises to reward her. The letter was meant to explain why those promises had not ripened into a contract. He was providing a basis for his right, his continuing freedom, as a testator to make whatever disposition of his property pleased him. In addition, he was characterizing his daughter as someone who had lost her moral claim on any inheritance or other compensation.

In 1949 the new New Jersey Supreme Court (after World War II, a new state constitution merged previously separated "law" and "equity" courts and created a state supreme court that replaced the previous

Court for the Correction of Errors and Appeals) divided on whether John Stertzer's letter would be admissible as evidence of his wishes and of the existence of an underlying contract between Margaret and her father. In the end, a majority on the court decided (over a forcefully expressed dissent by Chief Justice Vanderbilt) to exclude the letter. However, it did not really matter, for the whole court agreed that Margaret's claim that she had acquired a contractual right to Stertzer's estate failed both because he retained his freedom as a testator and because she had failed to take care of him for the rest of his life. It did not help her case that she had left him just as his need for care increased.[5]

Adult children who had not received an expected inheritance or other compensation had only one effective counter to the charge that they were nothing but ungrateful children—or worse—and that was to describe the care they had provided. In almost every trial, whether for *quantum meruit* or specific performance, testimony began with a description, usually by the plaintiff or petitioner, about the work the child had done. The lawyer would lead the witness through a description that emphasized what had made the work distinctive, exceptional, unusual, extraordinary, as something other than ordinary family labor. In doing so, lawyer and client were both marking the client's singularity, the client's right to special treatment within the moral universe of family solidarity and, at the same time, revealing the client as an autonomous, contractual actor. (It must have been telling that, when Margaret Robertson testified in support of her claim for a share of her father's estate, she did not begin by describing the work she had done.)[6] Lawyer and client worked to connect the client's life to still widely shared and culturally resonant understandings (we might call them "labor theories of value") that certain kinds of work done singularly entitled a client to property or to the benefits of a promise.[7]

In 1899, for example, Henry Cullen sued the estate of Asher Woolverton as the assignee of the *quantum meruit* claim of David Lawshe. Lawshe was married to Woolverton's stepdaughter; he had called

Woolverton "father," and Woolverton had treated him, he said, as a son. Testimony in the case began with Lawshe on the stand to tell his story about the work he had done for Woolverton.

Asher Woolverton may have been around eighty in 1893.[8] In January of that year, on a cold and foggy morning "just a little while before church-service time," he had fallen on a stone pavement and broken his hip. From then on he suffered from chronic trouble with his bowels and required frequent "injections" (enemas). Only Lawshe was allowed to help him. Frequently, while Lawshe was giving him his injections, Woolverton would say to him, "Dave, this is a very unpleasant job, and you shall be well paid for it."

What had Lawshe done for Woolverton? "Either the second or the third day after . . . this injury," a doctor gave Woolverton a "physic" to help him move his bowels. By evening, he was in distress because nothing was happening, "and of course I [Lawshe] had to give him the injection in the bed." Lawshe and others arranged clothes under Woolverton beforehand "so as to protect the bed as much as possible." But Woolverton was a "nervous, fidgety man," so Lawshe "had considerable trouble." "Of course he got himself pretty well smeared up, and of course the result was that I got my hands pretty well smeared up." The same process was repeated every three or four days for the next three years. "There was no regularity about just when the bowels would move after the physic was given."

Eventually the bowels began to operate on their own. After that Lawshe would help Woolverton out of bed and onto the commode and then give him "an injection." It was hard work to get him onto the commode since his hip was broken. In particular, Lawshe had to get the rubber tube between his legs. He would have to use his hand to get the tube into the rectum "to find just where to place the tube in pumping in the water." "Sometime his bowels would break loose before you would be able to get the rubber tube removed, and, of course, the result was your hands would be in a pretty bad condition. Of course, sometimes you wouldn't be able to get away." How had Lawshe helped then? He had gotten him back into bed after he was washed and cleaned. "I would stand him up and clean him in that position, standing up alongside the bed." Did he ever "cleanse his person by passing your hand in under him, between his legs, as he sat on the commode?" . . . "Yes, sir; I have done that."

Meanwhile, Lawshe also looked after Woolverton's farm and his quarries in Hunterdon County. He would get things for the household from the farm—potatoes, apples, and chickens—and also shoveled snow for Woolverton.[9]

What was such testimony supposed to prove? The simple answer is that it demonstrated that David Lawshe was not doing what a neighbor, friend, or household member ordinarily did. He was doing something peculiarly repellent, something that a man certainly, but a woman, too, would have been unlikely to do without a preexisting understanding, an agreement, a contract. Because of the exceptional nature of these tasks and because of his exceptional labors, he became something other than a member of Woolverton's household or a friend or neighbor. As the judge put it at the end of the trial when charging the jury, if what Lawshe had provided were "mere neighborly services that one man would render to another," then there could be no claim. But that was certainly not the case here. The jury gave a verdict for Cullen, Lawshe's assignee, for $975. (That verdict was reversed for technical reasons unrelated to the claim of work done. A second trial then took place, again with a verdict for Cullen, Lawshe's assignee, and that verdict was affirmed on appeal.)[10]

From the earliest U.S. case in which a court ordered specific performance for a promise of care, an 1846 New York case brought by one brother for the care of a brother subject to epileptic seizures, "exceptional" tasks or labors were mobilized to justify a right to compensation. (According to the assistant vice chancellor in the case, an agreement must have existed. Otherwise, why would the brother have stayed to provide services of "such a peculiar character" in a situation that was "harrowing to the mind, destructive to the peace and comfort of his family, and injurious to his own health"?)[11] In an equity case, in an action for specific performance, the exceptional was crucial to demonstrate the transformed life of the adult child. The caretaker was changed by having assumed exceptional tasks, which were by nature ones that could not easily or simply be reduced to "ordinary" payable work for which a cash equivalent could be determined. That explained why specific performance rather than damages offered the appropriate remedy for the wrong done. On the other hand, in *quantum meruit* cases, as in *Cullen v. Woolverton,* the exceptional explained why one was entitled to something more, to compensation in ways that differed from the ordinary compensation for having lived as a family member. In particular, at a time when nursing could mean either doing what family members ordinarily did for one another or a job (not yet a profession) that one had to pay someone to do, the "exceptional" moved the description into the second moral universe and away from the first.[12]

The "exceptional" also solved the problem of proving an underlying oral contract. Tasks that were exceptional, like those undertaken by David Lawshe, were not ones that could be explained except through the lens of contract. Ordinary household duties and routine care belonged presumptively to the realm of *Disbrow*'s "reciprocal acts of kindness and goodwill, which tend to mutual comfort and convenience." Not so, however, when care became intense, personal, and arduous, such as when older bodies and minds fell apart.

There is a certain mystery about what was recognized as an exceptional task. It is often hard to discern why a case came out as it did. Given nineteenth- and twentieth-century gender conventions, it is easy to imagine that David Lawshe would have been recognized as engaged in a peculiarly repellent and extraordinary nursing undertaking, certainly for a man. However, many of the cases leave the reader uncertain why work revealed by the testimony did or did not entitle the complainant or the plaintiff to special compensation. One is always left wondering what made this situation different from one that those who lived together in households ordinarily experienced, without expectations of special compensation. Why was the adopted son in *Van Duyne* understood as having done something exceptional in having stayed with his uncle or adoptive father? What made his life "exceptionally" difficult, unlike that of other informally adopted children who were understood as having benefited from their adoptions and as having done no more than what was predictable and expected of them? Likewise, why were the services that James W. Davison provided understood as of "such a peculiar character" that he would be recognized as entitled to an order for specific performance, one that restored him to the position of favored heir?

Sometimes, it is clear, the terms "extraordinary," "exceptional," and "peculiar" served ancillary judicial goals, justified actions and decisions intended to rectify unfairnesses. The terms became distinctively legal categories that were shorn of much of their social or cultural meaning. It was James Davison's father's probably demented claim that his wife had committed adultery with his nephew, followed by James and his family's unfair expulsion from his father's home, that made James Davison into someone who had worked exceptionally hard. It was not really that he had done anything that any son living at home might not have done. Moreover, the work his wife performed in her father-in-law's household was just what a daughter-in-law was expected to do (putting aside having to deal with James W.'s sexual innuendos). The terms became ways to conclude inquiries, to rationalize decisions made for other reasons. They were then not really descriptions of what made the work in these situations different from the work that family members routinely did.

Even so, even if much that was labeled extraordinary or exceptional was little different from what went on ordinarily when aged people were present within households, the language used still has surprising significance. In Anglo-American property law a standard understanding rests on a rejection of labor theories of value. "Labor might transform land, but it did not create the right to own it."[13] Yet, for adult children who stayed home to provide care and mixed their labor in the soil of the family, that was obviously a nonsensical understanding. Their work, certainly the peculiar or extraordinary conditions of their work in a world where adult children did not typically stay at home, meant that their labors ought to create a right to own it. Sometimes New Jersey's courts agreed.[14]

Adult children and the older people they cared for dealt with each other and with surrounding family members and wider communities in legal ways that changed only modestly between the mid-nineteenth and the mid-twentieth centuries. Continuities in legal practice and legal consciousness shaped the ways in which family members dealt with promises and caretaking, even as the processes of urbanization, economic change, mobility, and family dissolution entirely transformed the New Jersey in which these understandings operated. The cases brought by twentieth-century family members still reproduced older legal understandings and practices. Throughout a century of legal history, core understandings of entitlement, ownership, disposition, and family work—notions of testator's freedom, competence, undue influence, and legitimate and illegitimate uses of the power that accompanied ownership within a household—sustained themselves in testimony, in lawyer's briefs, and in judicial opinions.

Much, of course, did change between 1850 and 1950. In 1940 the particularities of the work done might have included telephoning and driving a car, as they did in *Ehling v. Diebert*, while in 1860, testimony would have instead emphasized mucking out the stable. (At all times, on the other hand, women might have found themselves scrubbing, cooking, or changing the sheets of the incontinent old.) By the 1940s it was, if the case records are at all representative of an underlying social history, more difficult than it had once been for older people to convince their own children or grandchildren to do the work of care. By then, most of the cases brought to enforce promises for land or other compensation were being brought by housekeepers, more distant relatives, friends, neighbors, or informally adopted children. Adult children were mobile in 1850, as they would be in 1950. However, in the mid-twentieth century, older people—or most of them—had apparently lost the capacity and perhaps the desire to draw those children back into the web of the household. They looked instead to others, and those others were more likely to understand themselves as employees.[15]

Over time, some of the routine work that women did—housework and nursing—gradually became tasks presumptively subject to market standards of compensation. That is, more of the work that women did as members of the households of others (whether those of their parents or of employers) gradually became understood as exceptional, unusual, unexpected, or explainable only by the presumption of a preexisting agreement.

The starting premise in the mid-nineteenth century had been an understanding that housework was just that, housework, all of a piece. Unless previously specified, there was no reason to distinguish one part of that complex whole from another. Furthermore, women who did the work for pay were expected to adjust to shifting demands and tasks as the needs and the requirements of the household changed.

So, Jane Voorhees lost in the late 1860s when she sued for extra compensation after the death of her employer, Princeton University professor John H. Woodhull. Woodhull was a very large man with very large appetites. In his last years, according to one witness, it took "two to lift him and another to wait on him." Jane Voorhees was his housekeeper, the only "white woman in the house." She was cook and housekeeper, and she had no chambermaid to assist her. She did everything but the washing, according to her witnesses. Mostly, she cooked. As Woodhull lay dying, he insisted on roast oysters throughout the night. He expected Mrs. Voorhees to prepare "birds, pidgeons [sic], squirrels, chickens, beef tea, etc. She prepared beef tea every day." According to one witness, "her cares were increased" by the doctor's sickness. Woodhull's own medical doctor testified that she had had to perform a great deal of extra work—nursing—due to Woodhull's sickness. She had always been paid a regular wage, but shortly before he died Woodhull had his financial agent write down a promise to give her an extra $500 for her care in his last illness.

When she appealed a judge's decision to nonsuit her, that is, to prevent a jury from considering her claim founded on that promise for extra pay, the Court for the Correction of Errors affirmed. According to the court, she had no right "to suppose that the family, in which she was to serve, would be exempt from the ills of life." All that she had done was "in the line of her regular duties." Her labors, whether "ordinary or extraordinary," would be satisfied by the payment of her salary.[16]

For most women, indeed, ordinary nursing was understood as a part of the package of goods and services that were incorporated into the generic term "housework," although what was ordinary and what was extraordinary was a matter of continuing litigation.[17] Nursing was both a general skill peculiarly identified with womanhood and, by the end of the nineteenth century, was becoming a distinct skill that had a clear and growing market value.

One result was a good deal of conflict over the rights of married women to charge for nursing services. In *Garretson v. Appleton* (1895), one case among several in which a wife insisted on separate compensation *quantum meruit* for nursing she had provided within her (or, more properly, her husband's) home, a wife brought a claim against an estate for nursing services. Peter Van Pelt had been the landlord of their house in Perth Amboy. He had moved in with them in 1891 to get a kind of "attendance" or care he could not get in his own home. The nursing that his tenant's wife, Christina Appleton, provided was, all agreed, "arduous, exacting, and sometimes of a repulsive character." She was, according to an attending doctor, an "excellent nurse." Van Pelt's dropsy meant that his testicles had swollen to huge dimensions, "as big as a small muskmelon" and "as black as ink." His scrotum and testicles needed constant washing and bandaging. She had to get him out of bed and to and from the "stool." For his sores his doctor gave her a liniment to give him made of alcohol and red peppers, which burned the skin off her own hands. What she did, according to another doctor, was worth around $3 a day. After a trial, a jury awarded her $964 for her labors.

The problem the case raised was that Van Pelt had made a bargain with Christina Appleton's husband when Van Pelt had first moved in with them. The contract, according to her and her husband, was only for board, meaning that they made no agreement for nursing. However, according to the other side, those who represented Van Pelt's estate, the bargain had been for both board and nursing. (Since he had moved in with them because he was not receiving appropriate care in his own home, it seems unlikely that nursing was not contemplated.) In light of that bargain, could she bring a separate cause of action apart from her husband?

According to Christina Appleton's lawyer, it was appropriate that she bring this case in her own name. The husband had done no nursing except for occasionally helping to move "the old man from bed to stool, as any husband would have done." He was an oysterman and a boatman, not a woman, not a nurse.

However, such facts were quite irrelevant, according to the defense. And the Court of Errors agreed, although for technical reasons the jury verdict in her favor would be confirmed. What she had done, the "services" she had "rendered," were "in the discharge of her duty as a wife" and thus were incorporated into the contract Van Pelt had made with her husband. A wife's right to her own earnings under the new statutes that limited coverture were restricted to those that derived from a "regular calling," and nursing in the home was not such. More, according to the defense, her husband had signed an agreement that "we" would bring no claim against Van Pelt's estate. (When the husband was asked whether the "we" meant that the wife accepted and signed as well, he answered "No sir; I never consult my wife about my business matters." He insisted that the "we" was a simple mistake.) Christina Appleton had apparently believed that Van Pelt would leave her the house and lot on which they lived. She was, as such, simply speculating on a legacy. Furthermore, what she had done for Van Pelt, if viewed as outside or beyond her marital duties, was properly understood as gratuitous and voluntary, not compensable. Her services were, at most or at best, just a gift she had given to Peter Van Pelt.[18]

Still, over time, nursing, which had long been understood as an undifferentiated part of the package of services that women as employees and as family members provided, became a specialized task and separately compensable work. The care and attention that disease, decrepitude, and dementia required were less likely to be viewed as predictable and ordinary family responsibilities. Nursing as such belonged to a labor market, and it could be measured and paid for with reference to that market. In addition, nursing and intimate bodily carework gradually ceased to be tasks that daughters, younger women, and ordinary domestic servants generally expected to assume as part of the unspoken understandings of their jobs within households.[19]

During the first half of the twentieth century, very few daughters appeared in the case records as petitioners or plaintiffs asking for compensation for having served as their parents' "nurses" or caretakers. We cannot know whether that is because they had already been paid, because they had been told in lawyer's offices that they would not be paid, or because there were simply fewer of them doing that kind of work. Instead, most of the cases between 1900 and 1950 seem to be about young men and women in complex relationships—sometimes blood relations, sometimes informally adopted, sometimes employees of one sort or another—with the older people they cared for.

After World War II, the ordinary activities involved in staying home to care for demanding elderly people—cleaning, cooking, comforting—became understood as exceptional in their nature, not as normal things for one (even daughters or daughters-in-law) to do for others in a household. Such activities presumed an underlying understanding that compensation would be paid. That is, courts were learning to view the undertaking to care for an older person as carrying with it a presumption that it must have been an activity premised on a promise to pay.

One might say that is the end of our story. The older understanding that work within the home constituted an exception to the presumption that all work was paid work was apparently no longer operative. Claimed promises that had once seemed unproven, unprovable, or legally uncompelling because they were made to a younger person who was doing what a younger person was expected to do had now became more believable and more legally compelling.

Thus, in 1952, a daughter-in-law's claim that she had been promised pay for the care she gave to her husband's parents over almost two decades seemed entirely believable to the New Jersey Superior Court. (Soon after her marriage in 1933, she began "going to the apartment of her in-laws, where she did the housework, shopped for the couple, cooked their meals[,] and acted as their practical nurse." Both "in-laws" were overweight and sickly, and the daughter-in-law cared "for them and their needs through the day.") Those who resisted her claim had argued that because the plaintiff was a daughter-in-law the services she had rendered must have been offered "without expectation of compensation." The court made short work of that argument by distinguishing the facts in this case from those in *Disbrow*. (The daughter-in-law had lived with her husband in their own apartment, unlike the sister in *Disbrow*. Thus, she had a separate residence and was not technically part of the same household as those she cared for.) Implicit in the decision was the court's belief that the in-laws must have expected, or had led her to believe they expected, to pay her. If she were not expecting to be paid, she would not have stayed to work and to care for them. No one, certainly no daughter-in-law, would have done so.[20]

In a second example, it may be that *Cooper v. Colson*, the 1903 case of the housekeeper who never received the farm she had been promised by her employer, was silently overruled in *Poloha v. Ruman* (1945). In *Poloha*, as in *Cooper*, a longtime housekeeper and nurse caretaker had been promised a house by her employer (and friend), Mrs. Ruman (or Rumane). Testimony revealed that Mrs. Poloha did "everything that was necessary to take care of Mrs. Ruman, cooked and took care of the house. . . . Gave her massages morning and night. . . . [W]as with her when she died." However, when Mrs. Ruman died and Mr. Ruman inherited Mrs. Ruman's estate and remarried, Mrs. Poloha, the housekeeper and nurse, was excluded. She got nothing. When Mrs. Poloha challenged that disposition, Vice Chancellor Lewis held that the promise of property had become an enforceable contract because the intimate care she had offered Mr. and Mrs. Ruman was explicable only through the lens of that promise. Why else would the housekeeper and nurse, an employee, have stayed without pay? She got the house.[21]

We are not yet in a normative universe—the New Jersey or the America familiar to us in the early twenty-first century—where direct care of the aged is presumptively provided by way of paid contracted work by strangers, many of whom will be employees of large corporations (e.g., health providers, nursing homes, insurance companies) or of governments. We are not yet in a normative universe where the needs of old people will be "serviced" by global armies of migratory workers who do the work of care that most family members no longer imagine doing. However, we are entering a normative universe in which the default rules have changed. After World War II, direct care of old people was not something done presumptively out of love, habit, or sense of duty, although this is not to say that there were not many who would continue to provide care for others out of love, habit, or sense of duty. Yet, in the courts—in the law—carework for the elderly was increasingly understood as belonging to a commoditized universe of pay for services, and to nowhere else.

Epilogue

Old age superbly rising! Ineffable grace of dying days!

Walt Whitman, *Leaves of Grass,* 1855

Over the course of the past half century, those of us in the Western world have witnessed extraordinary changes in the management, care, and financing of what is still crudely labeled "old age." Older people live differently from the way they did in the early twentieth century. Moreover, it is at least possible, as some have suggested, that these changes herald a major discontinuity in human history.

To write in broad and crude generalities: We and our parents and grandparents (not to mention our children, grandchildren, and great-grandchildren) live longer lives than previous generations. We also live healthier lives, although in the end we may also have to live longer with debilitating or disabling conditions. There is, as yet, no cure for mortality. Still, older people live today (and many even live well) with chronic illnesses that not so long ago would have killed them quickly and painfully. A number of conditions—some cancers and heart ailments—have become curable or manageable life circumstances. Older people are less likely to have been beaten down by their work lives.[1]

They live so much longer and so differently from earlier generations that it probably no longer makes sense to speak of a single "age" that is "old age." In France one hears people talk about "le troisième âge"—a

happy period beyond working life but before disability and dependence. Others imagine three stages of postworking life: an early stage
when "footloose" retirement decisions are made; a second, involving
moves closer to one's children; and a third, into institutional settings,
assisted care facilities, and nursing homes.[2]

Behind those demographic and medical transformations lie fiscal,
political, and institutional changes of equal or greater magnitude.
Old age is financed today, although still incompletely, through the
public sphere. Much of the financial health of retired old people comes
through programs—Social Security, as well as public and private
pensions—that depend variously on the statutory and contractually
mandated taxation of the work and the salaries of working people.
Core and crucial political decisions have "socialized" the financial
support of the old, have placed the costs of retirement and old-age care
on larger populations beyond the family, and have made us all effectively into participants in risk pools for the elderly. Meanwhile, the
elderly have come to understand themselves and to be understood as a
political constituency. As such, they have come to know themselves as
dependent on state-funded and state-mandated programs and as "entitled" as a class to public support and to a funded retirement and
health care. Whether this sense of entitlement is a realistic one for the
long-term economic health of the society is a matter of great uncertainty. As the number of retired older people surviving as costly non-
workers continues to grow, relative to a declining number of working
adults, many worry that the structures of support for the old will
become politically and economically unsustainable in the not-too-
distant future. However, at present the sense of entitlement is strong.[3]

The qualities and the terms of old age were once defined by where
and with whom the old person or old couple lived. The choices were
obvious and limited. A couple might live in their own house, with
children and others to attend them, or they might live in the homes of
those children, with less control or power. Worst of all, they might live

in the "poorhouse" or in some effectively similar "home for the aged," "alone" and isolated from family. (In reality, those who were in the poorhouse may have been there because they were without family.)

Today, however, the housing options of the old have multiplied: "Sun Belt" cities organized around the "needs" of older residents, adult communities, senior housing, assisted living residences, and nursing homes, to make an inadequate list of the more obvious possibilities. Many older people still work to remain in their own homes. That is, they remain in residences that they had lived in as working adults, often "assisted" by a range of services provided by agencies both public and private and by occasional or regular family help. For middle-class people, to find oneself living with one's children—in the children's home or with them in one's own—is often understood as a mark of failure or an indicator of particular difficulties or failures on the part of the old or of the adult young. There is a widespread belief that older people want to live with others of the same age, often in age-segregated communities, in what has been marketed as "splendid isolation" from their families. In those communities, they are attended to by "others," who are employees of the corporations and institutions that have marketed housing and care to them. Aside from spouses, family members are elsewhere, although sometimes nearby. It is apparent to many gerontological scholars that feelings of well-being are intimately tied to "independence," which is often interpreted as meaning living apart from family. "Privacy" is a particularly valued good.[4]

Where once a decent old age depended on the mobilization of family labor (always remembering the varieties of workers that could be contained within the category "family"), many of the core features of old-age life are now produced by large corporations who market goods to the old. Beginning in the late 1950s and early 1960s, businesses learned to chase after "this new class of mobile consumers called retirees." Older people became, both politically and economically, core members of the "consumers' republic" of post–World War II America.

Today, as any casual viewing of television advertisements will quickly reveal, older people—as individuals and as couples—are the subjects of sustained commercial attention. Companies—health care and drug companies, hospital systems, real estate developments, financial companies, and food producers—have targeted the old. Resources that once would have been "saved" as a legacy for family members are now understood, both by the older people and by their suppliers, as available or necessary to be consumed in life—before death.[5]

Throughout the consumers' republics of the Western world, the work of caregiving—nursing, as well as bodily care and much companionship and help with "activities of daily living" when needed—is done in the first instance by spouses. But then, perhaps after a spouse has died or departed, when a disabled or partially abled older person has been left "alone," the work is mostly done by a global army of contractual careworkers, the vast majority of whom are poor women. In some parts of the world, particularly in Europe and Israel, elder care has become a work specialty identified with Filipinas. In the United States, a variety of recent immigrants, both legal and undocumented, from the Caribbean, Central America, Eastern Europe, and Russia, have similarly assumed roles and labors that once belonged exclusively to family members. These people, certainly in the United States, are subject to much abuse, and their work circumstances are largely unregulated. It is likely that much labor law reform in the next years will revolve around efforts to organize such caregivers and to regularize and improve their working conditions, whether they are working for commercial agencies or corporations, for the state, or for families.[6]

In the American consumer's republic in which we live, inheritance is a sideshow for all but a few very rich people. Wealth exists to be consumed in life, not to be preserved as a legacy. Moreover, it certainly does not exist to solicit the caring labor of one's children. Inherited wealth is understood—both in everyday usage and, perhaps more important, in the tax code—as "unearned." Economists debate whether

Americans are saving enough to see them through retirement and old age, for life beyond a salary. This is apparently a matter of enormous disagreement within that discipline. Yet, the discipline conducts this debate using a common assumption that "enough" means that there will be sufficient funds to last until the old person (or the old person's spouse) dies, whenever that occurs. "Enough" means enough to last however many years the old person lives, a matter of enormous uncertainty in a world where people can often be kept alive by machines and drugs. However, only the very rich are thought to plan for an inheritance that will outlast them or, more precisely, outlast the surviving spouse of a couple. No one assumes that significant numbers save to leave a legacy.[7]

Many older people do share wealth they have accumulated with their children. Yet now, unlike in the past, they are more likely to do so with transfers earlier in life by paying for education and the purchase of a first house. Contributions provide "stakes" and capital (real and intellectual) for the young at a time when those stakes are most needed. Such transfers make sense in a demographic environment in which many older people will live significantly longer, on into the relative old age of their children. Still, such forms of family sharing also mark the differences between today's expectations and those that defined the behavior of families in the nineteenth and early twentieth centuries.[8]

More than twenty-five years ago, an economics article hypothesized that older people with wealth made bequests "strategically," to control and to achieve care from their children and other younger family members. (This was posed against a dominant economic understanding that considered inheritance through the lens of altruism.) In the years since, efforts have been made to test the hypothesis. There is evidence that some parents transfer preferentially to children who are lifetime caregivers. Yet, for the most part the so-called strategic bequest motive has come to seem empirically implausible as an interpretation of bequest behavior today.[9]

In the legal culture we live in now, in the legal culture which came into being after World War II, the transactions explored in this book no longer have a legal presence. They are certainly no longer a part of the everyday legal world of American courts, as they were throughout the prior century. No doubt some parents still say to their children, "Someday all this will be yours" if you stay and take care of me. Surely, that still happens. Older people who might say something like that would do so knowing that they still possessed the right, as a tacit and unquestionable feature of property ownership, to choose who should inherit. Testator's freedom remains a known and understood part of the legal culture. In addition, some children presumably still believe that in assuming responsibility for the financial, emotional, and physical care of their parents, they become entitled to a legacy. What is more, their assumptions may be reinforced or framed by promises made by their parents. However, those promises have largely disappeared from the case records of the law.

Indeed, today much legal attention is paid to a problem that might be understood as the precise opposite of the core legal problem that shaped the cases of the New Jersey courts from the mid-nineteenth to the mid-twentieth century. Then the core problem for someone who planned for old age was how to keep while apparently giving, how to promise an estate without actually giving it away, how to negotiate one's way through the King Lear dilemma. Now the equivalent problem is how to give away in order to gain access to Medicaid and other means-tested forms of support. "Keeping while giving" has become "giving in order to gain eligibility." The legal game of how to do that is fraught with complications. In 1996 it became a crime to transfer assets in order to become eligible for Medicaid. In 1997 that law was repealed and was replaced by a law that made it a crime for lawyers and accountants to advise clients on how to transfer assets to gain eligibility. The U.S. Justice Department refused to enforce that law, citing constitutional worries, and its refusal was supported by a court deci-

sion in 1998 that focused on the law's interference with the privacy of
the lawyer-client relationship. In 2005 the U.S. Congress extended
from three to five years the "look-back" period, during which asset
transfers would be scrutinized. The goal is to prevent older people from
"spending down" their estates to produce Medicaid eligibility. If a
transfer during that five-year period was made for which something
of equal value (and care is not a value) was not received, a penalty will
be applied, delaying Medicaid eligibility.[10]

Beyond the game of means-tested eligibility that some twenty-first-
century older people and their advisors play, consider the broader
public-policy question of whether public funds are today simply sub-
stituting for family resources that once defined old age. Are public and
commercialized forms of care "crowding out" family responsibilities,
leaving older people in the hands of bureaucratic and unloving institutions? Or, has there been an aggregate gain, a "crowding in," where
older people get public funding and access to a great variety of consumer goods that meet their many needs, and still retain and enjoy the
continuing love and attention of children, grandchildren, and other
family members? Do we live in a better and happier world where, as
one European study puts it, "professional providers take over the med-
ically demanding and regular physical care, whereas the family is more
likely to provide the less demanding, spontaneous help"? Do we really
live in a world today where "Everyone does what they do best"?[11]

In recent years, feminist legal theorists, memoirists, and a few social
scientists have worked to make visible the largely invisible situation of
those many family members who—for a wide variety of emotionally
and culturally laden reasons—still end up serving as the designated but
"unpaid" caretakers for older people and others who can no longer care
for themselves.[12]

What it means to take on such work in this new world is as complex and contradictory as it ever was. Some adult children will still move in with their elderly parents or take them into their homes. More than a few will still provide direct bodily care for older people. The latter is understood as "heroic" and exceptional (perhaps worthy of a memoir).[13] As states and insurers work to reduce the costs of the health care system, and as more and more medical care is shifted to homes away from hospitals, some caretakers are put in the position of managing "complex care technologies . . . [such] as catheters, intravenous tubes[,] and oxygen masks," technologies that older people need today, all of which may be sent home. One study finds that women who do such work "seldom define it as care," which means that such nursing work has tacitly been incorporated into their "housework tasks."[14] A few legal and political initiatives work to recognize and pay such kin as "caregivers," as contract employees, although strong contrary understandings remain. Many still believe that what family members do for one another is not done—and ought not to be done—with an expectation of pay.[15]

However, many caretakers today find mediating and middle-ground positions. They may do little or no intimate bodily care, no "caregiving" as such. Instead, they step in as decision makers when older people are no longer able to make important decisions. They become "responsible," often through powers of attorney and other forms of legal agency. What such caretakers do today, then, is intimately tied to an understanding of the conditions of life for the elderly (as for all of us), in which large institutions—state and nonstate—are central. Caretakers negotiate with those large institutions, so that pension checks keep coming and health care is paid for. They manage care; they make appointments and accompany the old on those appointments; they make sure medications are taken and diagnoses are kept up to date. They may, under constrained circumstances (public rules), hire and manage caregivers, those contractual workers who will do the actual bodily carework. They also counter loneliness and offer attention, often from afar. They visit; they make conversation.[16]

There may always be choice involved in the decision to become or to let oneself become what has been called "trapped kin," even as such caretaking family members often understand themselves as having been coerced by culture, gender socialization, love, or religious faith to have done what ought to be done. However, the choice as such is never framed as the consequence of a narrowly economic set of calculations. I have not read a justification for caretaking published in the last two decades that was based on an expectation of reward through inheritance. Furthermore, in the writings of those who have taken on these roles, staying home and providing care are never framed as defined by a preexisting contract, although doing so is often understood through the lens of reciprocity: of a giving back to those who once gave to you.[17]

In the early twenty-first century, as in the late nineteenth and early twentieth centuries, very few caregivers have been literally trapped. Even spouses know that they are free to abandon or free to put a declining or declined spouse into a nursing home. We all have available to us the option of behaving as the children did who allowed their mother to go "over the hill to the poor-house" in Will Carleton's poem from the early 1870s.

Who are those who become trapped kin in the early twenty-first century? With longer lives and with no adult children present, a spouse is most often the individual who lands in that situation. However, just as in the late nineteenth and early twentieth centuries, the caretaker who attends may be a child, a grandchild, a more distant relative, or no blood relation at all (a daughter-in-law, a stepchild, a neighbor, a lover, a younger friend).

To be trapped and to understand oneself as trapped are often relative and comparative judgments made in relation to other similarly situated kin—siblings, other relatives—who for diverse reasons do not experience any wish to be designated as a caretaker and who are not psychically trapped by familial obligations. Gender socialization, inherited understandings of birth-order obligations, duty, culture, and religious faith may all serve to explain why some become trapped kin, whereas others do not. Yet the awareness that others are similarly situated who do not feel trapped by a sense of duty and are not distracted by care from their "real" lives may well produce a sense of resentment.[18]

Why is "trap" the right word for the situation? The answer is that few believe they have chosen to take on the work of care. Caring for older people is not like caring for children, which, at least in our day, is usually understood as a chosen activity. The care of older relatives comes upon one unexpectedly. One is caught off guard by a sense of duty and by the needs of others. It can be scary, frustrating, unpredictable, and emotionally draining. It may also feel like a trap, that is, an inescapable situation. Further, taking care of an elderly person—not as a job but because the person is "family"—may feel like a distraction, a diversion, and a distortion of who one really is.

Perhaps that was not the case in the past. There was certainly a rhetoric—mostly religious, mostly female—throughout the nineteenth century and into the twentieth, that characterized unpaid carework as transcendent destiny, as offering a road to salvation, and as participating in a crucial and socially useful task. This rhetoric, which must at least sometimes have been felt, seems largely unavailable today, and when mobilized, it seems insincere, usually sexist, and mean spirited. As trapped kin, one may not want pay; one may discover enormous satisfaction in doing the work well; still, few are doing real work—following a calling or a destiny—when caretaking.

What connections can be drawn between the ways we experience old age and caretaking in the early twenty-first century and the family relations and inheritance conflicts that the late nineteenth- and early twentieth-century New Jersey records reveal? Do the medical, demographic, fiscal, and political novelties of the past two generations suggest that the relations and conflicts of earlier generations belonged to a lost world of family care?

All of the litigants, witnesses, lawyers, and judges who appeared in the New Jersey case records of the nineteenth and early twentieth centuries lived, as we do, in a capitalist legal culture defined by free labor and expectations of mobility. They understood and lived, as we do, the contradictions that attached to notions of family work in a culture where work was understood as separate from home life. As competent members of the legal culture, they recognized that young people had the right to seek their fortunes elsewhere, away from their families of origin. They understood, as we do, that parents could not presume that children would stay home to care for them out of unquestioning love, obedience, or duty. They knew that it would take work—contractual work, gift work, guilt work, love work—for older parents and others contemplating retirement and old age to ensure that they would be cared for. The forms of planning may have been different then, but the need to plan has been a constant.

Everyone knew then, as we do today, that part of what distinguished a household from other workplaces was the fact that the terms of employment, compensation, reward, and care would remain relatively unarticulated. Everyone knew (although, of course, they interpreted what they knew in dramatically varying ways) that family work meant something different from work outside of the home. Everyone knew that within the home workers sometimes ended up (and sometimes started out) caring for—even, loving—those they worked for. That emotional reality at minimum complicated their position as employees. Everyone knew that the processes by which some younger people became providers of care, while others did not, were a fertile source of family conflict.

For those family members who became litigants and for lawyers and judges, property ownership was both the field on which conflict occurred and, in theory, the means to avoid or to resolve conflict. From the mid-nineteenth to the mid-twentieth century, property ownership continued to serve as the primary way to recognize competence and autonomy within this legal culture. It offered some limited security within a mobile and speculative world in large part because property ownership and household headship carried with them the expectation that others within a household would serve, obey, and care for the head. Why those others did so was undoubtedly complicated. A few would have understood themselves as living out a contract of care for property, a contract for a legacy. Far more would have mixed an awareness of promises made with "inherited" understandings of duty and obligation. Over time, there would be fewer adult children and others available to be drawn into the net of service and care and the expectation of a legacy. More of those who took on the tasks of care did so as "mere" employees, without an expectation of a legacy. However, early and late, throughout a century of American legal history, many of those who served and provided care did so because of the hope of reward, the hope of a legacy. Older people could discipline and control those they used to provide care—could rely on them—because those who cared for them expected to inherit.

Throughout those years, testator's freedom reinforced the older property owner's capacity to produce a good old age by leaving the older property owner in control of who would be rewarded at the end. Notions of uncontracted family obligations and of family sharing of resources may have survived within some ethnic communities, but, in the courts, property was owned individually and offered decisional power to older individuals. Recurrent claims that a particular will was the product of undue influence or that the will writer had grown incompetent to make a will served structurally and ironically as ways to reinforce those understandings. Courts used such claims to mark and to protect the privileges and the rights of the modestly competent and the not unduly influenced older testator. They remained decidedly reluctant to challenge the dispositional decisions made by an older property owner. The burden of proof on those who challenged such decisions was at all times a heavy one.

How do the practices of that legal field—of that distant and seemingly lost world—connect to the law of old age in our day? Perhaps it is all a matter of emphasis, as easy to argue for continuity and gradual evolution as for radical change. In legal theory, the pensions, mutual funds, insurance policies, and other forms of property that older people may own today remain subject to rules of testation that have changed only modestly over the past half century. Within the confines of legal doctrine, one can imagine a great deal of continuity between twenty-first century estates and trust law and the nineteenth- and early twentieth-century world we have explored. Likewise, as much recent economic sociology reveals, family relations remains a field of tacit contractual relations, filled with varying and unsettled arrangements.[19] It is still a part of legal common sense that members of a family do not ordinarily help or care for one another with an expectation of pay. Households remain places that abound, as was said in 1892 in *Disbrow v. Durand*, "in reciprocal acts of kindness and goodwill, which tend to mutual comfort and convenience."

Yet, today, in a world where longer lives, new consumption practices, and enormous health-care costs are likely to deplete most estates well before death, the powers and the security that property ownership once gave to the old have largely disappeared. In addition, the statutes and regulations that today control or attempt to control age discrimination, pension funds, elder care, and so much else have effectively swallowed up the private law that once governed household life for the old. Those who provide direct care for old people are likely to be employed by agencies and institutions public and private. They may not be members of the older person's household, if the older person still possesses a household at all.

To put the argument for discontinuity in a slightly different way, the relationship of "the family" to "the state" has changed fundamentally in the past several generations. The consequences are deeply confusing and upsetting both for older people and for adult children who serve as caretakers. Once, as in Carleton's poem, "Over the Hill to the Poor-House," public assistance was a disastrous last resort, while family was the first and preferred solution. Today, public relief, through modalities of social security, Medicare, and Medicaid, among others, as well as the semipublic and certainly nonfamilial modalities of insurance and pension funds, is what most older people look to first to see them through years of relatively "independent" retirement. Only when older people have become "dependent" and can no longer care for themselves do they look to care from their families. For an older person, the turn to family members probably suggests "decline," "need," and, almost certainly, a growing inability to care for oneself. The turn to family is almost never, as it was for James W. Davison or Ruth Buzby, an expression or a reflection of one's power over others and one's wealth.

Meanwhile, for the family members who do become caretakers today, the situation must often be experienced as a disturbing one. Their obligations are unclear; they are not necessarily responsible (they are certainly not "in control"); there is not, as there once was, an obvious explanation of why they are doing what they are doing (there will probably not be an inheritance at the end), and it may be hard to see when they ought to take responsibility for the actions of a parent or other older person. Usually they get responsibility without power, and that responsibility likely comes without the prospect of economic reward. It is all very different from the way it once was.[20]

Nonetheless, let me end by turning the story around once again, back toward continuity. The changes in legal doctrine and in judicial language, not to mention the statutory, economic, medical, and demographic transformations of the past sixty years, may have produced a new landscape of old age. Yet those changes did not undo the fundamental and continuing emotional tensions—the existential dilemmas—that continue to shape family relations in the context of care of old people. Furthermore, when we reflect on the stories in the case records of the late nineteenth and early twentieth centuries, we still may resonate to the ambivalences and discomforts that litigants and other family members experienced. Those stories of family conflict and unhappiness seem linked to twenty-first-century lives by the ways they expose apparently fundamental and perhaps inescapable contradictions in our expectations of ourselves in relation to our families.[21]

Then, as now, we think we value the autonomy of old people. Then, as now, we know that the independence of the young and the middle aged is a fundamental premise of our moral and legal culture. And then, as now, for the young and the middle aged, autonomy has usually meant to live and work apart from the old, from one's parents. However, then, as now, when the independence of the old has come to an end, we expect that decision making and more will become the responsibility of family members, usually children.[22]

In spite of demographic and medical changes, people still grow old, and then, when they are old, they become frail, needy, and difficult to work with and for, before they finally die. Frailty and need do not arrive according to a schedule. Older people do not age predictably, unlike young children, who do age as expected (at least as we observe them), who are (at least sometimes) cute and lovable, and who offer emotional rewards to those who care for them. Usually the need for care for and attention to the old arrives at an inconvenient and unplanned moment. At that moment family members find themselves confused about what to do when the need arrives—perhaps now even more than in the past. They are hard pressed to understand what their responsibilities are: how to serve those needs, how to deal with the chaos of care, not to mention why they ought to serve those needs, that is, why they need to deal with the chaos. In addition, because the old are not like children—at least within the conventional wisdom of our legal or moral imaginations—no one is actually compelled to stay home and serve. To be a neglectful child to declining and needy parents is now, as it has long been, morally and legally something quite different from being a parent guilty of neglect.

We still have access to the anger and resentments that pervaded the nineteenth- and early twentieth-century New Jersey cases. We know that we, too, might have been driven to drink by the demands of a lonely and needy adoptive mother. We can experience the injustice of having committed one's life to a dreary existence in somebody else's home (not one's own, even if the owner is a mother or a father) and then discovering that promises made to us were not carried out. We understand how horrible it must have been to watch an older parent develop dementia in one's care and still not die. Particularly as we ourselves age, we can imagine the terror that one might be left isolated and lonely in old age, and we can conceive of the promises we would have made to forestall that ending. We can also recognize how much we would have resented having to make such promises.

Perhaps the real mystery is why some younger people still stay home to provide care, why families continue to work and to share, why adult children and old people still remain entangled, remain "family," now that the apparent and historically resonant explanation of inheritance has largely disappeared.

Notes · *Acknowledgments* · *Index*

Notes

Introduction

1. Lotz. v. Rippe, 2 N.J. Misc. 754 (Ch. 1924); Burns v. McCormick, 233 N.Y. 230; 135 N.E. 273 (1922). Joseph William Singer, *Property Law: Rules, Policies, and Practices*, Law School Casebook Series (Boston: Little, Brown, 1993). See generally Zechariah Chafee Jr. and Sidney Post Simpson, *Cases on Equity, Jurisdiction, and Specific Performance* (Cambridge, Mass.: The editors, 1934), 1121–1138. A case like *Burns* has survived in casebooks because it can serve as an introduction to core doctrinal concepts and underlying policies. In particular, it introduces the central policies of the Statute of Frauds, a famous seventeenth-century English statute, re-enacted in every U.S. jurisdiction, that made oral—nonwritten—promises to convey land void. Such a case also offers law teachers an opportunity to play the pedagogical game of "thinking like a lawyer." The teacher attacks students' predictable sympathy for younger persons (someone like John Martin Lotz) whose lives have been given determinative shape, perhaps ruined, by their acceptance of an offer made by an older relative. The teacher counters that "natural" or merely moral response with distinctively legal arguments. At the end of the classes devoted to such cases, students have become a bit more socialized into a professional legal culture that stands apart from ordinary moral intuitions and everyday life.

2. For a summary of relevant features of the New Jersey court structure, as fixed by the state constitution of 1844, a structure that continued until a new state constitution was enacted in 1947, see http://en.wikisource.org/

wiki/New_Jersey_Constitution_of_1844#JUDICIARY. The judges of the New Jersey Prerogative Court, known by the titles "the ordinary" and "the vice ordinaries," were in fact the chancellor and the vice chancellors of the New Jersey Court of Equity. The New Jersey Court for the Correction of Errors and Appeals was composed of the chancellor, the judges of the New Jersey Supreme Court, and six other judges (who were paid on a per-diem basis for attending the court). When there was an appeal from an equity order or a decree, the chancellor did not participate in the deliberations of the court of errors. Likewise, when there was an appeal from a supreme court decision, the judges involved in the decision did not participate. Until the 1844 constitution, the governor of the state served as the chancellor. *Journal of the Proceedings of the Convention to Form a Constitution for the Government of the State of New Jersey* (Trenton: Mills, 1844); *State of New Jersey Constitutional Convention* (New Brunswick, N.J.: The Convention, 1947), vol. 1; Edward Quinton Keasbey, *The Courts and Lawyers of New Jersey, 1661–1912* (New York: Lewis Historical Pub., 1912); John Whitehead, *The Judicial and Civil History of New Jersey Microform* (Boston: Boston History Co., 1897).

3. See Lawrence Meir Friedman, *Contract Law in America a Social and Economic Case Study* (Madison: University of Wisconsin Press, 1965). For other surveys of such cases, see Roscoe Pound, "The Progress of the Law, 1918–1919 (Concluded)," *Harvard Law Review* 33 (1920): 929, 933–950; Harold C. Havighurst, "Services in the Home—A Study of Contract Concepts in Domestic Relations," *Yale Law Journal* 41 (1932): 386–406. One should not attach particular significance to my focus on New Jersey. I might as easily have studied any of a number of other state systems. It may be that some southern jurisdictions made enforcement of such transactions by disappointed young people somewhat more difficult. Compare Hooks v. Bridgewater, 111 Tex. 122, 229 S.W. 1114 (1921) and Upson v. Fitzgerald, 129 Tex. 211, 103 S.W. 2d 147 (1937) with cases like Van Duyne v. Vreeland, 12 N.J.Eq. 142 (1858). However, everywhere in nineteenth- and early twentieth-century America, caretakers constantly tested their rights by bringing up for judicial scrutiny promises made by elderly people.

4. However, see Bente v. Bugbee, 4 N.J.Misc. 701; 134 A. 185 (Sup. Ct., 1925); rev'd, 103 N.J. 608; 137 A. 552, and 103 N.J.L. 696; 137 A. 554 (Ct. of Errors; 1927). My reading of these cases and of the doctrinal law they reveal may be contrasted with readings by legal historians of other bodies of

private law, readings that emphasize the "legal instrumentalism" of private law, the ways, at least sometimes, that private law served as an alternative mechanism for the formulation of public policy. See J. Willard Hurst, *Law and the Conditions of Freedom in the Nineteenth-Century United States* (Madison: University of Wisconsin Press, 1956); Morton Horwitz, *The Transformation of American Law* (Cambridge, Mass.: Harvard University Press, 1977).

5. See, likewise, Paul Johnson, "Historical Readings of Old Age and Ageing," in *Old Age from Antiquity to Post-Modernity,* ed. Paul Johnson and Pat Thane (London: Routledge, 1998), 1–18. As always in using the records of appellate cases, particularly the records that lay behind the New Jersey Court for the Correction of Errors and Appeals, there are selection effects. Most of the litigants who had lost in a lower court would not have chosen to continue to that final appeal. One would also expect to encounter some bias toward litigation where more wealth was at stake. There was surely a bias toward family disharmony. I also suspect that I see more adoption or semiadoption cases than were represented in the larger society because those constituted a distinctively murky legal arena throughout the period.

6. On cases of trouble, see Michael Grossberg, *A Judgment for Solomon* (Cambridge: Cambridge University Press, 1996); Karl N. Llewellyn and E. Adamson Hoebel, *The Cheyenne Way: Conflict and Case Law in Primitive Jurisprudence* (Norman: University of Oklahoma Press, 1941). On the idea of "tests," see Luc Boltanski and Laurent Thévenot, *On Justification: Economies of Worth,* trans. Catherine Porter (Princeton, N.J.: Princeton University Press, 2006). In my reading of "cases of trouble," I have attended to the multivocality of cases and trials, paying particular attention to the competing strategies and interpretations of lawyers and their clients. I have also resisted the impulse to resolve factual and legal ambiguities by finding a right answer lurking within the cases.

7. Here I remain indebted to the fundamental insight of Willard Hurst in Hurst, *Law.* This book offers an alternative but complementary formulation of how to understand "law and the conditions of freedom" in nineteenth-century America.

8. My notion of a "field" borrows from Sally Falk Moore, *Law as Process: An Anthropological Approach* (London: Routledge and Kegan Paul, 1978); Pierre Bourdieu, *The Logic of Practice* (Cambridge: Cambridge University Press, 1990).

9. Although fathers and sons in early America certainly negotiated over inheritance and care (See Philip J. Greven, Four Generations: Population, Land, and Family in Colonial Andover, Massachusetts [Ithaca, N.Y.: Cornell University Press, 1970]), I am skeptical about whether the legal practices we focus on here would have been available to New Jersey's family members prior to a world defined by free labor and mobility and the increasing commodification of real property, prior to what historians have called a "market revolution." Nor would those practices make much sense to most of us living today, in the early twenty-first century, although younger family members still do a great deal of caretaking of older family members.

10. See Oliver Wendell Holmes, "The Path of the Law," Harvard Law Review 10 (1897): 457.

11. Sometimes they also made legal distinctions that might not have had any significance in any court of law. One husband felt outraged at trial when his wife was called a "foster" child rather than an "adopted" child. "McTague v. Finnegan," Record and Briefs 228(4), Court of Errors and Appeals (New Jersey State Library, 1896–1897). That was not a meaningful distinction in the law at that time.

12. On family law and life in this period, see Michael Grossberg, Governing the Hearth: Law and the Family in Nineteenth-Century America (Chapel Hill: University of North Carolina, 1985); Ariela R. Dubler, "Governing through Contract: Common Law Marriage in the Nineteenth Century," Yale Law Journal 107(6) (April 1998): 1885–1920. On the practices of the early modern overseers of poor people, see Douglas Jones, "The Strolling Poor: Transiency in 18th Century Massachusetts," Journal of Social History 8 (1975): 18. Nina Dayton and Sharon Salinger, "Robert Love and His Warning Book: Searching for Strangers in Pre-Revolutionary Boston," book manuscript in progress. On the development of corporate welfare, see Jennifer Klein, For All These Rights: Business, Labor, and the Shaping of America's Public-Private Welfare State (Princeton, N.J.: Princeton University Press, 2003).

13. See Pound, "Progress of the Law, 1918–1919 (Concluded)."

14. Brian Gratton, "The Creation of Retirement: Families, Individuals, and the Social Security Movement," in Societal Impact on Aging: Historical Perspectives, ed. K. Warner Schaie and W. Andrew Achenbaum (New York: Springer, 1993), 45–73; Brian Gratton, "The Poverty of Impoverishment Theory: The Economic Well-Being of the Elderly, 1890–1950," Journal of Economic History 56(1) (March 1996): 39–61.

15. The poem was first published in newspapers in 1872. Carleton reprinted it a year later in a book of "farm ballads." Will Carleton, Charles Stanley Reinhart, and Sinclair Hamilton Collection of American Illustrated Books, *Farm Ballads,* illus. Charles Stanley Reinhart (New York: Harper and Brothers, 1873). There, Carleton added a second poem, "Over the Hill from the Poor House," which described the actions of the protagonist's sixth child, a prodigal son who returns from prison to save his mother from the poorhouse. For the song version, see David Braham, *Over the Hill to the Poor House: Song and Chorus* (New York: Pond, 1874). According to the IMDB database, film versions were made in 1908, 1911, 1917, 1920, and 1931. The 1920 version was one of the highest grossing silent films.

16. See, for example, Glenda Laws, "'The Land of Old Age': Society's Changing Attitudes toward Urban Built Environments for Elderly People," *Annals of the Association of American Geographers* 83(4) (December 1993): 672–693; Walter Gellhorn, "Poverty and Legality: The Law's Slow Awakening," *Proceedings of the American Philosophical Society* 112(2) (presented Nov. 10, 1967, at the Symposium on Law and Liberty) (April 1968): 107–116; Ollie A. Randall, "Old-Age Security at 'Home,'" *American Journal of Nursing* 37(5) (May 1937): 488–493; Clarke A. Chambers, "Toward a Redefinition of Welfare History," *Journal of American History* 73(2) (September 1986): 407–433; J. Douglas Brown, "The Birth of Old-Age Insurance, 1934–35" (delivered at a conference of Social Security District Office Managers in Yonkers, New York, May 17, 1963), http://www.ssa.gov/history/jdb4.html; Louella Parsons, "New York Is Killing Mary Pickford with Kindness," *New York Telegraph* (Sept. 18, 1921). On the phrase "over the hill" see "The Hill," *American Speech* 33(2), Part 2 (May 1958): 69–72.

17. Will Carleton, *Over the Hill to the Poor-House & Over the Hill from the Poor-House* (New York London: Harper and Brothers, 1904), preface.

18. Grossberg, *Governing;* Linda Gordon, *Heroes of Their Own Lives* (New York: Vintage, 1988); Hendrik Hartog, *Man and Wife in America: A History* (Cambridge, Mass.: Harvard University Press, 2000).

19. On the notion of a "character," see Amélie Oksenberg Rorty, *Mind in Action* (Boston: Beacon, 1988).

20. Loïc Trabut and Florence Weber, "How to Make Care-Work Visible? The Case of Dependence Policies in France," in Nina Bandelj, ed., *Economic Sociology of Work* (Bingley, U.K.: JAI Press/Emerald, 2009), 343–368.

21. On the market revolution, see Eric Foner, "Free Labor and Nineteenth-Century Political Ideology," in *The Market Revolution in America,* ed. Melvyn Stokes and Stephen Conway (Charlottesville: University Press of Virginia, 1996), 99–127; Susan B. Carter, Richard L. Ransom, and Roger Ransom, "Family Matters: The Life-Cycle Transition and the Antebellum American Fertility Decline," in *History Matters: Essays on Economic Growth, Technology, and Demographic Change,* ed. Timothy Guinnane (Stanford: Stanford University Press, 2003), 271–329; Charles Grier Sellers, *The Market Revolution: Jacksonian America, 1815–1846* (New York: Oxford University Press, 1991); Jeanne Boydston, "The Woman Who Wasn't There: Women's Market Labor and the Transition to Capitalism in the United States," in *Wages of Independence: Capitalism in the Early American Republic,* ed. Paul A. Gilje (Madison: Madison House, 1997), 23–47; Amy Dru Stanley, *From Bondage to Contract: Wage Labor, Marriage, and the Market in the Age of Slave Emancipation* (New York: Cambridge University Press, 1998); Allan Kulikoff, *From British Peasants to Colonial American Farmers* (Chapel Hill: University of North Carolina Press, 2000); Steven Ruggles, "Multigenerational Families in Nineteenth-Century America," *Continuity and Change* 18(1) (2003): 139–165.

22. E. Wayne Carp, ed., *Adoption in America Historical Perspectives* (Ann Arbor: University of Michigan Press, 2002); Barbara Melosh, *Strangers and Kin: The American Way of Adoption* (Cambridge, Mass.: Harvard University Press, 2002); Claudia Nelson, *Little Strangers: Portrayals of Adoption and Foster Care in America, 1850–1929* (Bloomington: Indiana University Press, 2003); Hendrik Hartog, "Someday All This Will Be Yours: Inheritance, Adoption, and Obligation in Capitalist America," *Indiana Law Journal* 79(2) (Spring 2004): 345–362.

23. See Joyce Appleby, *Inheriting the Revolution: The First Generation of Americans* (Cambridge, Mass.: Belknap, 2000), 170–174; Dylan C. Penningroth, *The Claims of Kinfolk: African American Property and Community in the Nineteenth-Century South* (Chapel Hill: University of North Carolina Press, 2003).

24. On work that questions these assumptions largely from the standpoint of the history of old age, see Steven Ruggles, "The Transformation of American Family Structure," *American Historical Review* 99(1) (February 1994): 103–128; Steven Ruggles, "Living Arrangements of the Elderly in America: 1880–1980," in *Aging and Generational Relations*

over the Life Course: A Historical and Cross-Cultural Perspective, ed. Tamara K. Hareven (Berlin: de Gruyter, 1996), 254–271; Ruggles, "Multigenerational Families in Nineteenth-Century America"; David I. Kertzer, "Toward a Historical Demography of Aging," in *Aging in the Past: Demography, Society, and Old Age*, ed. David I. Kertzer (Berkeley: University of California Press, 1995), 363–383; David I. Kertzer, "Living with Kin," in *The History of the European Family*, ed. David I. Kertzer and Marzio Barbagli (New Haven, Conn.: Yale University Press, 2001), 40–72; Tamara Hareven and Kathleen J. Adams, "The Generation in the Middle: Cohort Comparisons in Assistance to Aging Parents in an American Community," in *Aging and Generational Relations over the Life Course: A Historical and Cross-Cultural Perspective*, ed. Tamara K. Hareven (Berlin: de Gruyter, 1996), 272–293. Students of the inheritance practices of immigrant communities have explored some of the ways that adult children remained present in families. See Jon Gjerde, *The Minds of the West: Ethnocultural Evolution in the Rural Middle West, 1830–1917* (Chapel Hill: University of North Carolina Press, 1997); Sonya Salamon, *Prairie Patrimony: Family, Farming, and Community in the Midwest, Studies in Rural Culture* (Chapel Hill: University of North Carolina Press, 1992).

25. The privileging of these relational legal categories, which are rooted in the law of persons, bears a close relationship to the hierarchy of kinship relations explored and critiqued in recent anthropology. David M. Schneider, *American Kinship: A Cultural Account* (Chicago: University of Chicago Press, 1968).

26. Arthur Ripstein, "Private Order and Public Justice: Kant and Rawls," *Virginia Law Review* 92(7) (November 2006): 1391–1438.

27. Holly Brewer and the Omohundro Institute of Early American History and Culture, *By Birth or Consent: Children, Law, and the Anglo-American Revolution in Authority* (Chapel Hill: Published for the Omohundro Institute of Early American History and Culture, Williamsburg, Va., by the University of North Carolina Press, 2005); Steven Mintz, *Huck's Raft: A History of American Childhood* (Cambridge, Mass.: Belknap Press of Harvard University Press, 2004); Grossberg, *Governing*; Gordon, *Heroes of Their Own Lives*.

28. Christopher Lasch, *Haven in a Heartless World: The Family Besieged* (New York: Basic, 1979). On the meanings of "love," see Carol J. Greenhouse, "Lear and Law's Doubles: Identity and Meaning in a Time of

Crisis," *Law, Culture, and the Humanities* 2(2) (2006): 239–258. See also Talcott Parson's canonical description of the family as the prototypical home of "service." Talcott Parsons, "Service," in *Encyclopedia of the Social Sciences,* ed. Edwin Robert Anderson Seligman and Alvin Saunders Johnson, vol. 13 (New York: Macmillan, 1937), 672–674.

29. John Bouvier, *A Law Dictionary,* 1st ed. (Philadelphia: Lippincott, 1856); Noah Webster, *An American Dictionary of the English Language,* rev. Chauncey Goodrich (Springfield, Massachusetts: Merriam, 1856), 436.

30. See Stanley, *From Bondage.*

31. One might call this a strategy of methodological individualism. It is exemplified in Gordon, *Heroes of Their Own Lives.*

32. As Viviana Zelizer argues, a serious understanding of family work begins with the rejection—or bracketing off—of what she calls "nothing but" ideological frameworks that presume that love means the rejection of economic strategy and individual ambition and vice versa. Viviana Zelizer, *The Purchase of Intimacy* (Princeton, N.J.: Princeton University Press, 2005).

33. For surveys of the mostly European history of old age, see Peter Laslett, "Necessary Knowledge: Age and Aging in the Societies of the Past," in *Aging in the Past: Demography, Society, and Old Age,* ed. David I. Kertzer (Berkeley: University of California Press, 1995), 3–77; Pat Thane, "Social Histories of Old Age and Aging," *Journal of Social History* 37(1) (2003): 93–111. For a short moment nearly a generation ago, a few American scholars worked on the history of old age. David Hackett Fischer, *Growing Old in America* (New York: Oxford University Press, 1977); John P. Demos, "Old Age in Early New England," in *Turning Points: Historical and Sociological Essays on the Family,* ed. John P. Demos and S. S. Boocock (Chicago: University of Chicago Press, 1978), 248–287; W. Andrew Achenbaum, *Old Age in the New Land: The American Experience since 1790* (Baltimore: Johns Hopkins University Press, 1978). For a critique by a literary scholar of the uses made of death as a scholarly solution to the conundra of old age, see Kathleen M. Woodward, *Aging and Its Discontents: Freud and Other Fictions,* Theories of Contemporary Culture (Bloomington: Indiana University Press, 1991).

34. Roger L. Ransom, Richard Sutch, and Samuel H. Williamson, "Inventing Pensions: The Origins of the Company-Provided Pension in the United States, 1900–1940," in *Societal Impact on Aging: Historical*

Perspectives, ed. K. Warner Schaie and W. Andrew Achenbaum (New York: Springer, 1993), 1–38; Roger L. Ransom and Richard Sutch, "The Impact of Aging on the Employment of Men in American Working-Class Communities at the End of the Nineteenth Century," in *Aging in the Past: Demography, Society, and Old Age,* ed. David I. Kertzer (Berkeley: University of California Press, 1995), 303–327. Historians have emphasized the desires of elderly people to maintain their independence and to live in households apart from children and other relatives. Mark Thomas and Paul Johnson, "Paying for Old Age: Past, Present, Future," in *The Economic Future in Historical Perspective,* ed. Paul A. David and Mark Thomas (Oxford: Oxford University Press, 2003), 479–508. Pat Thane, *Old Age in English History: Past Experiences, Present Issues* (Oxford: Oxford University Press, 2000). Brian Gratton suggests that the desire for independence, combined with younger people's desire for disengagement from the affairs of the elderly, helps explain the passage of social security. Gratton, "Poverty of Impoverishment"; Gratton, "Creation of Retirement." My reading of the gerontological literature has been much shaped by Lawrence Cohen, *No Aging in India. Alzheimer's, the Bad Family, and Other Modern Things* (Berkeley: University of California Press, 1998); Haim Hazan, *Old Age Constructions and Deconstructions* (New York: Cambridge University Press, 1994); Haim Hazan, "Disposable Children: On the Role of Offspring in the Construction of Conjugal Support in Later Life," in *Global Aging and Challenges to Families,* ed. Vern L. Bengtson and Ariela Lowenstein (New York: de Gruyter, 2003), 159–171; Chris Phillipson, "From Family Groups to Personal Communities: Social Capital and Social Change in the Family Life of Older Adults," in *Global Aging and Challenges to Families,* ed. Vern L. Bengtson and Ariela Lowenstein (New York: de Gruyter, 2003), 54–74. On the emphasis on independence within the American family as seen from a European perspective, see Hervé Varenne, "Love and Liberty: The Contemporary American Family," in *A History of the Family,* vol. 2, *The Impact of Modernity,* ed. André Burguière, Christiane Klapisch-Zuber, Martine Segalen, and Françoise Zonabend and trans. Sarah Hanbury Tenison (Cambridge: Polity, 1996), 416–441.

35. The converse situation also plays a part throughout: that is, the familial origins of contract law and contractualism. This second paradox has played an important role in feminist legal theory and political

theory. See Carole Pateman, *The Sexual Contract* (Stanford: Stanford University Press, 1988).

36. Sloan v. Maxwell, 3 N.J.Eq. 563 (Prerogative Ct., 1831).

1. Of Helplessness and Power

1. James W. Davison was probably born in 1784 (see the 1860 census, although the 1850 census lists him as born in 1795). He served in the War of 1812. A history of the New Jersey coast describes him as having held "a position of trust." However, according to the pension records, he was a private. William Nelson, *The New Jersey Coast in Three Centuries: History of the New Jersey Coast with Genealogical and Historic-Biographical Appendix,* vol. 3 (New York: Lewis, 1902), 457. http:// search.ancestrylibrary.com/cgi-bin/sse.dll?db=pennj&so=2&rank=0 &gsfn=james&gsln=davison&sx=&gs1co=2%2cUSA&gs1pl=33 %2cNew+Jersey&year=&yearend=&sbo=0&sbor=&ufr=0&wp=4%3b _80000002%3b_80000003&srchb=r&prox=1&db=&ti=5542&ti.si=0 &gss=angs-c&o_iid=21416&o_lid=21416.

2. "Davison v. Davison," Records and Briefs, docket: 3 614 1860, 13-2510-20 c2-0507-20, Court of Chancery (New Jersey State Archives, 1861), testimony, June 12, 1860; "Davison v. Davison," petition of complainant. On the relative sizes and values of the brothers' farms, see the testimony of John, Reuben, and Joseph Davison, "Davison v. Davison," October 25 and 27, 1860.

3. Marriage records can be found at http://homepages.rootsweb.com/ ~genea/Dnjmgs.html. In the trial transcript, Jane is often referred to as Laura. To avoid confusion, I refer to her as Jane. The Perrines and the Davisons were much intermarried. See *Genealogies of New Jersey Families, from the Genealogical Magazine of New Jersey,* vol. 1 (New Brunswick, N.J.: Genealogical Society of New Jersey, 1996), 1:188–189.

4. "Davison v. Davison," Defendants' Response, Apr. 13, 1860; "Davison v. Davison," Testimony, May 29, 1860, and Sept. 12, 1860.

5. "Davison v. Davison," Testimony, Sept. 12, 1860.

6. "Davison v. Davison," Testimony, Oct. 12, 1860; June 12, 1860; October 27, 1860.

7. "Davison v. Davison," Testimony, June 12, 1860. If one relies on the records of the Perrineville cemetery, Jane had given birth to two children by 1860, neither of whom survived infancy. William Davison Perrine,

History of Perrineville and the Presbyterian Church, 1786–1935 (Princeton Junction, N.J., 1935). The first would have been conceived in March or April 1857, shortly after their marriage. Was James W. referring to another child conceived and born before the marriage of Jane and James? Or was he accusing Jane of having conceived one of the couple's two children with another man?

8. "Davison v. Davison," Records and Briefs, docket: 3 614 1860, 13-2510-20 c2-0507-20, Court of Chancery (New Jersey State Archives, 1861), Testimony, Oct. 25, 1860. Actually, Perrine had no right to bring suit in defense of his daughter once she was married. It was just talk on his part.

9. "Davison v. Davison," Testimony, Oct. 25, 1860.

10. Ibid.

11. Andrew J. King, "The Law of Slander in Early Antebellum America," *American Journal of Legal History* 35(1) (January 1991): 1–43; Andrew J. King, "Constructing Gender: Sexual Slander in Nineteenth-Century America," *Law and History Review* 13(1) (Spring 1995): 63–110. I have not been able to find any record of the slander suit in the Monmouth or Middlesex County court records.

12. "Davison v. Davison," Testimony, Oct. 25 and Oct. 27, 1860.

13. Davison v. Davison, 13 N.J. Eq. 246, 247 (Ch. 1861).

14. "Davison v. Davison," Testimony, June 12, 1860. In the 1860 census, James Davison and Jane Davison are listed as part of Peter Perrine's household. See http://content.ancestry.com/iexec/?htx=View&r=an& dbid=7667&iid=NJM653_699-0308&fn=James&ln=Davison&st=r& ssrc=&pid=54424587.

15. Davison v. Davison,13 N.J. Eq. 246 (Ch. 1861).

16. The essential starting point for the English history is Frederic William Maitland, *Equity, Also the Forms of Action at Common Law,* ed. A. H. Chaytor, two courses of lectures by F. W. Maitland (Cambridge, 1929), 1–11. The best source for the American history remains Zechariah Chafee Jr. and Sidney Post Simpson, *Cases on Equity, Jurisdiction and Specific Performance* (Cambridge, Mass.: The editors, 1934); Lawrence M. Friedman, *A History of American Law* (New York: Simon & Schuster, 2005), 80.

17. John Bouvier, *A Law Dictionary,* 1st ed. (Philadelphia: Lippincott, 1856). Maitland wrote: "No one could set any very strict limits to his [the chancellor's] power, but the best hint as to its extent . . . given by the words 'fraud, accident, and breach of confidence.'" Maitland, *Equity, Also the Forms of Action at Common Law,* 1–11.

18. "Davison v. Davison," Testimony, May 27, 1860; June 12, 1860.
19. Ibid., May 27, 1860. In cross-examination, both Reuben and Joseph conceded the point. Ibid., Oct. 25, 1860.
20. "Davison v. Davison," Response, Reuben, Joseph, and James W. Davison; "Davison v. Davison," Testimony, October 25, 1860.
21. He clearly did not consider the slander suit as constituting a breach of the contract between father and son.
22. Davison v. Davison, 13 N.J. Eq. 246 (Ch. 1861).
23. "Davison v. Davison."
24. *Genealogies of New Jersey Families*, vol. 1, 421. James and his father were both buried in the graveyard of the Perrineville Presbyterian Church. Their headstones are still visible. http://search.ancestrylibrary.com/cgi -bin/sse.dll?indiv=1&db=1870usfedcen%2c&rank=0&gsfn=james& gsln=davison&sx=&gs1co=2%2cUSA&gs1pl=33%2cNew+Jersey&year= &yearend=&sbo=0&sbor=&ufr=0&wp=4%3b_80000002%3b _80000003&srchb=r&prox=1&ti=5542&ti.si=0&gss=angs-d&o_iid= 21416&o_lid=21416&pcat=35&fh=3&h=24471364&recoff=1+2. See also, http://search.ancestrylibrary.com/cgi-bin/sse.dll?indiv=1&db=1880us-fedcen%2c&rank=0&gsfn=james&gsln=davison&sx=&gs1co=2 %2cUSA&gs1pl=33%2cNew+Jersey&year=&yearend=&sbo=0&sbor= &ufr=0&wp=4%3b_80000002%3b_80000003&srchb=r&prox=1&ti= 5542&ti.si=0&gss=angs-d&o_iid=21416&o_lid=21416&pcat=35&fh=2 &h=36399095&recoff=1+2. Nelson, *New Jersey Coast*, vol. 3, 457.
25. Carlisle v. Fleming, 1 Harrington 421 (Del. Ch. 1835). Rhodes v. Rhodes, 3 Sandf. Ch. 279 (N.Y. Ch. 1846). There were also a few early cases in which children (sometimes grandchildren or informally adopted children) sued estates for compensation *quantum meruit* for the work and services they had provided as a member of a household. Jacobson v. The Executors of La Grange, 3 Johns. 199 (N.Y. Sup. Ct. 1808), Patterson v. Patterson, 13 Johns. 379 (N.Y. Sup. Ct. 1816), Burlingame v. Burlingame, 7 Cow. 92 (NY Sup. Ct. 1827), Eaton v. Benton, 2 Hill 576 (NY Sup. Ct. 1842), Jack v. McKee, 9 Pa. St. 235 (1848).
26. The cases are Rue v. Rue, 21 N.J.L. 369 (Sup. Ct. 1848), Ridgway v. English, 22 N.J.L. 409 (Sup. Ct. 1850), Weart v. Hoagland, 22 N.J.L. 517 (Sup. Ct. 1850), France v. France, 8 N.J. Eq. 650 (Ch. 1852), Grandin v. Reading, 10 N.J. Eq. 370 (Ch. 1855), Van D[u]yne v. Vreeland, 11 N.J. Eq. 370 (Ch. 1857), Van Duyne v. Vreeland, 12 N.J. Eq. 142 (Ch. 1858), Updike v. Titus, 13 N.J. Eq. 151 (Ch. 1860), and Smith v. Administrators of

Smith, 28 N.J.L. 208 (Sup. Ct. 1860). (The first Van Duyne citation is to the chancellor's decision on a demurrer by the defendants.) It would be easy to connect the sudden appearance of these cases to the passage of a new New Jersey State Constitution in 1844, which, among other changes, made the chancellor into a professional judicial office, were it not for the fact that similar cases began springing up all over the country, including jurisdictions without separate equity courts.

27. David M. Schneider, *American Kinship: A Cultural Account* (Chicago: University of Chicago Press, 1968); Alan Macfarlane, *Marriage and Love in England* (Oxford: Blackwell, 1986); Michael Grossberg, *Governing the Hearth: Law and the Family in Nineteenth-Century America* (Chapel Hill: University of North Carolina, 1985).

28. See "Davison v. Davison," Testimony, Oct. 27, 1860.

29. Lisa Dillon, *The Shady Side of Fifty: Age and Old Age in Late Victorian Canada and the United States* (Montreal: McGill-Queen's University Press, 2008); Peter Laslett, "Necessary Knowledge: Age and Aging in the Societies of the Past," in *Aging in the Past: Demography, Society, and Old Age*, ed. David I. Kertzer (Berkeley: University of California Press, 1995), 3–77. See also L. A. Botelho, *Old Age and the English Poor Law, 1500–1700* (Woodbridge, Suffolk, UK: Boydell, 2004), 57.

30. Susan B. Carter, Richard L. Ransom, and Roger Ransom, "Family Matters: The Life-Cycle Transition and the Antebellum American Fertility Decline," in *History Matters: Essays on Economic Growth, Technology, and Demographic Change*, ed. Timothy Guinnane (Stanford: Stanford University Press, 2003), 271–329. See, for examples, Hermann Zeitlhofer, "Headship Succession and Retirement in South Bohemia, 1640–1840," in *Family Welfare Gender, Property, and Inheritance since the Seventeenth Century*, ed. David R. Green, Contributions in Family Studies (Westport, Conn.: Praeger, 2004), 73–96; Martin Kohli, M. Rein, A. Guillemard, and H. Van Gunsteren, eds., *Time for Retirement: Comparative Studies of Early Exit from the Labour Force* (Cambridge: Cambridge University Press, 1991); Carole Haber and Brian Gratton, *Old Age and the Search for Security: An American Social History* (Bloomington: Indiana University Press, 1994); Christoph Conrad, "The Emergence of Modern Retirement: Germany in International Comparison," *Population* (Paris: INED), English selection no. 3 (1991); Brian Gratton, "The Creation of Retirement: Families, Individuals, and the Social Security Movement," in *Societal Impact on Aging: Historical Perspectives*, ed. K.

Warner Schaie and W. Andrew Achenbaum (New York: Springer, 1993), 45–73.

31. Charles Grier Sellers, *The Market Revolution: Jacksonian America, 1815–1846* (New York: Oxford University Press, 1991); Eric Foner, "Free Labor and Nineteenth-Century Political Ideology," in *The Market Revolution in America*, ed. Melvyn Stokes and Stephen Conway (Charlottesville: University Press of Virginia, 1996), 99–127; Carter, Ransom, and Ransom, "Family Matters"; Allan Kulikoff, *The Agrarian Origins of American Capitalism* (Charlottesville: University Press of Virginia, 1992); Allan Kulikoff, *From British Peasants to Colonial American Farmers* (Chapel Hill: University of North Carolina Press, 2000).

32. David Braham [from old catalog], *Over the Hill to the Poor House: Song and Chorus* (New York: Pond, 1874).

33. William E. Schenck, ed. and comp., *Nearing Home: Comforts and Counsels for the Aged* (Philadelphia: Presbyterian Board of Publication, 1868), 51–52; Henry Ward Beecher, "Old Age," *Friends' Intelligencer* (American Periodicals Series Online) 25 (Mar. 14, 1868): 2; "The Editor's Fireside," *American Farmer; Devoted to Agriculture, Horticulture, etc.* (American Periodicals Series Online) 73 (May 1, 1892): 18; "Home Chats with Farmers' Wives: The Old Folks (American Periodicals Series Online)," *Michigan Farmer* 36 (Aug. 19, 1899): 128; "Care in Old Age (American Periodicals Series Online)," *Maine Farmer* 54 (Feb. 11, 1886): 3.

34. As one often-reprinted poem, first published in 1918, put it, it was not "fear of toil" or "love of dress" that had driven young men away. Rather, it was "just the methods of their dads." "Why He Left the Farm," *Indiana Farmer's Guide* (American Periodicals Series Online) 30–31 (Aug. 3, 1918): 9.

35. See "Young Folks from Home; Companion to Old Folks at Home," http://library.duke.edu/digitalcollections/hasm.no376/; "I Wonder How the Old Folks Are at Home," 1909, http://library.duke.edu/digital collections/hasm.ao276/; "Old Folks at Home; Ethiopian Melody," 1851, http://library.duke.edu/digitalcollections/hasm_no234/; "Where Are the Old Folks[?]" 1882, http://library.duke.edu/digitalcollections/hasm.a6570/. See likewise, "The Old Folks Are Gone" [n.d.], http://mem ory.loc.gov/cgi-bin/query/h?ammem/mussm:@field(NUMBER+@ band(sm1880+01903)).

36. Why was Martha Hancock taken in by them? Had her parents died? She was identified in testimony as the daughter of Lewis Hancock, but there are no Lewis Hancocks of the right age to be found in the New

Jersey records. However, there were many Hancocks living near the Buzbys. http://search.ancestrylibrary.com/cgi-bin/sse.dll?indiv=1&db= 1850usfedcenancestry%2c&rank=0&gsfn=martha&gsln=hancock&sx =&=%2c%2c1%2c+%2c%2c1%2c+&gs1co=2%2cUSA&gs1pl=33 %2cNew+Jersey&year=&yearend=&sbo=0&sbor=&srchb=r&prox=1& ti=5542&ti.si=0&gss=angs-d&pcat=35&fh=5&h=4596645&recoff=1+2.

37. For Asher Buzby's death, see http://wc.rootsweb.ancestry.com/cgi-bin/ igm.cgi?op=REG&db=gjohnston3&id=I18548. "Waddington v. Buzby," Record and Briefs, vol. 142 (6), Court of Errors and Appeals (New Jersey State Library, 1889), 54–61.

38. "Waddington v. Buzby," 17, 20–23.

39. For the death of Charles C. Gaskill, Beulah's husband, see *The Friend: A Literary and Religious Journal* 46 (Philadelphia, 1873): 128. One can track the changing dimensions of Ruth Buzby's household through the census. See http://search.ancestrylibrary.com/iexec/?htx=View&r=5542 &dbid=8054&iid=NJM432_462-0136&fn=Ruth&ln=Buzby&st=r&ssrc =&pid=4596643 (1850); http://search.ancestrylibrary.com/iexec/?htx= View&r=5542&dbid=7667&iid=NJM653_707-0350&fn=Ruth+W&ln= Buzby&st=d&ssrc=&pid=5500674a. (1860) http://search.ancestrylibrary .com/iexec/?htx=View&r=5542&dbid=6742&iid=NJT9_797-0305&fn =Ruth+W.&ln=Buzby&st=d&ssrc=&pid=28326793 (1880).

40. "Waddington v. Buzby," 35, 127, 131.

41. Ibid., 1–30.

42. Ibid., Will of Ruth W. Buzby, Deceased, 1–3.

43. Beulah Gaskill and Nathan Buzby Junior testified similarly. "Waddington v. Buzby," 30, 55–56, 40, Brief of Sinnickson, 2, 6–7.

44. Ibid., 11–39.

45. Ibid., Brief of Sinnickson, 7, 8, 10. (The treatise was Redfield on Wills.)

46. Ibid., Points of Appellant's Counsel, 7. On Hilliard's clerkship for Sinnickson, see John Whitehead, *The Judicial and Civil History of New Jersey Microform*, vol. 2 (Boston: Boston History, 1897), 414–415.

47. On the right to make unkind or immoral distributions, see Trumball v. Gibbons, 22 N.J.L. 117 (1849), to which Hilliard referred. On the issues that case raised, see Susanna L. Blumenthal, "The Deviance of the Will: Policing the Bounds of Testamentary Freedom in Nineteenth-Century America," *Harvard Law Review* 119 (February 2006): 959–1034.

48. "Waddington v. Buzby," Opinion of Reed, P.J., in Salem Orphan's Court, 1. Waddington v. Buzby, 43 N.J. Eq. 154; 10 A. 862 (Prerog. Ct. 1887).

49. Waddington v. Buzby, 45 N.J. Eq. 173, 16 A. 690 (E. & A. 1889).

50. Whitehead, *The Judicial and Civil History of New Jersey Micro-form*, vol.2, 414–415. In 1910 Martha Hancock was still living as an "aunt" in the household of Mary Buzby Waddington. See http://search.ancestrylibrary.com/cgi-bin/sse.dll?indiv=1&db=1910USCenIndex%2c&rank=0&gsfn=martha&gsln=hancock&sx=&gs1co=2%2cUSA&gs1pl=33%2cNew+Jersey&year=&yearend=&sbo=0&sbor=&ufr=0&wp=4%3b_80000002%3b_80000003&srchb=r&prox=1&ti=5542&ti.si=0&gss=angs-d&o_iid=21416&o_lid=21416&pcat=35&fh=0&h=16758028&recoff=1+3; see also http://search.ancestrylibrary.com/iexec/?htx=View&r=5542&dbid=1054&iid=NJV227_101-0177&fn=Martha+B&ln=Hancock&st=r&ssrc=&pid=111562.

51. David I. Kertzer, "Living with Kin," in *The History of the European Family*, ed. David I. Kertzer and Marzio Barbagli (New Haven, Conn.: Yale University Press, 2001), 40–72; David I. Kertzer, "Toward a Historical Demography of Aging," in *Aging in the Past: Demography, Society, and Old Age*, ed. David I. Kertzer (Berkeley: University of California Press, 1995), 363–383. On the concept of "family strategy," meaning the willingness of various members of a family (conceived as an intergenerational unit) to merge their goals and desires in pursuit of a common goal, see Jan Kok, "The Challenge of Strategy: A Comment," *International Review of Social History* 47 (2002): 465–484; Pier Paolo Viazzo and Katherine A. Lynch, "Anthropology, Family History, and the Concept of Strategy," *International Review of Social History* 47 (2002): 423–452.

52. For work that discusses the "nuclear disaster" hypothesis, the portrayal (initially by Peter Laslett) of old people in late medieval and early modern times in England and northern Europe as being without strong legal or cultural claims on their children and having instead to fend for themselves or to depend on the county and the poor law authorities, see David Thomson, "Generations, Justice, and the Future of Collective Action," in *Justice between Age Groups and Generations*, ed. Peter Laslett and James S. Fishkin (New Haven, Conn.: Yale University Press, 1992), 206–236; David Thomson, "Welfare of the Elderly in the Past: A Family or Community Responsibility," in *Life, Death, and the Elderly*, ed. M. Pelling and R. M. Smith (London: Routledge, 1991), 194–221; David Thomson, "'I Am Not My Father's Keeper': Families and the Elderly in Nineteenth-Century England," *Law and History Review* 2 (1984): 265–286; Richard M. Smith, "Ageing and Well-Being in

Early Modern England: Pension Trends and Gender Preferences under the English Old Poor Law c. 1650–1800," in *Old Age from Antiquity to Post-Modernity*, ed. Paul Johnson and Pat Thane (London: Routledge, 1998), 64–95; Macfarlane, *Marriage and Love in England*, 105–116; Renzo Derosas and Osamu Saito, "Introduction," in *When Dad Died: Individuals and Families Coping with Family Stress in Past Societies*, ed. Renzo Derosas and Michel Oris (Bern: Lang, 2002), 1–13. See Michel Oris and Emiko Ochiai, "Family Crisis in the Context of Different Family Systems: Frameworks and Evidence on 'When Dad Died,'" in *When Dad Died: Individuals and Families Coping with Family Stress in Past Societies*, ed. Renzo Derosas and Michel Oris (Bern: Lang, 2002), 49, for the argument that late marriage countered "nuclear hardship." Unmarried children played an important role in the economic support of elderly parents, but when these unmarried children reached old age, they stayed completely alone. Thus, those children were "sacrificed twice, early and at the end of life."

53. *Mills v. Wyman*, 20 Mass. 207 (1825). In theory, overseers of the poor could go after children who threw their parents on county poor relief—into the poorhouse. In practice, however, that was a meaningless coercion as even the most formalistic treatise writers recognized. James Schouler, *A Treatise on the Law of the Domestic Relations: Embracing Husband and Wife, Parent and Child, Guardian and Ward, Infancy, and Master and Servant*, 2d ed. (Boston: Little, Brown, 1874), 364–367. See Tapping Reeve, *The Law of Baron and Femme, of Parent and Child, Guardian and Ward, Master and Servant, and of the Powers of the Courts of Chancery; with an Essay on the Terms Heir, Heirs, Heirs of the Body*, ed. Amasa J. Parker and Charles Baldwin (Albany: Gould, 1862), 415. See also "Balance," "Reflections on the Greater Force of Parental Than of Filial Affection," *Weekly Visitor, or Ladies' Miscellany* (American Periodicals Series Online) 2 (June 16, 1804): 291.

54. Steven Ruggles, "Living Arrangements and Economic Well-Being of the Aged in the Past," *Population Bulletin of the United Nations* 42–43 (2001): 141–161; Steven Ruggles, "Multigenerational Families in Nineteenth-Century America," *Continuity and Change* 18(1) (2003): 139–165; Steven Ruggles, "Living Arrangements of the Elderly in America: 1880–1980," in *Aging and Generational Relations over the Life Course: A Historical and Cross-Cultural Perspective*, ed. Tamara K. Hareven (Berlin: de Gruyter, 1996), 254–271. Dillon, *Shady Side of Fifty*.

55. *Updike v. Ten Broeck,* 32 N.J.L. 105, 115 (1866); *Mott v. Mott,* 49 N.J. Eq. 192, 22 A. 997 (1891); *Carlisle v. Fleming,* 1 Harrington 421 (Del. Ch. 1835).

56. Blumenthal, "Deviance of the Will." Testator's freedom is intertwined with that other phrase used to express the significance of individual ownership, Blackstone's notion of "despotic dominion." See A. W. B. Simpson, "Land Ownership and Economic Freedom," in *The State and Freedom of Contract,* ed. Harry N. Scheiber (Stanford: Stanford University Press, 1998), 13–43. Carol M. Rose, "Canons of Property Talk, or, Blackstone's Anxiety," *Yale Law Journal* 108(3) (December 1998): 601–632. Locke described testator's freedom as "the power men generally have to bestow their estates on those who please them best." John Locke, *Two Treatises of Government,* rev. ed., revised and with an introduction by Peter Laslett (New York: New American Library, Mentor, 1963), 2d treatise, paragraph 73. "On those phrases as expressing a distinctively modern understanding of property relations, see John Brewer and Susan Staves, eds., *Early Modern Conceptions of Property* (London: Routledge, 1995); E. P. Thompson, "The Grid of Inheritance," in *Family and Inheritance: Rural Society in Western Europe 1200–1800,* ed. Jack Goody, Joan Thirsk, and E. P. Thompson (Cambridge: Cambridge University Press, 1976); E. P. Thompson, *Customs in Common* (New York: New Press, 1991). In general, see Orin K. McMurray, "Liberty of Testation and Some Modern Limitations Thereon," *Illinois Law Review* 14 (1919–1920): 96–123.

57. Johnson v. Hubbell, 10 N.J. Eq. 332, 66 Am. Dec. 773 (N.J. Ch., 1855). "Johnson v. Hubbell," Records and Briefs, docket #3, p. 52, Record Center Location Numbers: 13-2128-08, C2-0423-17, Court of Chancery (New Jersey State Archives, 1855).

58. Fritz v. Turner, 46 N.J. Eq. 515; 22 A. 125 (Prerogative Ct., 1890). See likewise "McTague v. Finnegan," Record and Briefs, vol. 228 (4), Court of Errors and Appeals (New Jersey State Library, 1896–1897), Brief of James R. English, 3–4. McTague v. Finnegan, 54 N.J. Eq. 454; 35 A. 542 (N.J. Eq., 1896); aff'd 55 N.J. Eq. 588; 39 A. 1114 (N.J. Ct. for the Correction of Errors, 1897).

59. Sloan v. Maxwell, 3 N.J. Eq. 563 (Prerogative Ct., 1831); Van Huss v. Rainbolt, 42 Tenn. 139 (1865). The converse was also true: In New Jersey, a contract to make a will might be enforceable in equity, as it was in *Davison.* However, putting aside a situation such as occurred in *Davison,* where the will writer tried to put his property into other

hands before death, one could not sue for specific performance under a will until the will writer was dead. The fact that the person had written a will that did not make provision for the promisee was not in itself a breach of the promise until the person had died. "No breach can be assured as long as she lives," for it was always possible to write a new will. Galloway v. Eichells, 1 N.J. Super. 584; 62 A. 2d 499 (1948). "Making and Breaking Wills," *Christian Advocate* (American Periodicals Series Online) 57 (Sept. 7, 1882): 1.

60. I have come to think of testator's freedom as central to what Pierre Bourdieu would have called the habitus within which New Jersey family members worked and lived. See Elles Bulder, *The Social Economics of Old Age: Strategies to Maintain Income in Later Life in the Netherlands, 1880–1940* (Amsterdam: Thesis Publishers and Tinbergen Institute, 1993); A. G. Roeber, *Palatines, Liberty, and Property: German Lutherans in Colonial British America* (Baltimore: Johns Hopkins University Press, 1993). Pierre Bourdieu, *The Logic of Practice* (Cambridge: Cambridge University Press, 1990); Pierre Bourdieu, *Masculine Domination*, trans. Richard Nice (Cambridge: Polity, 2001). On the political significance of testator's freedom, see Holly Brewer, "Entailing Aristocracy in Colonial Virginia: 'Ancient Feudal Restraints' and Revolutionary Reform," *William and Mary Quarterly*, 3rd ser. 54(2) (April 1997): 307–346.

61. Waiting too long might not be a disaster for the older person so long as younger caretakers had stayed until the end (and, in the case of older husbands, so long as they had made arrangements for the care of the widows). It was not always an unplanned disaster. Some parents relied on intestacy as a solution to claims they did not want to meet. In addition, sometimes lawyers advised elderly clients to wait and let the child or employee who stayed sue the administrators of the estate by *quantum meruit*. See De Camp v. Wilson, 31 N.J. Eq. 656 (Prerog. Ct., 1879).

62. Haberman v. Kaufer, 70 N.J. Eq. 381; 61 A. 976 (E. & A. 1905). The intention to leave an inheritance to someone was understood as a "merely voluntary" intention, one that could be replaced by a new intention as expressed in someone's final will. Anderson v. Eggers, 61 N.J. Eq. 278 (Ch. 1900); reversed, 63 N.J. Eq. 264; 49 A. 578 (E. & A. 1901). "Anderson v. Eggers," Record and Briefs, vol. 278 (2), Court of Errors and Appeals (New Jersey State Library, 1900/1901). Ackerman v. Ackerman's Executors, 24 N.J. Eq. 315 (Ch. 1873); aff'd 24 N.J. Eq. 585 (E.& A.1874); Fortunel v. Martin, 114 N.J. Eq. 235, 168 A. 393 (E. & A. 1933); "Fortunel

v. Martin," Record and Briefs, vol. 1275 (3), Court of Errors and Appeals (New Jersey State Library, 1933).

63. "Anderson v. Searles," Record and Briefs, vol. 779 (2), Court of Errors and Appeals (New Jersey State Library, 1919), 83–84.

64. Courts presumed that competent participants in the culture understood the freedom of the will writers to change their mind. See Fortunel v. Martin, 114 N.J. Eq. 235, 168 A. 393 (E. & A. 1933), in which the judge wrote the following: "He [the lawyer] knew, and the Martins are presumed to have known, that a verbal agreement of this kind was void under the statute of fraud . . . and that a will could be changed on the whim of the maker." In that case, the Martins were at best semiliterate. "Fortunel v. Martin."

65. 5. Hattersley v. Bissett, 50 N.J. Eq. 577, 25 A. 332 (Ch. 1892), aff'd 51 N.J. Eq. 597, 29 A. 187 (E. & A. 1893). In *Taylor v. Langenbacker,* a thirty-one-year-old nurse married a ninety-two-year-old man. He died in 1912, leaving her a $5 million estate, specifically excluding his relatives. At a family conference, his relatives threatened to bring suit charging the widow with "undue influence." Supposedly, they got her to agree to make a will in favor of her husband's grandchildren. However, when she died, nearly thirty years later, she had not done so. When the grandchildren sued to enforce the agreement she may have made at that conference, the court dismissed their case. She, too, like her long-dead husband, was free to do as she chose. The court also looked with "utmost suspicion" at oral agreements to make a will. 130 N.J. Eq. 59, 21 A.2d 219 (Ch. 1941). See also White v. Risdon, 140 N.J. Eq. 613; 55 A.2d 308 (Ch. 1947); Middleditch v. Williams, 45 N.J. Eq. 726, 729, 17 A. 826, 827 (Prerog. Ct. 1889); Davis v. Elliott, 55 N.J. Eq. 473, 36 A. 1092 (Prerog. Ct. 1897). On charitable giving as another expression of testator's freedom, see Mrs. L. H. Sigourney, *Past Meridian* (New York: Appleton), 208–209. In general see Blumenthal, "Deviance of the Will."

66. Hattersley v. Bissett, 50 N.J. Eq. 577, 25 A. 332 (Ch. 1892), aff'd 51 N.J. Eq. 597, 29 A. 187 (E. & A. 1893). Slack v. Rees, 66 N.J. Eq. 447 (E. & A. 1904); Mott v. Mott, 49 N.J. Eq. 192, 22 A. 997 (Prerog. Ct. 1891). In other cases, testimony would reveal that the child, servant, or adopted child who had received the land or estate had done nothing exceptional to earn a distinctive or enlarged or exclusive share; therefore, it was hard to avoid an implication of "undue influence." In situations in which the testator's intent was unclear, courts and lawyers reinforced the cultural

preference—emblazoned in intestacy statutes—for "equality" between similarly situated siblings. Speer v. Speer, 14 N.J. Eq. 240 (Ch. 1862); Ackerman v. Ackerman's Executors, 24 N.J. Eq. 315 (Ch. 1873); aff'd 24 N.J. Eq. 585 (E. & A. 1873).

Testator's freedom confused Alexis de Tocqueville. In volume 1 of *Democracy in America,* he argued, looking apparently only at statutory intestacy laws, that it was inheritance law that "caused the final advance of equality" in the United States by destroying family solidarity. He argued that U.S. law ordained the "equal sharing of a father's property among his children." One result was the undoing of family feeling. "Now, as soon as landowners are deprived of their strong sentimental attachment to the land, based on memories and pride, it is certain that sooner or later they will sell it, for they have a powerful pecuniary interest in so doing since other forms of investment earn a higher rate of interest, and liquid assets are more easily used to satisfy the passions of the moment." He continued: "Where family feeling is at an end, personal selfishness turns again to its real inclinations." A property owner "thinks about getting the next generation established in life, but nothing further." Finally, "Thus the law of inheritance not only makes it difficult for families to retain the same domains intact but takes away their wish to try to do so and, in a sense, leads them to cooperate with the law in their own ruin." However, in an appendix he acknowledged that equal shares became the rule only for those who did not write wills—through intestacy. "A Frenchman who studies the American law of inheritance is particularly struck to find that our laws on the same subject are infinitely more democratic even than theirs. American law divides a father's property equally, but only in the case where his will is not known: For each man. . . . 'shall have full and free liberty, power and authority to give, dispose, will or devise to any person or persons.' . . . 'by his last will and testament'" (quoting from New York's statute.) The somewhat strained conclusion he drew was that "in France democracy is still busy demolishing; in America it reigns in tranquility over the ruins." Alexis de Tocqueville, *Democracy in America,* ed. J. P. Mayer, trans. George Lawrence (Garden City, N.Y.: Doubleday, 1969), 51–55, 721–722.

67. Hattersley v. Bissett, 50 N.J. Eq. 577 (Ch. 1892); aff'd 51 N.J. Eq. 597 (E. & A. 1893); See Fortunel v. Martin, 114 N.J. Eq. 235, 168 A. 393 (E.& A. 1933).

68. Brick v. Brick, 44 N.J. Eq. 282, 15 A. 58 (E. & A.1888); Will of Eddy, 32 N.J. Eq. 701 (Prerog. Ct. 1880).

69. Middleditch v. Williams, 45 N.J. Eq. 726, 17 A. 826 (Prerog. Ct. 1889). The locus classicus of this rhetoric is the Gibbons case. See Blumenthal, "Deviance of the Will."

70. Waddington v. Buzby, 45 N.J. Eq. 173, 16 A. 690 (E. & A. 1889); Sloan v. Maxwell, 3 N.J. Eq. 563 (Prerog. Ct. 1831); Merrill v. Rush, 33 N.J. Eq. 537 (Prerog. Ct. 1881); Collins v. Johnson, 21 N.J. Eq. 353 (Prerog. Ct.1871), In re Humphrey's Will, 26 N.J. Eq. 513 (Prerog. Ct. 1875), aff'd, 27 N.J. Eq. 567 (E. & A. 1876); Will of Eddy, 32 N.J. Eq. 701 (Prerog. Ct. 1880); Whitenack v. Stryker, 2 N.J. Eq. 8 (Prerog. Ct. 1838); Lunacy Hearing of Abraham Whitenack, 2 N.J. Eq. 252 (Ch. 1834); Will of Lewis, 33 N.J. Eq. 219 (Prerog. Ct. 1880). Isaac F. Redfield, *The Law of Wills: Embracing the Jurisprudence of Insanity; the Making and Construction of Wills; and the Effect of Extrinsic Evidence upon Such Construction. With Forms and Instructions for Preparing Wills*, 4th ed. (Boston: Little, Brown, 1876), 94–106 (quoting Maverick v. Reynolds, 2 Bradf. Sur. 360 and Van Alst v. Hunter, 5 Johns. Ch. 148.).

71. Sloan v. Maxwell, 3 N.J. Eq. 563 (Prerog. Ct. 1831). See also Whitenack v. Stryker, 2 N.J. Eq. 8 (N.J. Prerog. Ct. 1838); in the matter of the alleged lunacy of Abraham Whitenack, 3 N.J. Eq. 252 (Ch. 1834).

72. Stackhouse v. Horton, 15 N.J. Eq. 202 (Prerog. Ct. 1854). See similarly, Will of Gleespin, 26 N.J. Eq. 523 (Prerog. Ct. 1875): "The unreasonableness of his prejudices and the unfairness of his disposition of his property cannot, of themselves alone, avail to induce the court to repudiate his will."

73. Den v. Van Cleve, 5 N.J.L. 589 (E. & A. 1819) (C. J. Kirkpatrick, in dissent).

74. Turner v. Cheesman, 15 N.J. Eq. 243 (Prerog. Ct. 1857).

75. In re Humphrey's Will, 26 N.J. Eq. 513 (Prerog. Ct. 1875); aff'd, 27 N.J. Eq. 567 (E & A. 1876). The headnote to Moore v. Blauvelt, 15 N.J. Eq. 367 (Prerog. Ct. 1862), describes what would be undue influence: "Threats of personal estrangement and non-intercourse, addressed by a child to a dependent parent, or threats of litigation between the children to influence a testamentary disposition of property by the parent, constitute undue influence." See "Will Kindness and Affection Coupled with Importunity Constitute Such Undue Influence as Will Be Sufficient to Set Aside a Will," *Central Law Journal* (American Periodicals Series Online) 62(2) (Jan. 12, 1906): 21–25.

76. Melanie B. Leslie, "Enforcing Family Promises: Reliance, Reciprocity, and Relational Contract," *North Carolina Law Review* 77 (1999): 551–636; Susanna L. Blumenthal, "The Default Legal Person," *UCLA Law Review* 54(5) (June 2007): 1135–1265.

77. Johnson v. Hubbell, 10 N.J. Eq. 332, 66 Am. Dec. 773 (Ch. 1855). On the other hand, see Anderson v. Eggers, 63 N.J. Eq. 264; 49 A. 578 (E. & A. 1901), for the proposition that petitioners had to know that testators had the right to change their will. See generally Bertel M. Sparks, *Contracts to Make Wills: Legal Relations Arising out of Contracts to Devise or Bequeath* (New York: New York University Press, 1956).

78. Amy Dru Stanley, *From Bondage to Contract: Wage Labor, Marriage, and the Market in the Age of Slave Emancipation* (New York: Cambridge University Press, 1998)

79. On the contrast between gifts and contracts, see Roy Kreitner, "The Gift beyond the Grave: Revisiting the Question of Consideration," *Columbia Law Review* 101(8) (December 2001): 1876–1955.

2. The Work of Promises

1. The same questions are pursued through the lens of "bait" in Stewart Macaulay et al., *Contracts: Law in Action* (Charlottesville: Michie, 1992), 250–401. What I am after bears a close relationship to what Jedediah Purdy identifies as the "circumstances of recruitment." Jedediah Purdy, *The Meaning of Property: Freedom, Community, and the Legal Imagination* (New Haven, Conn.: Yale University Press, 2010), 88.

2. Susan B. Carter, Richard L. Ransom, and Roger Ransom, "Family Matters: The Life-Cycle Transition and the Antebellum American Fertility Decline," in *History Matters: Essays on Economic Growth, Technology, and Demographic Change,* ed. Timothy Guinnane (Stanford: Stanford University Press, 2003), 271–329; Roger L. Ransom and Richard Sutch, *Did Rising Out-Migration Cause Fertility to Decline in Antebellum New England? A Life-Cycle Perspective on Old-Age Security Motives, Child Default, and Farm-Family Fertility,* Social Science Working Paper 610 (Pasadena: Division of the Humanities and Social Sciences, California Institute of Technology, 1986); P. David and W. A. Sundstrom, *Bargains, Bequests, and Births: An Essay on Intergenerational Conflict, Reciprocity, and the Demand for Children in Agricultural Societies,* Working Paper no. 12, Stanford Project on the History of Fertility Control (Palo

Alto, Calif.: Department of Economics, Stanford University, 1984); Michael S. Rendall and Raisa A. Bahchieva, "An Old-Age Security Motive for Fertility in the United States?" *Population and Development Review* 24(2) (June 1998): 293–307; J. B. Nugent, "The Old-Age Security Motive for Fertility," *Population and Development Review* 11(1) (1985): 75–97.

3. Lisa Dillon, *The Shady Side of Fifty: Age and Old Age in Late Victorian Canada and the United States* (Montreal: McGill-Queen's University Press, 2008). James W. Davison also conformed to a pattern that Toby Ditz has identified as "favored son plus burdens," with James as the favored son. Toby L. Ditz, *Property and Kinship: Inheritance in Early Connecticut, 1750–1820* (Princeton, N.J.: Princeton University Press, 1986); Susan Grigg, "Women and Family Property: A Review of U.S. Inheritance Studies," *Historical Methods* 22(3) (Summer 1989): 116–122. For an example of another estate shaped by the "favored son plus burdens" pattern, along with a story of a son's failure to satisfy the burdens, see Schanck v. Arrowsmith, 9 N.J. Eq. 314 (E. &. A. 1853).

4. "Waddington v. Buzby," Record and Briefs, vol. 142 (6), Court of Errors and Appeals (New Jersey State Library, 1889), 38. On the broader motives for doing so, see André Burguière and François Lebrun, "The One Hundred and One Families of Europe," in *A History of the Family*, vol. 2, *The Impact of Modernity*, ed. André Burguière, Christiane Klapisch-Zuber, Martine Segalen, and Françoise Zonabend and trans. Sarah Hanbury Tenison (Cambridge: Polity, 1996), 32–33.

5. Maria Ågren, *Domestic Secrets: Women and Property in Sweden, 1600–1857*, Studies in Legal History (Chapel Hill: University of North Carolina Press, 2009); Elles Bulder, *The Social Economics of Old Age: Strategies to Maintain Income in Later Life in the Netherlands, 1880–1940* (Amsterdam: Thesis Publishers and Tinbergen Institute, 1993); David Gaunt, "The Property and Kin Relationships of Retired Families in Northern and Central Europe," in *Family Forms in Historic Europe*, ed. R. Wall, J. Robin, and P. Laslett (Cambridge: Cambridge University Press, 1983), 249–280; David Gaunt, "Rural Household Organization and Inheritance in Northern Europe," in *Family History at the Crossroads*, ed. Tamara Hareven and Andrejs Plakans (Princeton, N.J.: Princeton University Press, 1987), 121–143; Beatrice Moring, "Conflict or Cooperation? Old Age and Retirement in the Nordic Past," *Journal of Family History* 28(2) (April 2003): 231–257; Beatrice Moring, "Systems of Survival: Continuities and Discontinuities after the Death of the

Household Head in Pre-Industrial Finland," in *When Dad Died: Individuals and Families Coping with Family Stress in Past Societies,* ed. Renzo Derosas and Michel Oris (Bern: Lang, 2002), 173–194; Pat Thane, "Old People and Their Families in the English Past," in *Charity, Self-Interest, and Welfare in the English Past,* ed. M. Daunton (New York: St. Martin's, 1996), 75; Richard M. Smith, "Ageing and Well-Being in Early Modern England: Pension Trends and Gender Preferences under the English Old Poor Law c. 1650–1800," in *Old Age from Antiquity to Post-Modernity,* ed. Paul Johnson and Pat Thane (London: Routledge, 1998), 64–95; Jack Goody, "Inheritance, Property, and Women: Some Comparative Considerations," in *Family and Inheritance: Rural Society in Western Europe, 1200–1800,* ed. Jack Goody, Joan Thirsk, and E. P. Thompson (Cambridge: Cambridge University Press, 1976), 10–36; Liam Kennedy, "Farm Succession in Modern Ireland: Elements of a Theory of Inheritance," *Economic History Review* 2d ser. 44 (1991): 477–499; Jill S. Quadagno, *Aging in Early Industrial Society: Work, Family, and Social Policy in Nineteenth-Century England* (New York: Academic Press, 1982); Alan Macfarlane, *Marriage and Love in England* (Oxford: Blackwell, 1986), 105–116; R. M. Smith, "The Manorial Court and the Elderly Tenant in Late Medieval England," in *Life, Death, and the Elderly: Historical Perspectives,* ed. M. Pelling and Richard M. Smith (London: Routledge, 1991), 39–61; Hermann Zeitlhofer, "Headship Succession and Retirement in South Bohemia, 1640–1840," in *Family Welfare: Gender, Property, and Inheritance since the Seventeenth Century,* ed. David R. Green, Contributions in Family Studies (Westport, Conn.: Praeger, 2004), 73–96; Henk de Haan, *In the Shadow of the Tree: Kinship, Property, and Inheritance among Farm Families* (Amsterdam: Het Spinhuis distribution, Nijhoff International, 1994), 88–89. Historians who have studied German and Scandinavian immigration to the United States (mostly the Midwest) have argued that such agreements were the norm throughout the nineteenth century, although they have focused less on the actual care of the elderly than on their general uses in family and community reproduction. They have mobilized these as a way to demarcate the continuing differences between ethnic Germans and Scandinavians and their Anglophone neighbors. Kenneth H. Parsons and Eliot O. Waples, *Keeping the Farm in the Family* (Madison: Wisconsin Agricultural Extension Service, 1945); Carl Wehrwein, "Bonds of Maintenance as Aids in Acquiring Farm Ownership," *Journal of Land and*

Public Utility Economics 8 (1932): 396–403; Robert C. Ostergren, "Land and Family in Rural Immigrant Communities," *Annals of the Association of American Geographers* 71 (1981): 400–411; Jon Gjerde, *The Minds of the West: Ethnocultural Evolution in the Rural Middle West, 1830–1917* (Chapel Hill: University of North Carolina Press, 1997); Sonya Salamon, *Prairie Patrimony: Family, Farming, and Community in the Midwest,* Studies in Rural Culture (Chapel Hill: University of North Carolina Press, 1992). For early America see David and Sundstrom, *Bargains, Bequests, and Births;* William A. Sundstrom and Paul A. David, "Old-Age Security Motives, Labor Markets, and Farm Family Fertility in Antebellum America," *Explorations in Economic History* 25 (1988): 164–197; Gloria L. Main, *Peoples of a Spacious Land: Families and Cultures in Colonial New England* (Cambridge, Mass.: Harvard University Press, 2001); Jack Resch, "Poverty, Patriarchy, and Old Age: The Households of American Revolutionary War Veterans, 1820–1830," in *Power and Poverty: Old Age in the Pre-Industrial Past,* ed. Susannah R. Ottaway, L. A. Botelho, and Katherine Kittredge (Westport: Greenwood, 2002), 31–47. For cautions against making inter vivos transfers to children, see Richard Grassby, *Kinship and Capitalism: Marriage, Family, and Business in the English-Speaking World, 1580–1740* (Cambridge: Cambridge University Press, 2001), 104.

6. See, for example, Butterhof v. Butterhof, 84 N.J.L. 285; 86 A. 394 (E. & A. 1913); "Butterhof v. Butterhof," Record and Briefs, vol. 570 (10), Court of Errors and Appeals (New Jersey State Library, 1913); Ochs v. Ochs, 122 N.J. Eq. 143, 192 A. 502 (E. & A.1937); "Ochs v. Ochs," Record and Briefs, vol. 1456 (3), Court of Errors and Appeals (New Jersey State Library, 1937); Arnwine v. Carroll, 8 N.J. Eq. 620 (Ch. 1852).

7. Schutt v. Missionary Society, 41 N.J. Eq. 115 (Ch. 1886); Kastell v. Hillman, 53 N.J. Eq. 49 (Ch. 1894). See generally A. G. Roeber, *Palatines, Liberty, and Property: German Lutherans in Colonial British America* (Baltimore: Johns Hopkins University Press, 1993). On the other hand, there were instances of a husband leaving a will that left property to children on condition that they provide space and resources for a widow and offered her care. See Schanck v. Arrowsmith, 9 N.J. Eq. 314 (Ch. 1853); Van Duyne v. Van Duyne, 14 N.J. Eq. 49 (Ch. 1861).

8. "Van Duyne (Van Dyne) v. Vreeland," Records and Briefs, vol. 8 (8), Court of Errors and Appeals (New Jersey State Library (also available in manuscript at New Jersey State Archives), 1857), 108–116. David Braham (from old catalog), *Over the Hill to the Poor House: Song and Chorus*

(New York: Pond, 1874); "The Editor's Fireside," *American Farmer; Devoted to Agriculture, Horticulture, etc.* (American Periodicals Series Online) 73 (May 1, 1892): 18; *Warning to the Aged: A Story Founded on Fact,* American Broadsides and Ephemera, ser. 1 (Boston: Clapp, 1820), http://infoweb.newsbank.com/iw-search/we/Evans/?p_product=EAIX &p_theme=eai&p_nbid=R4AX48JCMTMwNDcxMDAyNi4xOT-M3ODU6MToxMzoxMjguMTEyLjcwLjU5&p_action=doc&p_query-name = 21 & p _docref = v2:0F2B1FCB879B099B@EAIX -10F453CD34180F40@2495-10DE1E1677770150@1.

9.   For an example of older people who were caught by having formalized an agreement too soon, see Hill v. Ribble, 132 N.J. Eq. 486, 28 A. 2d 780 (Ch. 1942). Occasionally courts would undo a conveyance on grounds of undue influence. See Chapter 4, this volume.

10. For an example of a father who did commit a promise to writing but managed to sustain the ambiguity, see *Rue v. Rue,* 21 N.J.L. 369 (Sup. Ct.1848).

11. Van Horn v. Demarest, 76 N.J. Eq. 386, 77 A. 354 (Ch. 1910); aff'd 77 N.J. Eq. 264; 77 A. 369 (E. & A. 1910).

12. 76 N.J. Eq. 386, 77 A. 354.

13. When one older neighbor asked Garret how they were doing, Garret replied, "First class. . . . [G]ood workers both of them, John outside and his wife indoors." Several witnesses spoke of John as the only, or the best, farmer in the family. Several witnesses also spoke of how well Louisa took care of the house and the old people. "Van Horn v. Demarest," Record and Briefs, vol. 485 (5), Court of Errors and Appeals (New Jersey State Library, 1910), 280–290.

14. "Van Horn v. Demarest," 200–209, 439–440, 465–472.

15. Ibid., 429–435.

16. Ibid., 146–147, 153, 158, 178–180, 188–192, 242, 279, 289.

17. In 1910 John and Louisa Van Horn were living in Ocean County, New Jersey. http://search.ancestrylibrary.com/cgi-bin/sse.dll?indiv=1&rank =0&db=1910USCenIndex&gsfn=john&gsln=van+horn&gsico=2 %2cUSA&gsipl=33%2cNew+Jersey&sbo=0&ufr=0&wp=4%3b_ 80000002%3b_80000003&srchb=r&prox=1&ti=5542&ti.si=0&o_iid= 21416&o_lid=21416&gss=angs-d&pcat=35&fh=11&h=16660545&re coff=1+3+4&fsk=CIAAHswFGcHc&bsk=&pgoff=.

18. "Updike v. Ten Broeck," Will of John Ten Broeck (1858), Somerset County Wills, Microfilm: Box 903566 103, Orphans Court (New Jersey State Archives, 1866).

19. "Updike v. Ten Broeck," Case Files 1860s, 1532 (New Jersey State Archives, 1866). Updike v. Ten Broeck, 32 N.J.L. 105 (Sup. Ct. 1866).

20. Vreeland v. Vreeland, 48 N.J. Eq. 56 (Ch. 1891); Vreeland v. Vreeland, 49 N.J. Eq. 322 (E & A. 1892); Vreeland v. Vreeland, 53 N.J. Eq. 387 (Ch. 1895).

21. 48 N.J. Eq. 56, 62–3. Two of the deeds were recorded soon thereafter, at least according to the testimony in the case.

22. 48 N.J. Eq. 56 (Ch. 1891); 49 N.J. Eq. 322 (E. & A. 1892).

23. See *The Yearbook of the Holland Society of New York: 1896. In Memoriam.* http://search.ancestrylibrary.com/cgi-bin/sse.dll?db=nyholsoc1896&so=2&rank=0&gsfn=pierson&gsln=vreeland&sx=&=%2c%2c1%2c+%2c%2c%2c1%2c+%2c%2c%2c%2c%2c1%2c+%2c%2c&gs1co=2%2cUSA&gs1pl=1%2cAll+States&year=&yearend=&sbo=0&sbor=&ufr=0&wp=4%3b_80000002%3b_80000003&srchb=r&prox=1&db=&ti=5542&ti.si=0&gss=angs-b.

24. 53 N.J. Eq. 387, 393–396.

25. Van Dyne v. Vreeland, 11 N.J. Eq. 370 (Ch. 1857); Van Duyne v. Vreeland, 12 N.J. Eq. 142 (Ch. 1858); "Van Duyne v. Vreeland," 50. Hendrik Hartog, "Someday All This Will Be Yours: Inheritance, Adoption, and Obligation in Capitalist America," *Indiana Law Journal* 79(2) (Spring 2004): 345–362.

26. Dusenberry v. Ibach's Executors, 99 N.J. Eq. 39, 133 A. 186 (Ch. 1925); aff'd 100 N.J. Eq. 345, 134 A. 916 (E & A.1926). "Dusenberry v. Ibach," Record and Briefs, 1008 (2), Court of Errors and Appeals (New Jersey State Library, 1926), 2–3.

27. Hirschberg v. Horowitz, 105 N.J.L. 210; 143 A. 351 (E. & A. 1928). "Hirschberg v. Horowitz," Record and Briefs, 1072(3), Court of Errors and Appeals (New Jersey State Library, 1928), 18, 22, 24, 56–57.

28. Epstein v. Fleck, 141 N.J. Eq. 486; 57 A.2d 395 (E & A. 1948). "Epstein v. Fleck," Record and Briefs, vol. 1871 (1), Court of Errors and Appeals (New Jersey State Library, 1948), 128, 259–260.

29. Reva Siegel, "Home as Work: The First Woman's Rights Claims concerning Wives' Household Labor, 1850–1880," *Yale Law Journal* 103 (March 1994): 1073–1217; Amy Dru Stanley, *From Bondage to Contract: Wage Labor, Marriage, and the Market in the Age of Slave Emancipation* (New York: Cambridge University Press, 1998).

30. "Dusenberry v. Ibach," Brief of Respondent, St. Joseph's Hospital Edgar-Andre Montigny, *Foisted upon the Government: State Responsibilities, Family Obligations, and the Care of the Dependent Aged in Late*

Nineteenth-Century Ontario (Montreal: McGill-Queen's University Press, 1997), 44–45, 73. See also Jane Grey Swisshelm, *Half a Century*, 2d ed. (Chicago: Jansen, 1880); Tamara Hareven and Kathleen J. Adams, "The Generation in the Middle: Cohort Comparisons in Assistance to Aging Parents in an American Community," in *Aging and Generational Relations over the Life Course: A Historical and Cross-Cultural Perspective*, ed. Tamara K. Hareven (Berlin: de Gruyter, 1996), 272–293.

31. *Ridgway v. English*, 22 N.J.L. 409, 416, 422–423 (Sup. Ct. 1850). It is worth noting that in this case, like several others, it appears that the moving party in the suit was the daughter's new husband. Whether the wife-daughter would have otherwise sued remains unclear.

32. Frances E. Olsen, "The Family and the Market: A Study of Ideology and Law Reform," *Harvard Law Review* 96 (1982–1983): 1497–1578.

33. She married two days after her father's death. "Hattersley v. Bissett," Records and Briefs, Court of Errors and Appeals (New Jersey State Library, 1892), 27–31, 41, 62. Hattersley v. Bissett, 50 N.J. Eq. 577, 25 A. 332 (Ch. 1892), aff'd 51 N.J. Eq. 597, 29 A. 187 (E. & A. 1893). Similarly, see "Petty v. Young," Record and Briefs, vol. 190 (15), Court of Errors and Appeals (New Jersey State Library, 1887); Petty v. Young, 43 N.J. Eq. 654 (E. & A.1887); "Dodson v. Severs," Record and Briefs, vol. 206 (12), vol. 345 (6), vol. 359 (1), Court of Errors and Appeals (New Jersey State Library, 1896); De Camp v. Wilson, 31 N.J. Eq. 656 (Prerog. Ct. 1879).

34. Avner Offer, *The Challenge of Affluence: Self-Control and Well-Being in the United States and Britain since 1950* (New York: Oxford University Press, 2006), 91. Similarly, see Jane Adams, *The Transformation of Rural Life: Southern Illinois, 1890–1990* (Chapel Hill: University of North Carolina Press, 1994); Viviana A. Zelizer, *The Social Meaning of Money* (New York: Basic Books, 1994). These patterns challenge the economic historians' model of a shift from children to other "assets," with the end of the old-age security motive. See Carter, Ransom, and Ransom, "Family Matters"; Ransom and Sutch, *Did Rising Out-Migration Cause Fertility to Decline?;* David and Sundstrom, *Bargains, Bequests, and Births;* Rendall and Bahchieva, "An Old-Age Security Motive for Fertility in the United States"; Nugent, "Old-Age Security Motive for Fertility."

35. "Mulrooney v. O'Keefe," Record and Briefs, 906(6), Court of Errors and Appeals (New Jersey State Library, 1923), 18–35.

36. "Cooper v. Colson," Record and Briefs, vol. 320 (6), Court of Errors and Appeals (New Jersey State Library, 1904), 27,31–37, 42, 46, 66, 70–74.

Cooper v. Colson, 66 N.J. Eq. 328 (E. & A. 1903). See, likewise, Stone v. Todd, 49 N.J.L. 274; 8 A. 300 (Sup. Ct. 1887).

37. De Camp v. Wilson, 31 N.J. Eq. 656 (Prerog. Ct. 1879).

38. We might then consider care a form of "special money." Zelizer, *Social Meaning of Money*.

39. "Cooper v. Colson," 60–61. Once in litigation, though, informally adopted children could become "servants" to justify the payment of compensation. See "Waddington v. Buzby" (with regard to Martha Stewart).

40. There is more to be written about the ways in which will writing became an avocation for older Americans, particularly for older men. See "Van Duyne v. Vreeland" for an extended example. See, likewise, "Anderson v. Searles," Record and Briefs, vol. 779 (2), Court of Errors and Appeals (New Jersey State Library, 1919), 71–82, 94–103.

41. See Van Dyne v. Vreeland, 11 N.J. Eq. 370 (Ch. 1857); Van Duyne v. Vreeland, 12 N.J. Eq. 142 (Ch. 1858); "Van Duyne v. Vreeland." "Anderson v. Searles"; "Van Horn v. Demarest." In a few cases older people were coerced into writing a will or making a deed. See "Anderson v. Eggers," Record and Briefs, vol. 278 (2), Court of Errors and Appeals (New Jersey State Library, 1900/1901); Anderson v. Eggers, 61 N.J. Eq. 278 (Ch. 1900); 63 N.J. Eq. 264; 49 A. 578 (E. & A. 1901). Collins v. Collins, 45 N.J. Eq. 813; 18 A. 860 (E. & A. 1889).

42. Laune v. Chandless, 99 N.J. Eq. 186, 131 A. 634 (Ch. 1926).

43. Turner v. Cheesman, 15 N.J. Eq. 243 (Prerogative Ct., 1857); In re Humphrey's Will, 26 N.J. Eq. 513 (Prerogative Court, 1875); aff'd, Jenkin v. Moore, 27 N.J. Eq. 567 (Ct. of Errors, 1876); Byard v. Conover, 39 N.J. Eq. 244 (Prerogative Ct., 1884); Le Gendre v. Goodridge, 46 N.J. Eq. 419; 15 A. 543 (Equity, 1890).

44. Scott v. Beola, 111 N.J. Eq. 215; 161 A. 822 (Ch. 1932).

45. That was apparently the reason Ruby Prenowitz never wrote a will. "Epstein v. Fleck," 263. See also Klockner v. Green, 54 N.J. 230; 254 A.2d 782 (1969). For the argument that will writing serves as a way to control death, see Thomas L. Shaffer, *Death, Property, and Lawyers* (New York: Dunellen, 1970).

46. "Ehling v. Diebert," Record and Briefs, vol. 1623 (4), Court of Errors and Appeals (New Jersey State Library, 1941), 54–55, 99. Ehling v. Diebert, 129 N.J. Eq. 11; 17 A. 2d 777 (E. & A. 1941), affirming 128 N.J. Eq. 115; 15 A 2d 655 (Ch. 1940). Similarly, Boulanger v. Churchill, 86 N.J. Eq. 96; 97 A. 947 (Ch. 1916).

3. Keeping Them Close

1. "Roberts-Horsfield v. Gedicks," Record and Briefs, vol. 935 (4), Court of Errors and Appeals (New Jersey State Library, 1922), 1–3. Frances stayed in contact with her birth father, who contributed to her support, and she was certainly never formally adopted by her uncle and aunt. At trial, she claimed that her father furnished all of her clothing except what her aunt could get at wholesale through her place of business. When the court asked for the relevance of this, her lawyer Joseph T. Hague replied that he wanted to show that the Gedickses had not fully supported her. The court dismissed the claim: "She lived with her [her aunt] and was raised by her." "Roberts-Horsfield v. Gedicks," 64.

2. "Roberts-Horsfield v. Gedicks," 62–63, 81, 133, 138, 153–155.

3. According to Francis, her aunt made the initial payments, and her aunt's check was put into the record. Evidently her aunt relied on Francis to write her checks for her. "Roberts-Horsfield v. Gedicks," 64–67, 2, 131–132.

4. Ibid., 2–3.

5. Ibid., 3–4, 68, 75.

6. Ibid., 123. See *The Groszmann School for Nervous and Atypical Children: Maximilian P. E. Groszmann, Director* (Plainfield, N.J., 1905).

7. "Roberts-Horsfield v. Gedicks," 68–74.

8. Ibid., 68, 105–108, 97.

9. Ibid., 69–72.

10. Ibid., 138–156.

11. Ibid., 108.

12. Ibid., 74, 75.

13. Ibid., 28–30.

14. Ibid., 68, 74–75, 148. It may be that Blatt knew that her birth father was still a presence in her life.

15. Ibid., 79–80.

16. Ibid., 32, 145, 5.

17. Ibid., 7–8, 15, 36, 80–81.

18. Horsfield v. Gedicks, 94 N.J. Eq. 82, 118 A. 275 (Ch. 1922); aff'd, as Roberts-Horsfield v. Gedicks, 96 N.J. Eq. 384, 124 A. 925 (E & A. 1924).

19. Mrs. L. H. Sigourney, *Past Meridian* (New York: Appleton; Boston: Jewett, 1854), 136–140.

20. William E. Schenck, ed. and comp., *Nearing Home: Comforts and Counsels for the Aged* (Philadelphia: Presbyterian Board of Publication,

1868), 45–52, 115–124, 142–150, 183–191, 288–301, 355–363, 443–449; Rev. S. G. Lathrop, *Fifty Years and Beyond, or, Gathered Gems for the Aged,* with an introduction by Rev. Arthur Edwards (Chicago: Revell, 1881), 151–155; Henry Ward Beecher, "Old Age," *Friends' Intelligencer* (American Periodicals Series Online) 25 (Mar. 14, 1868): 2; S.L.R., "Christian Old Age," *Christian Advocate* (American Periodicals Series Online) 7 (Apr. 1, 1829): 155; Margaret E. White, ed. and comp., *After Noontide* (Boston: Houghton, Mifflin, 1907), 40–42 (quoting Frederick William Faber). See also Charles Wesley's 1788 lyric, which in the mid-nineteenth century was set to music: "In age and feebleness extreme, / Who shall a helpless worm redeem? / Jesus, my only hope Thou art, / Strength of my failing flesh and heart: / O could I catch one smile from Thee, / And drop into eternity!" http://wesley.nnu.edu/wesleyctr/books/2301-2400/HDM2309.pdf (page 22).

21. Lydia Maria Child, *Looking toward Sunset* (Boston: Ticknor and Fields, 1865), 332–33. See also Amelia E. Barr, *Three Score and Ten; a Book for the Aged* (New York: Appleton, 1915); Sigourney, *Past Meridian;* Beecher, "Old Age."

22. Child, *Looking toward Sunset,* 1–36.

23. This was also true in the more orthodox literature. See Schenck, *Nearing Home.*

24. In re Humphrey's Will, 26 N.J. Eq. 513 (Prerog. Ct. 1875); aff'd, 27 N.J. Eq. 567 (E. & A. 1876).

25. Annette B. Weiner, *Inalienable Possessions: The Paradox of Keeping-While-Giving* (Berkeley: University of California Press, 1992); Roy Kreitner, *Calculating Promises: The Emergence of Modern American Contract Doctrine* [electronic and print resource] (Stanford, Calif.: Stanford University Press, 2007).

26. On consideration, see Kreitner, *Calculating Promises.* But see "Fee v. Sharkey," Record and Briefs, vol. 258 (1), Court of Errors and Appeals (New Jersey State Library, 1900); Fee v. Sharkey, 59 N.J. Eq. 284; 44 A. 673 (Ch. 1900); aff'd 60 N.J. 446; 45 A. 1091 (E. & A. 1900) (where a neighboring father and son had not spoken to one another for more than a dozen years).

27. France v. France, 8 N.J. Eq. 650 (Ch. 1852); "France v. France," Records and Briefs, Enrolled Decree: 03, 836, Court of Chancery, New Jersey State Archives (1852).

28. France v. France, 8 N.J. Eq. 650 (Ch. 1852); "France v. France," Enrolled Decree: 03, 836 (New Jersey State Archives, 1852), Court of Chancery.

29. For a portrait of Harmony in Warren County, see the model Harmony Township site at http://www.historicsitesnj.com/sub.cfm?cs=harmony. The Hoff-Vannatta Farmstead, which the town's historical commission is reconstructing, is located very near where Henry Young and his sons farmed, and the buildings on that site are probably very like those found on Jacob Young's farm.

30. *Warren Journal,* Belvidere, Warren County, N.J. (Feb. 8, 1849): "In New York, on Tuesday, 30th ult., by the Rev. McCregh, Jacob Young, of Harmony, Warren County, N.J., to Huldah, daughter of Dr. Wm. Miller, of New York city." http://raub-and-more.com/warrenjournal/journal marriages4849.html.

31. "Young v. Young," Records and Briefs, Docket: v. 11 576 Dis. B #395 Record Center Location Number: 13-2026-21 C1-1622-22, Court of Chancery (New Jersey State Archives, 1879–1893), Bill for relief, filed Apr. 28, 1886.

32. Huldah B. Young, William Young, and New Jersey. Prerogative Court, *William Young, Appellant, and Huldah B. Young, Administratrix of Jacob Young, Deceased, Exceptant, Appellee: On Appeal from Decree of Orphans' Court* (Phillipsburg, N.J.: Warren Democrat Print, 1879). The printing was done at William's request. The murder was covered by newspapers in New Jersey and New York. See *Trenton Daily True American* (Monday, Apr. 10, 1876), p. 3; *Hunterdon Democrat* (Apr. 11, 1876:; "A Wealthy Farmer Murdered," *New York Times* (Apr. 7, 1876); *Hunterdon Democrat* (Apr. 25, 1876): "Suicide in Warren County . . . A miller named Theodore Garren, aged about 50 years, committed suicide by suspending himself by the neck from a beam in his barn, near Hutchinson's station, on the Belvidere Delaware Railroad, Warren County, Monday morning last. A letter written by him was subsequently found, setting forth that the people had suspected him of having been connected with the murder of Jacob Young, which took place in Warren county a few weeks ago." See also http://njsuttonfamily.org/Newspaper/jan1876.htm.

33. He later brought an action against the estate of Jacob Young on a "note" he claimed to have found. See Huldah B Young, William Young, and New Jersey. Prerogative Court, *William Young, Appellant, and Huldah B. Young, Administratrix of Jacob Young, Deceased, Exceptant, Appellee: On Appeal from Decree of Orphans' Court.* Also, *New York Times* (Oct. 28, 1879). On Mackey, see John Whitehead, *The Judicial and Civil History of New Jersey Microform,* vol. 2 (Boston: Boston History, 1897), 427.

34. See *New York Times* (Oct. 28, 1879). Huldah B. Young, William Young, and New Jersey. Prerogative Court, *William Young, Appellant, and Huldah B. Young, Administratrix of Jacob Young, Deceased, Exceptant, Appellee: On Appeal from Decree of Orphans' Court*. Warren County Circuit Court Minutes, microfilm box 960902 125. "Young v. Young." Young v. Young, 32 N.J. Eq. 275 (Ch. 1880); Young v. Young, 45 N.J.L. 197 (Sup. Ct.1883).

35. Huldah's involvement in conflicts over the intergenerational transmission of property extended to her family of origin. See *Hunterdon Democrat* (Oct. 23, 1888).

36. "Young v. Young." According to them, Huldah brought "a small outset," that is, chairs, bureau, and other furniture to the new household. Probably, they added, she also brought about $150 to the marriage, money she had received from her grandfather's estate.

37. Young v. Young, 45 N.J. Eq. 27 (Ch. 1889). Note that, according to the 1880 census, William was in possession of the property.

38. Young v. Young, 51 N.J. Eq. 491 (Ch. 1893). A longer version of the opinion, including a full review of all the evidence, including the varying advice she received from various lawyers, can be found at "Young v. Young," 16b–16f, opinion. In the 1900 census, Benjamin and Dorothea McCord are found living with their children in Newark. See http://search.ancestrylibrary.com/iexec/?htx=View&r=5542&dbid= 7602&iid=004120419_00123&fn=Benjamin&ln=McCord&st=r&ssrc= &pid=65680596.

39. "Danenhauer v. Danenhauer," Record and Briefs, vol. 1160 (6), Court of Errors and Appeals (New Jersey State Library, 1930–1931). See General Alumni Catalogue of the University of Pennsylvania, 1922 (Google Books).

40. "Danenhauer v. Danenhauer," 46.

41. "Danenhauer v. Danenhauer," 18–38. See Record Unit 7335, S. Stillman Berry Papers, 1880–1984, Smithsonian Institution Archives. The online *Eureka Iris Spelling Dictionary* includes many irises identified as produced by Danenhauer, most of which are dated as having been created in 1934. See *Eureka Hosta/Iris Reference Guide*.

42. "Danenhauer v. Danenhauer," 80, 84, 89, 93–94, 97, 101, 105.

43. Danenhauer v. Danenhauer, 105 N.J. Eq. 449, 149 A. 390 (Ch. 1930); aff'd 107 N.J. Eq. 597, 153 A. 906 (E. & A.1931); "Danenhauer v. Danen-

hauer." The terms of the will suggest that it was either a mistake or rewritten in a fit of pique. After the life estates for the two brothers, the will divides the property into two halves, with the $5,000 for Lee's son coming out of one half, but each half ends up going to George's children. One suspects that it had been expected to be written to give one half to George's children and one half to Lee's, but that would still have been unacceptable to Lee.

44. "Danenhauer v. Danenhauer," 66–70, 122. (Note: I have been unable to find anything more on the divorce or on Lee's first wife. A Howard Lee Danenhauer, who was born in Pennsylvania in 1910, would die in Riverside, California, in 1973.)

45. Ibid., 181–187, 122–124.

46. Ibid., 156, 176–177. His wife's testimony repeated the story. She had the mother saying that she "will settle this once for all." The place "will never belong to Katherine." Ibid., 191.

47. Danenhauer v. Danenhauer, 105 N.J. Eq. 449, 149 A. 390 (Ch. 1930).

4. Things Fall Apart

1. "Dodson v. Severs," Record and Briefs, vol. 206 (12), vol. 345 (6), vol. 359 (1), Court of Errors and Appeals (New Jersey State Library, 1896), 130, 154.

2. McTague v. Finnegan, 54 N.J. Eq. 454; 35 A. 542 (Ch. 1896); aff'd 55 N.J. Eq. 588; 39 A. 1114 (E. & A. 1897). "McTague v. Finnegan," Record and Briefs, vol. 228 (4), Court of Errors and Appeals (New Jersey State Library, 1896–1897), 368–371.

3. Cooper v. Colson, 66 N.J. Eq. 328 (E. & A. 1903); Pflu[e]gar v. Pultz, 43 N.J. Eq. 440 (Ch. 1887); Poloha v. Ruman, 137 N.J. Eq. 167, 44 A.2d 411 (E. & A. 1945); Stone v. Todd, 49 N.J.L. 274; 8 A. 300 (Sup. Ct. 1887); Voorhees v. Combs, 33 N.J.L. 482 (Sup. Ct. 1868); 33 N.J.L. 494 (E. & A. 1869); Westcott v. Sheppard, 51 N.J. Eq. 315 (E. & A.1893); affirming Hampton v. Westcott, 49 N.J. Eq. 522 (Ch. 1892).

4. Gay v. Mooney, 67 N.J.L. 27, 50 A. 596 (Sup. Ct. 1901); aff'd 67 N.J.L. 687, 52 A. 1131 (E. & A. 1902); "Gay v. Mooney," Record and Briefs, vol. 292 (7), Court of Errors and Appeals (New Jersey State Library, 1901); Fortunel v. Martin, 114 N.J. Eq. 235, 168 A. 393 (E. & A. 1933); "Fortunel v. Martin," Record and Briefs, vol. 1275 (3), Court of Errors and Appeals (New Jersey State Library, 1933).

5. Winfield v. Bowen, 65 N.J. Eq. 636 (Ch. 1903). Bryson v. McShane, 48 W.V.R. 126 (Sup. Ct. of Appeals, 1900). In one case, a relatively wealthy man who felt abandoned by his family just took to the road. One morning a farmer found him in his barn. He told the farmer that if he would take care of him for the rest of his life, he would give him his whole estate. In that case, the old man followed through on his promise and changed his will. Nonetheless, the farmer lost because the old man's relatives succeeded in demonstrating that he had been subject to "undue influence." Davenport v. Cole, 6 N.J. Eq. 522 (Ch. 1847); aff'd Cole v. Cook's Adm'rs, 6 N.J. Eq. 627 (E. & A. 1848).

6. Steven Ruggles, "Multigenerational Families in Nineteenth-Century America," *Continuity and Change* 18(1) (2003): 139–165; Martha Fineman, *The Neutered Mother, the Sexual Family, and Other Twentieth-Century Tragedies* (New York: Routledge, 1995); Martha Albertson Fineman, *The Autonomy Myth: A Theory of Dependency* (New York: New Press, 2004). On the choice to live with one child's family, see Ely v. Ely, 50 A. 657 (Ch. 1901), aff'd 64 N.J. Eq. 796, 53 A. 1125 (E. & A. 1902).

7. However, see Robert C. Ellickson, *The Household: Informal Order around the Hearth* (Princeton, N.J.: Princeton University Press, 2008).

8. By "love," I mean a historically contingent and complicated set of emotional understandings. See Carol J. Greenhouse, "Lear and Law's Doubles: Identity and Meaning in a Time of Crisis," *Law, Culture, and the Humanities* 2(2) (2006): 239–258; Viviana A. Zelizer, *The Purchase of Intimacy* (Princeton, N.J.: Princeton University Press / Basic Books, 2005).

9. I am grateful to Deborah Becher for suggesting this analysis.

10. This was a danger for nonblood relatives in households as well. See "Frean v. Hudson," Record and Briefs, 636 (5), Court of Errors and Appeals (New Jersey State Library, 1915).

11. Lawrence Cohen, *No Aging in India: Alzheimer's, the Bad Family, and Other Modern Things* (Berkeley: University of California Press, 1998), 51. On the historians' tendency to overstate the agency of those who are their subjects, see Walter Johnson, "On Agency," *Journal of Social History* 37(1) (Fall 2003): 113–124.

12. Mott v. Mott, 49 N.J. Eq. 192, 22 A. 997 (Ch. 1891). Le Gendre v. Byrnes, 44 N.J. Eq. 372 (Ch. 1888); Fritz v. Turner, 46 N.J. Eq. 515; 22 A. 125 (Prerog. Ct. 1890); Slack v. Rees, 66 N.J. Eq. 447 (E. & A. 1904). In Haydock v. Haydock, 33 N.J. Eq. 494 (Prerog. Ct. 1881); affirmed 34 N.J. Eq. 570 (E. & A. 1881), the court applied the same analysis of the parent-child

relationship to the husband-wife relationship. It found undue influence because the wife (who was twenty years younger than her husband) had become the powerful one in the relationship.

13. A number of cases involve younger people who were persuaded to take care of older people by promises of an inheritance and who arrived just as the older person died. Was there still an enforceable contract if no work had been done? *Davis v. Jacoby*, 1 Cal. 2d 370, 34 P. 2d 1026 (1934).

14. Slack v. Rees, 66 N.J. Eq. 447 (E. & A. 1904). The vice chancellor's opinion can be found at "Slack v. Rees," Records and Briefs, vol. 334 (1)*, Court of Errors and Appeals (New Jersey State Library, 1904), 218–220. Henry D. Phillips was an active member of the Trenton bar and a Princeton graduate. He seems to have made a specialty out of helping Civil War veterans obtain their pensions. He also appeared frequently in the federal courts on behalf of veterans. See Phillips v. Ballinger, 37 App. D.C. 46 (App. D.C., 1911), In re O'Shea, 166 F. 180 (1908), U.S. v. Ware, 189 U.S. 507 (1903), U.S. v. Hitchcock, 19 App. D.C. 503 (App. D.C., 1902), Evans, Commissioner of Pensions, v. U.S. ex rel. Phillips, 19 App. D.C. 202 (App. D.C., 1902). *Slack* was not the only time he was singled out by the New Jersey courts for criticism. See Phillips v. Phillips, 81 N.J. Eq. 459, 86 A. 949 (Ch. 1913).

15. "Slack v. Rees," 37, 46–49, 53–70, 89–94.

16. Ella Rees and her husband, Albert, are listed as part of her father's household in the 1880 census and in the 1895 New Jersey census. http://search.ancestrylibrary.com/iexec/?htx=View&r=5542&dbid=6742&iid=4242286-00247&fn=George+H.&ln=Slack&st=r&ssrc=&pid=36375106; http://search.ancestrylibrary.com/iexec/?htx=View&r=5542&dbid=1054&iid=NJV227_89-0276&fn=George+H&ln=Slack&st=r&ssrc=&pid=1010349. "Slack v. Rees," 50, 57–68, 76–79, 119–120, 160–175.

17. "Slack v. Rees," 37–56.

18. Ibid., 73, 68, 178, 87. The 1900 census has Albert, Ella, and their daughter, Caroline, living apart from Ella's parents.

19. Ibid., 120, 73–82.

20. Ibid., 45–49, 94.

21. Ibid., 75–76.

22. Ibid., 83.

23. Claffey v. Ledwith, 56 N.J. Eq. 333, 38 A. 433 (Prerog. Ct. 1897). In this case, as in several others, issues of competence and undue influence were merged and confused.

24. Ibid. At the same time that this suit was going on, Mary Ledwith, the daughter-in-law, sued in New York for partition of the real estate located there. There was a jury verdict in her favor, and Annie Claffey's appeal was denied. Once again, a court ruled that the will was caused by Annie's undue influence. Ledwith v. Claffey, 18 A.D. 115 (App. Div., 1897); aff'd 18 A.D. 628; 45 N.Y.S. 1143 (1897). I am grateful to Risa Goluboff for suggesting this analysis.

25. "Waldron v. Davis," Record and Briefs, vol. 338 (3), Court of Errors and Appeals (New Jersey State Library, 1904), 9–17, 39. Waldron v. Davis, 70 N.J.L. 627; 58 A. 293 (E. & A. 1904).

26. Garretson v. Appleton, 58 N.J.L. 386 (E. & A.1895); "Garretson v. Appleton," Record and Briefs, vol. 205 (11), Court of Errors and Appeals (New Jersey State Library, 1895), 9. See Schanck v. Arrowsmith, 9 N.J. Eq. 314 (Ch. 1853), in which a widow had to leave her son's home when he became intemperate.

27. Collins v. Collins, 45 N.J. Eq. 813; 18 A. 860 (E.& A.1889). To the court, this language showed that father and son had dealt with each other as fully contractual actors. "No presumption of undue influence should rest upon the fact of family relationship in view of such language— more brutal frankness could not have existed between total strangers."

28. Michael Grossberg has identified such practices as expressions of a "judicial patriarchy." Michael Grossberg, *Governing the Hearth: Law and the Family in Nineteenth-Century America* (Chapel Hill: University of North Carolina, 1985).

29. Mott v. Mott, 49 N.J. Eq. 192, 22 A. 997 (Ch. 1891.). Other important cases include Soper v. Cisco, 95 A. 1016, 85 N.J. Eq. 165 (E. & A. 1915) and In re Fulper's Estate, 132 A. 834, 99 N.J. Eq. 293 (Prerog. Ct.1926).

5. A Life Transformed

1. These arguments were all made (unsuccessfully) by the brothers of the daughter who had been given a deed by their father in "Hattersley v. Bissett," Records and Briefs, Court of Errors and Appeals (New Jersey State Library, 1892). Hattersley v. Bissett, 50 N.J. Eq. 577, 25 A. 332 (Ch. 1892), aff'd 51 N.J. Eq. 597, 29 A. 187 (E. & A. 1893). See, likewise, "Petty v. Young," Record and Briefs, vol. 190 (15), Court of Errors and Appeals (New Jersey State Library, 1887). Petty v. Young, 43 N.J. Eq. 654 (E. &

A.1887). "Dodson v. Severs," Record and Briefs, vol. 206 (12), vol. 345 (6), vol. 359 (1), Court of Errors and Appeals (New Jersey State Library, 1896).

2. In the real world of nineteenth- and early twentieth-century lawyering, no lawyer could have spent this much time and effort, certainly not for mundane legal problems of relatively little monetary value. To do so would have been a recipe for bankruptcy. In addition, much of what this chapter explores might have seemed too obvious to need attention or exploration because the issues would have belonged to realms of tacit knowledge and thus needed little, if any, explication.

3. For an introduction to the national story, see Lawrence M. Friedman, *A History of American Law* (New York: Simon and Schuster, 2005), 97–99. Federal Writers Project, *New Jersey, a Guide to Its Present and Past* (New York: Viking, 1939), 165–166. For the text of the 1844 constitution, see http://en.wikisource.org/wiki/New_Jersey_Constitution_of_1844#JUDICIARY. On the early history of "specific performance," see Zechariah Chafee Jr. and Sidney Post Simpson, *Cases on Equity, Jurisdiction, and Specific Performance* (Cambridge, Mass.: Editors, 1934), 245–247.

4. Scott v. Beola, 111 N.J. Eq. 215, 161 A. 822 (Ch. 1932); Burdick v Grimshaw, 113 N.J. Eq. 591, 602 A. 186 (Ch. 1933).

5. Philip Hamburger, "The Conveyancing Purposes of the Statute of Frauds," *American Journal of Legal History* 27(4) (October 1983): 354–385. The statute was in its inception a form of state building, directed to achieve royal control over land transactions at a time when the early modern land market was growing. Its explicit policy goal was to shape the behavior of those who conveyed land. The statute, which was taken verbatim from the English statute, was first enacted in New Jersey in 1794. See New Jersey Law Revision Commission, *Report and Recommendations relating to the Statute of Frauds* (Newark: Author, 1998).

6. John Norton Pomeroy, *A Treatise on the Specific Performance of Contracts as It Is Enforced by Courts of Equitable Jurisdiction in the United States of America*, 3d ed., ed. John Norton Pomeroy Jr. and John C. Mann (Albany: Banks, 1926), 234. The reasons for Southern hostility to the doctrine of part performance deserve further study. "Part performance" created something like a labor foundation for entitlement, work producing a right to property. One can well imagine that slave owners in the South would have found that entirely untenable.

7. Joseph Story, *Commentaries on Equity Jurisprudence as Administered in England and America*, 2d ed. (London: Maxwell, 1839), 434–435.

8. Causten Browne, *A Treatise on the Construction of the Statute of Frauds, as in Force in England and the United States, with an Appendix, Containing the English and American Statutes*, 4th ed. (Boston: Little, Brown, 1880), 524–525 (quoting William Roberts, *A Treatise on the Statute of Frauds, as It Regards Declarations in Trust, Contracts, Surrenders, Conveyances, and the Execution and Proof of Wills and Codicils: To Which Is Prefixed, a Systematic Dissertation upon the Admissibility of Parol and Extrinsic Evidence, to Explain and Controul Written Instruments* [London: Butterworth, 1805], 135). Pomeroy, *Specific Performance*, 108 (259). Roscoe Pound, "The Progress of the Law, 1918–1919 (Concluded)," *Harvard Law Review* 33 (1920): 929, 933–950.

9. Henry Reed, *A Treatise on the Law of the Statute of Frauds, and of Other Like Enactments in Force in the United States of America, and in the British Empire* (Philadelphia: Kay and Brother, 1884),vol. 2, 175–176; Browne, *Statute of Frauds*, 146, 507–535. Some judges and treatise writers believed that the good that the statute produced was dependent on "the understanding that the doctrine of part performance" went with it. One needed the one to prevent the misuse of the other. John Norton Pomeroy and Spencer W. Symons, *A Treatise on Equity Jurisprudence as Administered in the United States of America Adapted for All the States and to the Union of Legal and Quitable Remedies under the Reformed Procedure* (San Francisco: Bancroft-Whitney, 1941), 1056–1057; Reed, *Treatise on the Law*, vol. 1, 14–16; Umberto-Igor A. Stramignoni, "At the Dawn of Part Performance: A Hypothesis," *Journal of Legal History* 18(2) (August 1997): 32–46. One of the drafters of the original English statute was the chancellor of England at the time. From that Stramignoni infers that equity was always intended as a counter to or a brake on rigorous enforcement of the statute. See Joseph Story, *Commentaries on Equity Jurisprudence as Administered in England and America*, 14th ed., ed. W. H. Lyon Jr. (Boston: Little, Brown, 1918), 416.

10. Pound, "Progress of the Law"; Pomeroy, *Specific Performance*, 238–239. One treatise included all of the negative commentary on the malevolent consequences of the doctrine of part performance in one volume and then explained to lawyers how to use the doctrine in the next. Lawyers obviously carefully selected the part they drew on, depending on which side they found themselves representing. Reed, *Treatise on the Law*, vols. 1 and 2.

11. Johnson v. Hubbell, 10 N.J. Eq. 332, 66 Am. Dec. 773 (Ch. 1855); Van Dyne v. Vreeland, 11 N.J. Eq. 370 (Ch. 1857); Van Duyne v. Vreeland, 12 N.J. Eq. 142 (Ch. 1858); Davison v. Davison, 13 N.J. Eq. 246 (Ch. 1861). See Pomeroy, *Specific Performance,* 276–283. Note that in *France v. France* the Statute of Frauds was not raised.

12. Eyre v. Eyre, 19 N.J. Eq. 42, 102 (Ch. 1868); Petrick v. Ashcroft, 19 N.J. Eq. 339 (Ch. 1868); aff'd as modified, 20 N.J. Eq. 198 (E. & A. 1869). Fifteen years later, two brothers sued to gain title to land that their father had promised them. The lawyers for the brothers worked to analogize their case to the situation in *Davison v. Davison* and other early New Jersey equity cases in which "part performance" had proven the existence of a contract. But the vice chancellor was unpersuaded. Larison v. Polhemus, 36 N.J. Eq. 506 (Ch. 1883); aff'd, 39 N.J. Eq. 303 (E. & A. 1884).

13. Morton J. Horwitz, *The Transformation of American Law, 1870–1960: The Crisis of Legal Orthodoxy* (New York: Oxford University Press, 1992); Roy Kreitner, *Calculating Promises: The Emergence of Modern American Contract Doctrine* (electronic resource) (Stanford, Calif.: Stanford University Press, 2007); Thomas C. Grey, "Langdell's Orthodoxy," *University of Pittsburgh Law Review* 45(1) (Fall 1983): 1–54.

14. According to Pomeroy, "Part performance . . . assumes such a change in the relation of the parties that a restoration of their previous condition is impracticable, and a refusal to go on and complete the engagement would be a virtual fraud upon one of the parties." Pomeroy, *Specific Performance,* 101 (245).

15. Haberman v. Kaufer, 70 N.J. Eq. 381, 385; 61 A. 976 (Ch. 1905). See also Haberman v. Kaufer, 60 N.J. Eq. 271, 47 A. 48 (Ch. 1900). In this case, the complainant was the residual legatee of the estate, but he went to equity to complain that if the estate paid the legacies his parents had specified, there would not be enough left for him. He lost.

16. "Van Duyne (Van Dyne) v. Vreeland," Records and Briefs, vol. 8 (8), Court of Errors and Appeals (New Jersey State Library, 1857), 13–26 (also available in ms. at New Jersey State Archives); Hendrik Hartog, "Someday All This Will Be Yours: Inheritance, Adoption, and Obligation in Capitalist America," *Indiana Law Journal* 79(2) (Spring 2004): 345–362.

17. Van Dyne v. Vreeland, 11 N.J. Eq. 370, 379–380 (Ch. 1857).

18. 12 N.J. Eq. 142 (Ch. 1858). Note that the chancellor found the hardest part of the case the actual construction of the remedy since John Vreeland was still alive. It helped that Vreeland's stepdaughter and stepson-in-law were not bona fide purchasers without notice.

19. See, for example, McTague v. Finnegan, 54 N.J. Eq. 454; 35 A. 542 (Ch. 1896); aff'd 55 N.J. Eq. 588; 39 A. 1114 (E. & A. 1897). The trial in McTague is a repository of the confusions in the late nineteenth century about the meaning of "adoption." "McTague v. Finnegan," Record and Briefs, vol. 228 (4), Court of Errors and Appeals (New Jersey State Library, 1896–1897). The decision in the case might be understood as a reversal of *Van Duyne* at least on the question of the significance of adoption. However, see Van Tine v. Van Tine, 15 A. 249 (Ch. 1888). For the later cases see Dusenberry v. Ibach's Executors, 99 N.J. Eq. 39, 133 A. 186 (Ch. 1925); aff'd 100 N.J. Eq. 345, 134 A. 916 (E. & A.1926); Hirschberg v. Horowitz, 105 N.J.L. 210; 143 A. 351 (E. & A. 1928); Di Girolamo v. Di Matteo, 108 N.J. Eq. 592 (Ch. 1931); Scott v. Beola, 111 N.J. Eq. 215; 161 A. 822 (Ch. 1932); Elmer v. Wellbrook, 110 N.J. Eq. 15; 158 A. 760 (Ch. 1932); Burdick v. Grimshaw, 113 N.J. Eq. 591, 168 A. 186 (Ch. 1933). Hartog, "Someday All This Will Be Yours"; Claudia Nelson, *Little Strangers: Portrayals of Adoption and Foster Care in America, 1850–1929* (Bloomington: Indiana University Press, 2003).

20. For the vice chancellor's summary, see "Cooper v. Colson," Record and Briefs, vol. 320 (6), Court of Errors and Appeals (New Jersey State Library, 1904), 120–122. In the 1900 census, when Sayre and Colson were living in Woodstown, she is listed as the "head" of the household: http://search.ancestrylibrary.com/iexec/?htx=View&r=5542&dbid=7602&iid=004119929_00823&fn=Margaret+H&ln=Sayre&st=r&ssrc=&pid=32022094. For the boom in the marl business, see the *New York Times* (July 2, 1869), 2.

21. Cooper v. Colson, 66 N.J. Eq. 328 (E. & A. 1903).

22. 65 N.J. Eq. 636 (Ch. 1903).

23. Laune v. Chandless, 99 N.J. Eq. 186, 131 A. 634 (Ch. 1926). Her relationship to Chandless was not mentioned in the opinion, but she was identified as a sister-in-law in the 1910 census. See http://search.ancestrylibrary.com/cgi-bin/sse.dll?db=1910USCenIndex&indiv=try&h=16476037.

24. Boulanger v. Churchill, 86 N.J. Eq. 96; 97 A. 947 (Ch. 1916). See, likewise, McNamara v. Bohn, 108 A. 764 (Ch. 1919).

25. Johnson v. Wehrle, 9 N.J. Misc. 939 (Ch. 1931). See, likewise, White v. Risdon, 140 N.J. Eq. 613; 55 A.2d 308 (Ch. 1947). Pound, "Progress of the Law."

26. We first met Bertha Kulat, the butcher's widow, in the context of her unwillingness or inability to make a will in time. The reconstruction

that follows is drawn from "Ehling v. Diebert," Record and Briefs, vol. 1623 (4), Court of Errors and Appeals (New Jersey State Library, 1941).

27. On Hershenstein, see http://www.cityofjerseycity.org/hague/boss/the-boss8_2.shtml. Hague v. C.I.O., 337 US 541 , 543 (1949). On Bertha Kulat's net worth, see "Ehling v. Diebert," Bill of Complaint, 7, 141.

28. "Ehling v. Diebert," 1–15.

29. Drewen was the Hudson County prosecutor. It would be possible to read the lawyers' contrasting arguments through a political lens intertwined with attitudes toward drink.

30. "Ehling v. Diebert," 15–23.

31. Ibid., 45–74.

32. Ibid., 110, 155, 186.

33. Ehling v. Diebert, 128 N.J. Eq. 115; 15 A 2d 655 (N.J. Eq., 1940).

34. Hershenstein's brief began with a preliminary plea that probably revealed his own doubts about his ability to win the case for specific performance. He read the vice chancellor's dismissal as founded on two merged conclusions: first, that the proof presented did not carry the burden necessary to establish an agreement between Bertha Kulat and Frank Ehling, and, second, that there was insufficient "performance" to take the agreement out of the operation of the Statute of Frauds. Hershenstein wanted the Court of Errors to distinguish and separate those two in order to save the possibility that, even if he ultimately lost on the equity argument for specific performance, he could still bring a later case for damages *quantum meruit*.

35. "Ehling v. Diebert," Brief of Complainant-Appellant.

36. Ibid., Brief of Defendant-Appellee. Ehling v. Diebert, 129 N.J. Eq. 11; 17 A. 2d 777 (E. & A. 1941).

37. See www.familysearch.org/Eng/Search/AF/individual_record.asp?recid=13450907&lds=0&region=-1&regionfriendly=&frompage=99.

6. Compensations for Care

1. See John Bouvier, *A Law Dictionary,* 1st ed. (Philadelphia: Lippincott, 1856).

2. W. W. Thornton, "Quantum Meruit—Services," *Central Law Journal* 20(17) (1885): 326; Gavin Wright, *Slavery and American Economic Development* (Baton Rouge: Louisiana State University Press, 2006), 52–55.

3. Updike v. Titus, 13 N.J. Eq. 151 (Ch. 1860).
4. John D. Lawson, *The Law of Presumptive Evidence, including Presumptions Both of Law and of Fact, and the Burden of Proof Both in Civil and Criminal Cases, Reduced to Rules* (Littleton, Colo.: Rothman, 1982), 75–76.
5. This implication did not mean that the worker would actually be paid. As of the mid-nineteenth century, the core unsettled legal question in what was still called the "law of master and servant" was whether workers who quit before the end of their term were entitled to wages for the time actually worked. Robert J. Steinfeld, *The Invention of Free Labor: The Employment Relation in English and American Law and Culture* (Chapel Hill: University of North Carolina Press, 1991), 147–172; Christopher L. Tomlins, *Law, Labor, and Ideology in the Early American Republic* (New York: Cambridge University Press, 1993), 273–279; Peter Karsten, *Heart versus Head: Judge-Made Law in Nineteenth-Century America* (Chapel Hill: University of North Carolina Press, 1997), 157–189; Robert J. Steinfeld, *Coercion, Contract, and Free Labor in the Nineteenth Century* (Cambridge: Cambridge University Press, 2001), 295–311; James D. Schmidt, *Free to Work: Labor Law, Emancipation, and Reconstruction, 1815–1880* (Athens: University of Georgia Press, 1998), 203–205.
6. For expressions of the rhetoric, usually with regard to the uncompensated labors of wives and young children, see Reva Siegel, "Home as Work: The First Woman's Rights Claims concerning Wives' Household Labor, 1850–1880," *Yale Law Journal* 103 (March 1994): 1073–1217; Jeanne Boydston, *Home and Work: Housework, Wages, and the Ideology of Labor in the Early Republic* (New York: Oxford University Press, 1990); Amy Dru Stanley, *From Bondage to Contract: Wage Labor, Marriage, and the Market in the Age of Slave Emancipation* (New York: Cambridge University Press, 1998); Barbara Ryan, *Love, Wages, Slavery: The Literature of Servitude in the United States* (Urbana: University of Illinois Press, 2006); Holly Brewer and Omohundro Institute of Early American History and Culture, *By Birth or Consent: Children, Law, and the Anglo-American Revolution in Authority* (Chapel Hill: Published for the Omohundro Institute of Early American History and Culture, Williamsburg, Va., by the University of North Carolina Press, 2005).

7. 15 N.J.L. 27 (Sup. Ct. 1835). There is a largely unstudied case literature on responsibility for funerals and burials.

8. Laura F. Edwards, *The People and Their Peace: Legal Culture and the Transformation of Inequality in the Post-Revolutionary South* (Chapel Hill: University of North Carolina Press, 2009).

9. Williams v. Barnes, 14 N.C. 348 (1832).

10. Hauser v. Sain, 74 N.C. 552 (1876).

11. Guild v. Guild, 32 Mass. 129, 133 (1833).

12. Ridgway v. English, 22 N.J.L. 409, 422–423 (Sup. Ct., 1850).

13. "Petty v. Young," Record and Briefs, vol. 190 (15), Court of Errors and Appeals (New Jersey State Library, 1887), Appellant's Points, 3. This was once again a case coming out of little Harmony Township in Warren County.

14. Carol Sanger and Eleanor Willemsen, "Minor Changes: Emancipating Children in Modern Times," *Michigan Journal of Law Reform* 25 (1991): 239–355; Howard P. Chudacoff, *How Old Are You? Age Consciousness in American Culture* (Princeton, N.J.: Princeton University Press, 1989).

15. Petty v. Young, 43 N.J. Eq. 654 (E. & A. 1887).

16. Reinhart Koselleck, *The Practice of Conceptual History: Timing History, Spacing Concepts* (Stanford, Calif.: Stanford University Press, 2002), 248–255; Brewer and Omohundro Institute, *By Birth or Consent*; André Burguière and François Lebrun, "The One Hundred and One Families of Europe," in *A History of the Family*, vol. 2, *The Impact of Modernity*, ed. André Burguière, Christiane Klapisch-Zuber, Martine Segalen, and Françoise Zonabend and trans. Sarah Hanbury Tenison (Cambridge: Polity, 1996), 11–94.

17. Koselleck, *Practice of Conceptual History*. On manumission, see Orlando Patterson, *Freedom* (New York: Basic Books, 1991). Some sons and daughters had always defied parental authority, for example, by running away. However, only in the eighteenth century were such acts reinterpreted as acts of self-emancipation as opposed to acts of insubordination or petit treason. In that sense, in running away from his apprenticeship in Boston and achieving independence in Philadelphia, Benjamin Franklin was doing something relatively novel.

18. Sons or daughters who went off to find work or to live with others were presumptively emancipated from their parents. Parents were usually

no longer responsible for their support. However, as a correlative matter, the parents would also have lost a right to demand the children's wages from their employers. See Wood v. Gill, 1 N.J.L. 512 (1795). Michael Grossberg, *Governing the Hearth: Law and the Family in Nineteenth-Century America* (Chapel Hill: University of North Carolina, 1985). James D. Schmidt, "'Restless Movements Characteristic of Childhood': The Legal Construction of Child Labor in Nineteenth-Century Massachusetts," *Law and History Review* 23(2) (Summer 2006): 315–350.

19. Overseers of the Poor of Alexandria v. Overseers of the Poor of Bethlehem, 16 N.J.L. 119 (Sup. Ct. 1837).

20. Ridgway v. English, 22 N.J.L. 409 (Sup. Ct. 1850).

21. On presumptions see Lawson, *Presumptive Evidence;* Theophilus Parsons, *The Law of Contracts,* 7th ed., ed. William V. Kellen (Boston: Little, Brown, 1883), vol. 2, 46–48; James Schouler, *A Treatise on the Law of the Domestic Relations: Embracing Husband and Wife, Parent and Child, Guardian and Ward, Infancy, and Master and Servant,* 2d ed. (Boston: Little, Brown, 1874), 372; Coley v. Coley, 14 N.J. Eq. 350 (Ch. 1862).

22. Brown v. Ramsay, 29 N.J.L. 117 (Sup. Ct. 1860) (citing *Ridgway* and Prickett v. Prickett's Administrators, 20 N.J. Eq. 478 [Prerog. Ct. 1869]).

23. "Updike v. Ten Broeck," Case Files 1860s, 1532 (New Jersey State Archives, 1866). When Van Dyke had filed suit, his lawyer had asked for $7,500: $2,000 for "work and labor . . . done, performed, and bestowed in and about" John's business, $1,000 that Van Dyke had supposedly given John to use during his lifetime, $1,000 that John had received during his life for the use of Van Dyke, and $1,500 in interest accumulated in the years since Van Dyke had left the farm, plus $2,000 on account between them. Given that so much of the claim was clearly founded on debts that would have been beyond the statute of limitations, Van Dyke was probably lucky to be awarded $1,100.

24. Updike v. Ten Broeck, 32 N.J.L. 105, 115 (Sup. Ct. 1866).

25. Brown v. Ramsay, 29 N.J.L. 117 (Sup. Ct. 1860).

26. Gardner's Administrator v. Schooley, 25 N.J. Eq. 150 (Ch. 1874). See likewise, Brown v. Welsh, 27 N.J. Eq. 429 (Ch. 1876); Miller v. Sauerbier, 30 N.J. Eq. 71 (Ch. 1878).

27. De Camp v. Wilson, 31 N.J. Eq. 656 (Prerog. Ct. 1879).

28. See Brewer and Omohundro Institute, *By Birth or Consent.*

29. See Linda Gordon, *Heroes of Their Own Lives* (New York: Vintage, 1988); David S. Tanenhaus, "Between Dependency and Liberty: The Conundrum of Children's Rights in the Gilded Age," *Law and History Review* 23(2) (Summer 2005): 351–385; Michael Grossberg, "A Protected Childhood: The Emergence of Child Protection in America," in *American Public Life and the Historical Imagination*, ed. Wendy Gamber, Michael Grossberg, and Hendrik Hartog (Notre Dame, Ind.: University of Notre Dame Press, 2003), 213–239; Lea VanderVelde, "The Legal Ways of Seduction," *Stanford Law Review* 48(4) (April 1996): 817–901; Jane Larson, "'Even a Worm Will Turn at Last': Rape Reform in Late Nineteenth-Century America," *Yale Journal of Law and the Humanities* 9, no. 1 (Winter 1997): 1–72.

30. Dodson v. Severs, 54 N.J. Eq. 305; 38 A. 28 (Ch. 1896) (but actually July 1894). Reversed on other grounds, Severs v. Dodson, 53 N.J. Eq. 633; 33 A. 7 (E. & A. 1895). My reconstruction of the story is drawn from "Dodson v. Severs," Record and Briefs, vol. 206 (12), vol. 345 (6), vol. 359 (1), Court of Errors and Appeals (New Jersey State Library, 1896). Other moments in the litigation can be found at Dodson v. Taylor, 53 N.J.L. 200; 21 A. 293 (Sup. Ct. 1890); Dodson v. Taylor, 56 N.J.L. 11; 28 A. 316 (Sup. Ct. 1893); Dodson v. Severs, 52 N.J. Eq. 611; 30 A. 477 (Ch. 1894); Dodson v. Severs, 53 N.J. Eq. 347; 33 A. 388 (Ch. 1895). On early Trenton potters, including James Taylor and Isaac Davis, see http://www.ellarslie.org/about_pottery.htm; http://www.potteriesoftrentonsociety.org/publish/Vol%207%20Iss%203%20September%202006%20newslette.pdf. I have not been able to establish when Isaac Davis died, but his absence from the trial, combined with the fact that Ella's siblings and parents were understood as the beneficiaries of her estate, require the conclusion that he had died before then.

31. There was litigation in the Mercer County Orphan's Court between Ella and James Taylor's children, including Ella's parents. James Taylor's children had challenged his will, alleging undue influence. Their "caveat" had eventually been withdrawn. "Dodson v. Severs," 60.

32. Ibid., 131–134, 73–76, 10, 60, 72, 150–159.

33. Ibid., 35–43, 156, 162–168, 178.

34. Dodson v. Severs, 54 N.J. Eq. 305; 38 A. 28 (Ch. 1896), quoting from Disbrow v. Durand, 54 N.J.L. 343, 24 A. 545 (Ch. 1892).

35. In the final act of this drama, the Court for the Correction of Errors decided that Taylor's responsibility for Davis's debt was too attenuated

to prevent him from making a gift to his granddaughter, and it reversed the vice chancellor on those narrow grounds. 53 N.J. Eq. 633; 34 A. 7 (E. & A. 1895).

36. This understanding of the modern, nonagricultural household is entwined with emergent understandings of modern marriage and heterosexuality. See Nancy Cott, *Public Vows: A History of Marriage and the Nation* (Cambridge, Mass.: Harvard University Press, 2000); Margot Canaday, *The Straight State: Sexuality and Citizenship in Twentieth-Century America* (Princeton, N.J.: Princeton University Press, 2011). It also expresses the conventional wisdom of kinship. See David M. Schneider, *American Kinship: A Cultural Account* (Chicago: University of Chicago Press, 1968). The actual diversity of kinship and households in modern America was suppressed. See Hendrik Hartog, "Romancing the Quotation," in *Law in the Liberal Arts,* ed. Austin Sarat (Ithaca, N.Y.: Cornell University Press, 2004).

37. "Disbrow v. Durand," Record and Briefs, vol. 169 (4 and 5), Court of Errors and Appeals (New Jersey State Library, 1892), 1–4. Any possible recovery would be limited by the statute of limitations to the last six years of her brother's life. Disbrow v. Durand, 54 N.J.L. 343, 24 A. 545 (Ch. 1892). She had married George Washington Disbrow in 1841. Disbrow had died in 1842, leaving her with one son. Sarah had then lived with her mother until her mother's death, when she moved to Smith Noe's house.

38. "Disbrow v. Durand," 3–4.

39. Ibid., 2, 4–9, 14.

40. In a slightly later case, a sister claimed she had been defrauded by her brother because she had trusted him as a brother should be trusted. However, the court was unconvinced and held that the sister had a husband, in whom she ought properly to put her trust and who was there to advise her. The situation between the siblings was "the ordinary one" between parties "competent to contract" with one another. *Lozier v. Hill,* 68 N.J. Eq. 300, 59 A. 234 (Ch. 1904). For a case in which *Disbrow* was invoked but the court allowed compensation to the sister who had cared for her brother, see *Steuler v. Hansen,* 6 N.J. Misc. 208, 140 A. 401 (Sup. Ct. 1928).

41. In re Mullen's Estate, 134 A. 360 (Essex Orphans 1924).

42. See In re McDonald's Estate, 4 N.J. Misc. 542; 133 A. 884 (Prerog. Ct. 1926). By the twentieth century, the New Jersey Supreme Court found

it easy to hold that farming did not constitute such services. Waker v. Bergen, 4 N.J. Misc. 332, 132 A. 669 (Sup. Ct. 1926).

43. "Gay v. Mooney," Record and Briefs, vol. 292 (7), Court of Errors and Appeals (New Jersey State Library, 1901), 8.

44. Ibid., 12–16.

45. Ibid., 49–57.

46. Ibid., Brief for Plaintiff in Error, Brief for Defendant in Error. Gay v. Mooney, 67 N.J.L. 27, 50 A. 596 (Sup. Ct. 1901); aff'd 67 N.J.L. 687, 52 A. 1131 (E. & A. 1902).

47. "Frean v. Hudson," Record and Briefs, 636 (5), Court of Errors and Appeals (New Jersey State Library, 1915), Appellant's Brief, 70, 71, 87–89. Statutes of limitations precluded her from asking for more than six years' worth of work.

48. Ibid., 5–6, 8–9 She was listed as a part of Cornelia's household in both the 1900 and 1910 censuses.

49. Ibid., 12–47.

50. Ibid., 48–59.

51. Ibid., 65–106.

52. Frean v. Hudson, 87 N.J.L. 244, 93 A. 582 (E. & A. 1915). See generally Viviana A. Zelizer, *The Purchase of Intimacy* (Princeton, N.J.: Princeton University Press; Basic Books, 2005).

53. See Cerria v. De Fazio, 19 N.J. Super. 482; 88 A. 2d 643 (Superior Ct. 1952).

54. "Anderson v. Searles," Record and Briefs, vol. 779 (2), Court of Errors and Appeals (New Jersey State Library, 1919), 82–86.

55. Anderson v. Searles, 93 N.J.L. 227, 107 A. 429 (E. & A. 1919).

56. See Steffler v. Schroeder, 12 N.J. Super. 243, 79 A. 2d 485 (Superior Ct. 1951). "Steffler v. Schroeder," Record and Briefs, vol. 100, 1949–1950 (3), Superior Court, Appellate Division (New Jersey State Library, 1951).

7. Paid Work

1. "Hattersley v. Bissett," Records and Briefs, Court of Errors and Appeals (New Jersey State Library, 1892), 40–41.

2. "Hattersley v. Bissett"; "Cooper v. Colson," Record and Briefs, vol. 320 (6), Court of Errors and Appeals (New Jersey State Library, 1904); "Petty v. Young," Record and Briefs, vol. 190 (15), Court of Errors and Appeals (New Jersey State Library, 1887); Ridgway v. English, 22 N.J.L. 409 (Sup. Ct.1850).

3. Alexis de Tocqueville, *Democracy in America,* ed. J. P. Mayer, trans. George Lawrence (Garden City, N.Y.: Doubleday, 1969), 51–55. On justification within moral universes, see Luc Boltanski and Laurent Thévenot, *On Justification: Economies of Worth,* trans. Catherine Porter (Princeton, N.J.: Princeton University Press, 2006).

4. "Robertson v. Hackensack Trust Company," Record and Briefs, vol. 6 (3), Supreme Court (New Jersey State Library, 1949), 68a–69a; Robertson v. Hackensack Trust Company, 1 N.J. 304, 63 A.2d 515 (1949).

5. Robertson v. Hackensack Trust Co., 1 N.J. 304; 63 A.2d 515 (1949).

6. "Robertson v. Hackensack Trust Company," 23a–34a. An old friend of Stertzer did describe her as doing "housework, cleaning and dusting and the cooking," but continued: "I guess that is about all there was to be done." She did, he added, drive her father places, and she took care of her mother when she was sick. It is hard to say whether she lost because of these sketchy descriptions, but the absence of more surely did not help.

7. "Nor is it so strange . . . that the property of labour should be able to overbalance the community of land, for 'tis labour indeed that puts the value on every thing." John Locke, *Two Treatises of Government,* rev. ed., rev. and introd. by Peter Laslett (New York: New American Library, Mentor, 1963), paragraph 40. See, generally, Amy Dru Stanley, *From Bondage to Contract: Wage Labor, Marriage, and the Market in the Age of Slave Emancipation* (New York: Cambridge University Press, 1998); Barbara H. Fried, *The Progressive Assault on Laissez Faire: Robert Hale and the First Law and Economics Movement* (Cambridge, Mass.: Harvard University Press, 1998).

8. "Cullen v. Woolverton," Record and Briefs, vols. 255 (2), 269 (2), 279 (2)*, Court of Errors and Appeals (New Jersey State Library, 1900), 15–19. Woolverton was described in the testimony as eighty-four when he died. On the other hand, an Asher Woolverton is listed as born in 1831 in the 1880 census list for Kingwood, Hunterdon, N.J. http://search. ancestrylibrary.com/cgi-bin/sse.dll?indiv=1&db=1880usfedcen%2c& rank=0&gsfn=asher&gsln=woolverton&sx=&gs1co=2%2cUSA&gs1pl =1%2cAll+States&year=&yearend=&sbo=0&sbor=&ufr=0&wp=4 %3b_80000002%3b_80000003&srchb=r&prox=1&ti=5542&ti.si=0& gss=angs-d&o_iid=21416&o_lid=21416&pcat=35&fh=0&h=28116984 &recoff=1+3.

9. "Cullen v. Woolverton," 15–22, 31–32, 94–96, 125–132.

10. "Cullen v. Woolverton," 149. This verdict was reversed on the grounds that the assignee had not furnished Woolverton, the administrator of the estate, a copy of the assignment. Cullen v. Woolverton, 63 N.J.L. 644, 44 A. 646 (E. & A. 1899). Cullen v. Woolverton, 65 N.J.L. 279; 47 A. 626 (E. & A. 1900).

11. Rhodes v. Rhodes, 3 Sandf. Ch. 279 (N.Y., 1846).

12. On the history of nursing, see Emily K. Abel, *Hearts of Wisdom: American Women Caring for Kin, 1850–1940* (Cambridge, Mass.: Harvard University Press, 2000); Kathleen M. Brown, *Foul Bodies: Cleanliness in Early America,* Society and the Sexes in the Modern World (New Haven, Conn.: Yale University Press, 2009); Susan Reverby, *Ordered to Care: The Dilemma of American Nursing, 1850–1945,* Cambridge History of Medicine (Cambridge: Cambridge University Press, 1987).

13. David A. Chang, *The Color of the Land: Race, Nation, and the Politics of Landownership in Oklahoma, 1832–1929* (Chapel Hill: University of North Carolina Press, 2010).

14. English equity courts never acknowledged such a right. See Maddison v. Alderson, Law Reports, 8 Appeal Cases 467 (House of Lords, 1883).

15. Between 1932 and 1952, of seventeen such cases, only two (three, if one counts a daughter-in law) were brought by children or grandchildren. By contrast, between 1850 and 1870, of fourteen such cases, eight (nine, if one counts a son-in-law) were brought by children or grandchildren. But see Tamara Hareven and Kathleen J. Adams, "The Generation in the Middle: Cohort Comparisons in Assistance to Aging Parents in an American Community," in *Aging and Generational Relations over the Life Course: A Historical and Cross-Cultural Perspective,* ed. Tamara K. Hareven (Berlin: de Gruyter, 1996), 272–293.

16. "Voorhees v. Combs," Record and Briefs, vol. 21 (22), Court of Errors and Appeals (New Jersey State Library, 1869), 2,5; Voorhees v. Combs, 33 N.J.L. 482 (Sup. Ct. 1868); 33 N.J.L. 494 (E. & A. 1869).

17. See, for example, "Waldron v. Davis," Record and Briefs, vol. 338 (3), Court of Errors and Appeals (New Jersey State Library, 1904), 9–17. Waldron v. Davis, 70 N.J.L. 627; 58 A. 293 (E. & A. 1904).

18. "Garretson v. Appleton," Record and Briefs, vol. 205 (11), Court of Errors and Appeals (New Jersey State Library, 1895), 1–23; Garretson v. Appleton, 58 N.J.L. 386 (E. & A. 1895). The Court of Errors agreed with the defense that Christina Appleton should have been understood as working as a wife, and thus her suit should have been precluded.

However, the court split on the question of whether that understanding could be raised on appeal since it had not been raised at trial. As a result, the jury's verdict was affirmed. See generally Reva B. Siegel, "The Modernization of Marital Status Law: Adjudicating Wives' Rights to Earnings, 1860–1930," *Georgetown Law Journal* 82(7) (September 1994): 2127–2211.

19. Wives, on the other hand, might still be understood as assuming a duty to care for husbands, a duty implicit in the marriage contract. See Borelli v. Brusseau, 12 Cal. App. 4th 647, 16 Cal. Rptr. 2d 16 (1993). In recent years throughout the developed world, spouses have assumed responsibility for core caregiving. Haim Hazan, "Disposable Children: On the Role of Offspring in the Construction of Conjugal Support in Later Life," in *Global Aging and Challenges to Families*, ed. Vern L. Bengtson and Ariela Lowenstein (New York: de Gruyter, 2003), 159–171.

20. Cerria v. De Fazio, 19 N.J. Super. 482; 88 A. 2d 643 (1952).

21. "Poloha v. Ruman," Record and Briefs, vol. 1833 (2), Court of Errors and Appeals (New Jersey State Library, 1944–1945), 44; Poloha v. Ruman, 137 N.J. Eq. 167, 44 A. 2d 411 (E. & A. 1945).

Epilogue

1. Peter Laslett, "Necessary Knowledge: Age and Aging in the Societies of the Past," in *Aging in the Past: Demography, Society, and Old Age*, ed. David I. Kertzer (Berkeley: University of California Press, 1995), 3–77; Robert William Fogel, "Changes in the Process of Aging during the Twentieth Century: Findings and Procedures of the *Early Indicators* Project," in *Aging, Health, and Public Policy: Demographic and Economic Perspectives*, ed. Linda J. Waite (New York: Population Council, 2004), 19–47. *The Cambridge Handbook of Age and Ageing*, ed. Malcolm L. Johnson (Cambridge: Cambridge University Press, 2005).

2. Peter Laslett, *A Fresh Map of Life: The Emergence of the Third Age*, with a new preface by the author (Cambridge, Mass.: Harvard University Press, 1991); David A. Plane and Jason R. Jurjevich, "Ties That No Longer Bind? The Patterns and Repercussions of Age-Articulated Migration," *Professional Geographer* 61(1) (February 2009): 4–20.

3. Mark Thomas and Paul Johnson, "Paying for Old Age: Past, Present, Future," in *The Economic Future in Historical Perspective*, ed. Paul A. David and Mark Thomas (Oxford: Oxford University Press, 2003), 479–508;

Andrew Mason and Georges Tapinos, eds., *Sharing the Wealth: Demographic Change and Economic Transfers between Generations* (Oxford: Oxford University Press, 2000); Linda Gordon, *Pitied but Not Entitled: Single Mothers and the History of Welfare* (New York: Free Press, 1994).

4. Glenda Laws, "'The Land of Old Age': Society's Changing Attitudes toward Urban-Built Environments for Elderly People," *Annals of the Association of American Geographers* 83(4) (1993): 672–693; Irene Hardill, "Introduction: Geographies of Aging," *Professional Geographer* 61(1) (February 2009): 1–3; Plane and Jurjevich, "Ties That No Longer Bind?"; Kevin E. McHugh and Elizabeth M. Larson-Keagy, "These White Walls: The Dialectic of Retirement Communities," *Journal of Aging Studies* 19(2) (May 2005): 241–256; Gary V. Engelhardt, Jonathan Gruber, and Cynthia D. Perry, "Social Security and Elderly Living Arrangements: Evidence from the Social Security Notch," *Journal of Human Resources* 40(2) (Spring 2005): 354–372 (University of Wisconsin Press); Haim Hazan, *Old Age: Constructions and Deconstructions* (New York: Cambridge University Press, 1994), 14.

5. McHugh and Larson-Keagy, "These White Walls"; Kevin E. McHugh and Ann M. Fletchall, "Memento Mori: The 'Death' of Youngtown," *Professional Geographer* 61(1) (February 2009): 21–35; Lizabeth Cohen, *A Consumers' Republic: The Politics of Mass Consumption in Postwar America* (New York: Knopf, 2003).

6. Eileen Boris and Jennifer Klein, *Caring for America: How Home Health Workers Became the New Face of Labor* (New York: Oxford University Press, 2012).

7. Damon Darlin, "Your Money: A Contrarian View: Save Less and Still Retire with Enough," *New York Times* (Jan. 27, 2007), Business, 1. On inheritance generally, see Carole Shammas, Marylynn Salmon, and Michel Dahlin, *Inheritance in America: From Colonial Times to the Present* (New Brunswick, N.J.: Rutgers University Press, 1987); Jens Beckert, *Inherited Wealth*, trans. Thomas Dunlap (Princeton, N.J.: Princeton University Press, 2008); Lawrence M. Friedman, *Dead Hands: A Social History of Wills, Trusts, and Inheritance Law* (Stanford, Calif.: Stanford Law Books, 2009); Sigrid Weigel, "Inheritance Law, Heritage, Heredity: European Perspectives," *Law and Literature* 20(2) (Summer 2008): 279–287; T. P. Schwartz, "Durkheim's Prediction about the Declining Importance of the Family and Inheritance: Evidence from the Wills of Providence, 1775–1985," *Sociological Quarterly* 36(3)

(1996): 503–519; Janet Finch, Lynn Hayes, Jennifer Mason, Judith Masson, and Lorraine Wallis, *Wills, Inheritance, and Families,* Oxford Socio-Legal Studies (Oxford: Clarendon, 1996).

8. John H. Langbein, "The Twentieth-Century Revolution in Family Wealth Transmission," *Michigan Law Review* 86 (1988): 722–751.

9. B. Douglas Bernheim, Andrei Shleifer, and Lawrence H. Summers, "The Strategic Bequest Motive," *Journal of Political Economy* 93(6) (December 1985): 1045–1076; Meta Brown, "Informal Care and the Division of End-of-Life Transfers," *Journal of Human Resources* 41(1) (2006): 191–219; Alan Booth, ed., *Intergenerational Caregiving* (Washington, D.C.: Urban Institute Press, 2008), 263.

10. See New York State Bar Association v. Reno, 999 F. Supp. 710 (N.D. New York, 1998); Marshall B. Kapp, *Legal Aspects of Elder Care* (Sudbury, Mass.: Jones and Bartlett, 2010), 221–223; Harry S. Margolis, general ed., *The ElderLaw Portfolio Series* (Boston: Little, Brown, 1993), vol. 1, portfolio 2, 46–51; portfolio 9, 40–41.

11. Martina Brandt, Klaus Haberkern, and Marc Szydlik, "Intergenerational Help and Care in Europe," *European Sociological Review* 25(5) (2009): 585–601; Pat Thane, "Social Histories of Old Age and Aging," *Journal of Social History* 37(1) (2003): 93–111; Marco Albertini, Martin Kohli, and Claudia Vogel, "Intergenerational Transfers of Time and Money in European Families: Common Patterns, Different Regimes?" *Journal of European Social Policy* 17 (2007): 319–334.

12. Loïc Trabut and Florence Weber, "How to Make Care-Work Visible? The Case of Dependence Policies in France," Nina Bandelj, ed., *Economic Sociology of Work* (Bingley, U.K.: JAI Press/Emerald, 2009), 343–368; Florence Weber, "Care for the Elderly: Obligations, Feelings, and Payments. Some Ethnographic French Evidence" (Princeton University, Dec. 1, 2003). See http://elias.ens.fr/~weber/ $; Martha Albertson Fineman, *The Autonomy Myth: A Theory of Dependency* (New York: New Press, 2004); Kathy J. Phillips, *The Moon in the Water: Reflections on an Aging Parent* (Nashville: Vanderbilt University Press, 2008); Katherine S. Newman, "Responsible to Whom? The Boundaries of Community in a Racially Divided Society," in *Legality and Community: On the Intellectual Legacy of Philip Selznick,* ed. Robert A. Kagan, Martin Krygier, and Kenneth Winston (Lanham, Md.: Rowman and Littlefield, 2002), 335–355.

13. See Clark Freshman, "Re-Visioning the Dependency Crisis and the Negotiator's Dilemma: Reflections on the Sexual Family and the Mother-Child Dyad," *Law and Social Inquiry* 22 (1997): 97–130; Phillips, *Moon in*

the Water; John Borneman, "Caring and Being Cared for: Displacing Marriage, Kinship, Gender, and Sexuality," in *The Ethics of Kinship: Ethnographic Inquiries,* ed. James D. Faubion (Lanham, Md.: Rowman and Littlefield, 2001), 29–46.

14. Viviana Zelizer, "Caring Everywhere," in *Intimate Labors: Cultures, Technologies, and the Politics of Care,* ed. Eileen Boris and Rhacel Salazar Parreñas (Stanford, Calif.: Stanford Social Sciences, 2010), 267–279.

15. Boris and Klein, *Caring for America.*

16. See the lovely descriptions in Phillips, *Moon in the Water.* For France, see Trabut and Weber, "How to Make Care-Work Visible?"; Weber, "Care for the Elderly"; also, Brandt, Haberkern, and Szydlik, "Intergenerational Help and Care in Europe."

17. See Marilynne Robinson, *Home* (New York: Farrar, Straus, and Giroux, 2008). The term "trapped kin" comes from Trabut and Weber, "How to Make Care-Work Visible?"

18. Haim Hazan, "Disposable Children: On the Role of Offspring in the Construction of Conjugal Support in Later Life," in *Global Aging and Challenges to Families,* ed. Vern L. Bengtson and Ariela Lowenstein (New York: de Gruyter, 2003), 159–171.

19. Viviana A. Zelizer, *The Purchase of Intimacy* (Princeton, N.J.: Princeton University Press, 2005).

20. I am indebted to Risa Goluboff for this point.

21. Michael G. Peletz, "Ambivalence in Kinship since the 1940s," in *Relative Values: Reconfiguring Kinship Studies,* ed. Sarah Franklin and Susan McKinnon (Durham: Duke University Press, 2001), 413–444.

22. Tamara Hareven and Kathleen J. Adams, "The Generation in the Middle: Cohort Comparisons in Assistance to Aging Parents in an American Community," in *Aging and Generational Relations over the Life Course: A Historical and Cross-Cultural Perspective,* ed. Tamara K. Hareven (Berlin: de Gruyter, 1996), 272–293; Albertini, Kohli, and Vogel, "Intergenerational Transfers"; Cassandra Rasmussen Dorius and Laura Wray-Lake, "Expanding the Horizon: New Directions for the Study of Intergenerational Care and Exchange," in *Intergenerational Caregiving,* ed. Alan Booth (Washington, D.C.: Urban Institute Press, 2008), 351–381; Brandt, Haberkern, and Szydlik, "Intergenerational Help and Care in Europe."

Acknowledgments

This was a difficult book to write: difficult because I began with a particular kind of source rather than a theme, difficult because what I found in those sources connected so intimately to issues in my own life, issues about care, caretaking, and old age (Early on, Joyce Appleby commented, "You baby boomers! Always writing about your own lives."), and difficult because the stories I eventually drew from the sources were so dark, much more so than I had expected. (Oh, for some ordinary criminal violence, some rapacious capitalism, some slavery, the stuff of "regular" history.)

I am grateful to the wonderful librarians and archivists at the New Jersey State Archives and the New Jersey State Library. At the former, Betty Epstein was particularly helpful. Firestone Library of Princeton University offered the distinctive and important pleasures of the open stacks of a great library. How else would I have learned about the history of old age except through the unexpected joy of walking face forward into a stack with those holdings?

It took friends—honest, brilliant, and critical readers—to help me figure out what I was doing in this book: what I had found in the archives and what I was trying to say about what I had found. They are obviously not responsible for its continuing failures. However, I am more grateful to them than I can express, particularly to Nancy Hartog, who combined her usual critical gifts with wide reading and experience "in the field" and who struggled through drafts early and late, and to Amy Dru Stanley, who was willing to talk me through a very early version and to challenge me to try to make sense of what I was doing. I am also grateful to Risa Goluboff, Jonathan Levy, Margot Canaday, and Viviana Zelizer, each of whom raised anxieties and helped me find some answers and forms of expression at later points in this process. Likewise, I thank Steven Wilf, Sarah Seo, Maribel Morey, Susie Blumenthal, and Alix Lerner. Other conversations, early and late, with Dylan Penningroth, Mary Anne Case, Rebecca Scott, Carol Sanger, David Fischer, Florence Weber, Emma Rothschild, Roy Kreitner, Debbie Becher, Laura Weinrib, Dan Rodgers, Vicki Schultz, Liz Magill, Barbara Yngvesson, Jessica Lowe, and Howie Erlanger made an enormous difference. Stewart Macaulay gave me the run of the Wisconsin casebook and provided a model of how to think about contract law. Marni Sandweiss taught me about ancestry.com and reminded me that Tocqueville had said something interesting about wills. Heather Hendershot gets much of the credit for the title. Barbara Welke offered pointed comments on an early paper drawn from what would later become a portion of a chapter, and her own work modeled for me what one can do with trial transcripts. Amy Dru Stanley also served as an outside reviewer for Harvard University Press, as did John Demos. I am grateful to both for helping to bring a draft to something like a conclusion.

Early versions of chapters of this book were presented as a Centennial Lecture at the Chicago-Kent Law School, at the NYU Legal History Colloquium, the Harvard Legal History Colloquium, a workshop at the University of Virginia Law School, and workshops at Stanford Law School, Temple Law School, the University of Wisconsin Law School, and the Modern America Workshop of Princeton's Department of History. Thanks to the kindness of Jean-Louis Halperin I gave a workshop on a chapter at l'École Normale Supérieure in Paris, and thanks to the kindness of Roy Kreitner and others in Israel, I gave workshops at Tel Aviv University Law School.

Joyce Seltzer was, as before, the right editor for me—brutally honest, relentless, and uncompromising, but also a supportive friend. Carla La-Roche, Farah Peterson, and Alix Lerner provided research assistance. Alix, in particular, did the hard work of checking my quotations and citations. The Westchester Book Group scrupulously edited the book for Harvard University Press, along with the copyediting help of Maribel Morey and Sarah Seo.

Twenty-eight years ago, at the end of an earlier book project, I thanked my children for being there; now, it is the grandchildren, Naomi, May Alice, Elias, and Cole, who may someday enjoy seeing their names in print. It is not much, but someday all this will be theirs. I hope in a better world.

Index